ABOUT THE TEXT...

"Prof. Karenga has written the most comprehensive, theoretical and intellectual conception to date of Black Studies as a discipline. He has taken many general pronouncements about Black Studies and skillfully grouped them into a persuasive new clarity. He gives us a model of Black Studies as a logical system with its own principles, purposes, drives and philosophy."

Prof. William Strickland, Associate Professor, Political Science, W.E.B. DuBois Department of Afro-American Studies, University of Mass., Amherst.

"Prof. Karenga has provided a much-needed volume, the only of its kind. It is not doctrinaire and it presents Black Studies as an interdisciplinary academic field that challenges and broadens the traditional disciplines."

Dr. Johnnella Butler, Chairperson, Department of Afro-American Studies, Smith College

"Dr. Karenga's work represents the most important and comprehensive treatment of Black Studies as a discipline that has been published since the beginning of the Black Studies Movement. It is critical and thought-provoking and serves as an excellent foundation for students enrolled in Black Studies courses who need a single substantive reference in the discipline."

Dr. William Nelson, Chair, Black Studies Department, Ohio State University Columbus

"Dr. Karenga's book is the best available introductory text in Black Studies. It is excellent for beginning students who need a comprehensive and critical survey of the discipline. Moreover, it is especially valuable to students with assimilated backgrounds who have deficient grounding in the Black experience. For it allows them to experience vicariously the initial political and academic thrusts of Black Studies."

Dr. Bertha Maxwell, Frank Porter Graham Professor and Director, Afro-American and African Studies Program, University of North Carolina, Charlotte

Also by MAULANA KARENGA

- *Selections From The Husia: Sacred Wisdom of Ancient Egypt (Selected and Retranslated) (1984)*
- *Kawaida Theory: An Introductory Outline (1980)*
- *Essays on Struggle: Position and Analysis (1978)*
- *Kwanzaa: Origins, Concepts, Practice (1977)*
- *Afro-American Nationalism: An Alternative Analysis (forthcoming)*

INTRODUCTION TO
BLACK STUDIES

MAULANA KARENGA

Kawaida Publications
Los Angeles, California

Cover design: Tiamoyo Karenga.
Sculptured Head: Pharoah Thutmose III

First Printing: August, 1982
Second Printing: August, 1983
Third Printing: October 1984

LIBRARY OF CONGRESS CATALOG NUMBER: LCN: 82-81921

ISBN 0-943412-00-5

To the Black students, Black organizations
and Black people in the 60's who dared leave
the legacy of Black Studies and to those who
dare to sustain, enrich and expand this legacy.

CONTENTS

PREFACE

This text is essentially a contribution to the efforts to develop a standard body of discipline-specific literature for Black Studies. Its basic aim is to offer a definitive introduction to the discipline. Moreover, as an introductory text, it seeks to provide the student with a concise but substantive intellectual base for a critical understanding and discussion of Black Studies. Although a survey approach is employed, stress is placed on inquiry and analysis as key to building the student's intellectual base in the discipline.

Toward achieving this basic aim, several objectives have guided the preparation of this text: (1) to introduce and define the origins, relevance and scope of Black Studies; (2) to introduce, define and discuss critically the seven core subject areas of Black Studies, i.e., Black History, Black Religion, Black Social Organization, Black Politics, Black Economics, Black Creative Production and Black Psychology; (3) to introduce and define key concepts in the discipline and each subject area; (4) to delineate fundamental issues and areas for critical discussion in the discipline and its subject areas; (5) to introduce and discuss critically major challenges facing Black Studies; (6) to introduce fundamental literature in the discipline of Black Studies and its core subject areas; and (7) to raise provocative questions about the Black experience which cultivate the use of and an appreciation for inquiry and analysis as indispensable tools to an effective grasp and critical discussion of Black Studies.

This text then, is structured around these objectives. The first chapter introduces the discipline as a whole through discussion of its origins, relevance and scope. The main body of the text follows and is organized into seven chapters, each of which discusses critically one of the seven core subject areas of Black Studies and thus introduces the student to the basic internal dialogue of each subject area. The final chapter raises and examines the major challenges facing Black Studies and includes suggestions of how they might be met. At the end of each chapter are study questions and references aimed at encouraging and facilitating inquiry and analysis by the student.

This enterprise is self-consciously Afro-centric, critical and corrective in response to the internal demands of the discipline itself, whose subject matter and academic and social mission clearly demand this approach. An Afro-centric approach is essentially intellectual inquiry and production centered on and in the image and interest of African peoples. This responds to the early and continuing demands for academic and social relevance of the educational process and its contents. The critical thrust is the advancing of severe and ongoing criticism of the established order of things in order to negate myths, mystifications and insubstantialities of traditional white studies on Blacks, society and the world. And the corrective thrust is the correlative discovery and affirmation of the truth of the Black experience in its current and historical unfolding. It also means posing correctives to problems internal to the discipline of Black Studies as well as to those which confront Black people, themselves.

Several other points should be made about the book. First, I have self-consciously used abundant references to introduce the student to the literature in the field and provide him/her with a bibliography which will facilitate research for term papers in Black Studies and its seven core subject areas. Secondly, in citations, I have not used the first names of the authors in hopes that this will encourage use of the bibliography. Thirdly, I have written an admittedly long chapter on Black History in order to give the student a general panoramic view and sense of the origins, challenges and achievements of Black people as a backdrop for the discussions in the particular areas which follow.

Moreover, I tried to deal substantively with vital issues and questions often raised by students but not normally dealt with at length or in a systematic Afro-centric manner by other texts, i.e., resistance in slavery, the DuBois-Garvey conflict, the fall of African societies, Black scientific achievements, and of course the dynamics and legacy of the Sixties. Fourthly, an attempt has been made to avoid negative categories and introduce proactive and positive ones. Therefore, the word "negro" except when it is part of a title is replaced with Black, African, Afro-American, etc. in parenthesis and *the text focus is on Black struggle and achievement rather than on victimization.*

By way of acknowledgements, I owe a great debt to Tiamoyo, my wife, who lived up to her name "she who inspires." For she inspired, typed, proofread, xeroxed, edited, researched, raised questions, took notes and dictation, and understood and appreciated the limitations on my time during the writing.

Special thanks go to Chimbuko Tembo and Limbiko Tembo who did research, xeroxed, compiled bibliographies and supported the effort in other ways. Thanks goes to Jitahadi Imara, my administrative assistant, who conducted classes, seminars and forums for me while I was writing and to the other Executive Council members of Us, who shared other responsibilities to free me to finish this book. Thanks go to Ralph Tulivu who helped edit and Chanzo Ndoto and Salimu Logan for the long and many hours spent at the libraries on several campuses collecting needed material for me. Great thanks go to the founders of the Kawaida Groundwork Commitee (Us) who supported my theoretical and practical efforts to preserve and expand the legacy of the 60's out of which this book grew, i.e., Tiamoyo Karenga, W. Sikivu Kabaila, Mark Tangulifu, Chimbuko Tembo, Subira Kifano, Ujima Goode and Nzinga Ratibisha.

In addition to the founders, I am also grateful to other advocates whose critical questions in our regular discussions and at seminars and institutes sponsored by the Institute of Pan-African Studies helped lay the basis for this book. These are Chanzo Ndoto, Brent Mshindaji, Jitahadi Imara, Robert Mpinduzi, Limbiko Tembo, Imani Imara, Gerold Msadiki, Kweli Walker, Robert Tambuzi, Salimu Logan, Haiba Collier, Nyenyekevu Kumbufu, Arnold Kumbufu, Ralph Tulivu, Kamilisha Angalifu, Andrew Angalifu, Jifunza Pinkston, Muhebi James and supporters, Walter Jitahidi and Joel Mjengaji.

I am indebted to the many students who took my classes and listened to my lectures on the many campuses at which I have taught and lectured and who also raised critical questions about Black life, history and struggle which this book seeks to answer. Special thanks to my friend and colleague, Professor Amen Rahh, whose Afro-centric stress complements and reinforces mine; to Haki Madhubuti, Kalamu ya Salaam, Segun Shabaka, Mansong Kulubally and Kamau Tyehimba for intellectual exchange and support; to Eunice, my sister and Chestyn my brother, whose support has always been strong and timely; and to Clentine, my sister, for whom the finishing of this book was a last aspiration.

I am indebted also to the Black scholars in these pages whose works provide the substance of Black Studies.

But the greatest debt is to Black people whose lives, achievements and aspirations fill this book and give it whatever message and meaning it has.

Maulana Karenga

Inglewood, California
July, 1982

I
INTRODUCTION

From its inception, Black Studies has had both an academic and social thrust and mission. It grew out of one of the most important, politically active and successful periods of Black history in the U.S. and cannot be separated from it without severe damage to analytical clarity. Black Studies is rooted in the social visions and struggles of the 60's which aimed at Black power, liberation and a higher level of human life. If Black Power is defined as the collective capacity of Black people to define, defend and develop their interests, Black Studies and the students it develops obviously have a role in the definition, defense and development of those interests. Thus, to clearly understand the relevance, objectives and developmental direction of Black Studies, a critical review of its history is imperative.

ORIGINS OF THE DISCIPLINE

Black Studies, as an academic discipline, began as a political demand which had its origin in both the general Student Movement and the social struggles of the 60's out of which the Student Movement evolved (Brisbane, 1974; Pinkney, 1976: McEvoy and Miller, 1969). The 60's was a time of upheaval and confrontation and students, Third World and white, were at the center of the struggles which produced this process. Beginning first off campus in a struggle against the racist structure and functioning of society, students began to see the university as a key institution in the larger system

17

of coercive institutions created by the established order to maintain and perpetuate its role. Pictured as a microcosm of society, the
university was defined as racist, sick, unresponsive, rigid and supportive of war, exploitation, oppression and exclusion of Blacks,
other Third World peoples and the poor from the social knowledge, wealth and power of U.S. society. The decision was then
made to take up the struggle against society at the point of its
"brain," or put another way, at its "intellectual factory" which
produced both its leaders and followers and cherished social myths
(McEvoy and Miller, 1969).

The Student Movement expressed itself in four different thrusts,
the latter thrust being the one which more directly demanded and
achieved Black Studies. The first thrust of the Student Movement
began in 1960 with Black students who played a central and indispensable role in the Civil Rights Movement in the South. Essentially,
the Movement sought to: 1) break down the barriers of legal segregation in public accommodations; 2) achieve equality and justice
for Blacks; and 3) organize Blacks into a self-conscious social force
capable of defining, defending and advancing their interests. The
Student Non-Violent Coordinating Committee (SNCC) was
obviously the vanguard group in the Civil Rights struggle and the
Student Movement. As vanguard, SNCC not only mobilized,
organized and politicized thousands of Black students, but also
politicized many white students and their leaders thru recruiting
and training them and bringing them to the South to work in the
struggle. As Carson (1981:129) notes, white summer volunteers in
Mississippi "who returned home greatly influenced by their experiences...would bring a measure of SNCC radicalism into the student's rights and antiwar movements." This link would prove
valuable for joint action later.

The second thrust of the Student Movement began with the
Free Speech Movement at UC Berkeley in 1964. It was essentially
white student protest against the rigid, arbitrary, restrictive and

unresponsive character of the university, in a word, a demand for civil rights on campus (Draper, 1965; Lipset and Wolin, 1965). Mario Savio who had been one of the SNCC summer volunteers in Mississippi was the leader of this movement and expressed a link between the civil rights struggle on campus and in the larger society. He posed the Free Speech Movement on UC Berkeley's campus as "another phase of the same struggle," i.e., the civil rights struggle in the larger society and expressed the similarity of suppression of powerless Blacks and students by the established order (Carson, 1981:129).

The third thrust of the Student Movement began in 1965 which was the general student protest against the Vietnam war and university complicity in it thru its cooperation with the government (McEvoy and Miller, 1969). The anti-war movement was launched by New Leftists at the University of Michigan with a teach-in which was duplicated across the nation. On April 17, the largest New Left organization, the Students for a Democratic Society (SDS), held a massive anti-war demonstration at the Washington Monument in D.C. SNCC, which inspired leaders of SDS to organized activism, supported the demonstration and participated in it. New Leftists like Casey Hayden, Bob Zellner, Betty Garman, Maria Varela and Jim Monsonis had been SNCC workers. In 1962 SDS at its annual convention drafted the Port Huron Statement, which acknowledged their debt to the Black struggle in the South and SNCC in particular for their new consciousness and activism.

Tom Hayden, who had met with SNCC workers in McComb, Mississippi in 1961 and helped write the Port Huron Statement, was also very impressed with the achievements of SNCC and the possibility of its model. Likewise, other white activists and scholars on the Left such as Staughton Lynd and Howard Zinn were impressed with and inspired by the SNCC model. Thus, the student protest against the Vietnam war and university complicity was lead by the white

Left but informed and supported by SNCC and its theoretical and practical criticism of U.S. society.

To SDS and others, "selective service regulation and revocation of student deferments for dissent, military recruiting and R.O.T.C., corporate recruiting by Dow (Chemical Company) and other military suppliers and traditional recruitment by the Pentagon" were all evidence of university collusion with the government's war effort (McEvoy and Miller, 1969:4). SNCC supported the anti-war movement, not only from a student position, but also from a Black and Third World position. Thus, SNCC's opposition was to: 1) the government's war against Third World liberation movements and peoples in general and Vietnam in particular; 2) the threat draft posed to its male personnel not covered by student deferment and especially vulnerable in the South, and; 3) fighting an unjust war for a nation depriving Blacks of basic civil and human rights. It was Bob Moses, one of SNCC's most distinguished leaders, who represented SNCC at both the Washington massive demonstration and a subsequent one at Berkeley, outlining this basic position and making the link between the southern struggle, Third World Liberation and SNCC's opposition to the war (Carson, 1981:183-185). As Carson also reports, Jim Forman, another major SNCC leader, led SNCC's early opposition to the war criticizing "American involvement in Vietnam at a time when the federal government was unwilling to intervene on behalf of southern civil rights workers."

The importance of this third thrust of the Student Movement against the war and university complicity and unresponsiveness is that it included a general criticism of and struggle against the very structure and functioning of the university itself. This, in turn, had three basic results which were contributive to the Black Studies Movement: 1) it further exposed the university's political character and its reflection of social structure and power; 2) it revealed the university's vulnerability to student power; and 3) it suggested the possibility of an expanded struggle to change the way the university related to Black students and the Black community as well as to other Third World students and communities. Thus, social change was linked to university change and the students again moved into the vanguard.

The final thrust of the Student Movement which led directly to the establishment of Black Studies began in 1966 at San Francisco State College (SFSC) and was again initiated and led by Blacks. It came at the rising tide of the Black Power Movement and reflected its sense of social mission and urgency. By 1966, the Watts Revolt and the Black Power Movement had ushered in a more racially self-conscious and assertive activism and Black students at SFSC and on other campuses began to respond to this resurgence of nationalist activism. Thus, in 1966, the Negro Students Association changed their name to the Black Student Union (BSU) to indicate a new identity and direction. And in the fall of the same year, the BSU produced a document arguing for and demanding the first Department of Black Studies. Continuing their thrust, they established a Black arts and culture series in the Experimental College which was also created in 1966 and became involved in SFSC's tutorial program for the surrounding community. This and other community service activities signalled the social commitment and service Black Studies advocates would place at the center of the academic and social mission of Black Studies.

Since the Experimental College was set up with student money, there was no serious resistance to it, but the demand by the BSU for a legitimate Black Studies Department funded by the college and controlled by Black people brought stiff resistance. Moreover, the BSU demanded a special admissions program which would waive entrance requirements for a given number of Black students. This also was resisted, even though Black enrollment had been reduced drastically from over a thousand to a few hundred by the College's tracking system.

By 1968 the situation had escalated to the point where the BSU launched a strike on November 6th around a series of demands including a Black Studies Department, special admissions, financial aid and decisions on personnel. Influenced by Fanon's, SNCC's and the Black nationalist emphasis on Third World solidarity, other Third World groups joined with the BSU under the umbrella organization, the Third World Liberation Front. These other Third World groups included the Mexican American Student Confederation (MASC), the Asian-American Political Alliance (AAPA), the Intercollegiate Chinese for Social Action (ICSA), the Phillipine American Collegiate Endeavor (PACE) and the Latin American Student Organization (LASO). Reflecting a common concern for Third World students and Third World Studies, they issued fifteen demands which served as a model for other Black Studies struggles. The SDS, Peace and Freedom Party and white students from the Experimental College formed a strike support committee and worked to join the struggle of Third World students with the struggle against the war, ROTC on campus and other issues which linked the university with the government. In this student thrust, however, it was Blacks (and other Third World students) who again led the way and the whites supported, as in the first thrust in the early 60's.

On February 9, 1968, Dr. Nathan Hare had been appointed as coordinator of Black Studies and been given the task of formulating an autonomous Black Studies Department. By April 16, he had completed his proposal which included, not only the structure for the department, but special admission for Black students, and a B.A. degree in Black Studies. However, the board of trustees continually delayed implementation of the program and it is this which led to the November 6th strike. The school was closed; students clashed with police; presidents were changed with regularity; and the community became involved in the campus struggle in a way it had never done. Eventually, the students won at the end of 1968 and San Francisco State became the first institution to establish a Black Studies program and department.

As Brisbane (1974:228) notes, Black students paid close attention to the struggle at State and were impressed with the capacity of students to win concessions from the administration. Thus, already "by fall of 1968, the experiences of San Francisco State were being duplicated on dozens of campuses throughout the country." On every occasion, these struggles were seen as linked to the overall struggle for Black liberation and was often led by Black nationalists or Black Power advocates. Among these were members of SNCC, Us and other Kawaida formations on the West and East coasts, the BPP, CORE and smaller local nationalist formations. As Pinkney (1976:177) observed, the struggle for Black Studies was "seen as a necessary component of Black liberation" and white resistance seen "as an attempt to preserve (Black) subordinate status in society...." It became important then to break the white monopoly on knowledge and its manipulation and create a new context for the creation and dissemination of a new knowledge directed toward service to the community rather than toward its suppression.

Thus, the struggle to win Black Studies coincided with the general student revolt against the structure and functioning of the university and at the beginning often was supported by other Third World students and whites. Eventually, however, the Black students would reject cooperation with whites and thus, leave only the Black Panther Party, which changed its nationalist philosophy, to deal with their new-found allies. Nevertheless, as a result of countless struggles and negotiations, most of the major colleges and universities agreed to establish some form of Black Studies by 1969.

The Black Studies struggle extended also to Black colleges which had prided themselves on being pioneers in teaching the Black Experience. What they actually taught was "negro history" which both in content and consciousness was different from the liberational thrust for which Black Studies advocates struggled. Brisbane (1974:238-239) lists three reasons the Black colleges resisted the challenge: 1) alleged financial problems; 2) assumption that only a militant faction advocated it; and 3) the "bourgeois mentality" of the staff which was "committed to working within the system (and) completely rejected the notion of Black liberation." However, after a series of struggles and after "Harvard, Yale and Columbia universities provided 'legitimacy' by the adoption of such programs," leading Black institutions like Atlanta, Fisk, Howard, Lincoln, Morgan and Tuskegee initiated Black Studies Programs by fall of 1969.

RELEVANCE OF THE DISCIPLINE

One of the most important concepts in the general Student Movement and especially in the Black Student Movement which waged the struggle for Black Studies was the concept of relevance, a concept which had both academic and social dimensions. Relevance, as a fundamental category, was inevitably defined as emanating from education's contribution to liberation and a higher level of life for Blacks. Thus, Hare (1969:42), one of the guiding theorists and founders of the Movement, argued for an Afro-American education, which would contribute to solving "the problems of the race" by producing "persons capable of solving problems of a contagious American society." Moreover, he concluded, "a Black education which is not revolutionary in the current day is both irrelevant and useless." It is this stress on academic and social relevance of education that not only gave Black Studies its raison d'etre, but also brought it its major opposition.

The push for relevant education in the university was thus joined with a thrust by Black Studies to establish and maintain its own relevance as both an academic and social project. Therefore, in developing a relevant Black Studies, Black Studies advocates expressed two sets of basic concerns, i.e., academic and social ones (Robinson, 1969; Blassingame, 1973). On the academic level, they were concerned first with the quality and usefulness or relevance of traditional white studies. White studies was seen as incorrect, incomplete and exclusive of the majority of humankind, especially the fathers and mothers of humankind and human civilization, Blacks. Secondly, Black Studies advocates perceived white studies for the most part as so much propaganda for the established order which not only posed the white paradigm as the most definitive of human life and society, but also discouraged study and development of Third World models. Finally, the Black Studies advocates saw white studies as resistant or negative to social change inquiries and models. This they felt could only be countered by a self-conscious and viable discipline of Black Studies which would not only seek to study society and the world, but also to change them.

The social concerns of Black Studies centered around the questions of exclusion, treatment on campus, academic conversions and production of a conscious, committed and capable intelligentsia and on what all this meant for the Black community. Black Studies advocates were first concerned with the low number of Blacks on campus which they saw as a racist exclusion to maintain the white monopoly on critical knowledge and to thwart the rise of a Black intelligentsia capable of effectively leading and serving Blacks. Thus, one of their first demands was special admission and recruitment efforts to correct this problem. Secondly, Black Studies advocates were concerned with treatment of Black students on campus. In fact, a key set of grievances and incidents on San Francisco State's campus centered around what was considered racist treatment of Black students in terms of news reports, counselling, instruction, representation on decision-making bodies, etc. The concern was to make Blacks respected and politically effective on campus and in campus politics in the broadest sense of the word. (Hare 1972:33).

Thirdly, Black Studies advocates were concerned about what they conceived as white academic conversion, i.e., transformation of Blacks into vulgar careerists with no sense of social commitment. Equally feared was that Black students would become what Fanon called obscene caricatures of Europe, pathetic imitators of their oppressors. Finally, Black Studies advocates were concerned with the social problems of the Black community and how Black students and Black Studies could address them.

It is around these general concerns that Black Studies advocates across the country laid out some basic academic and social objectives which interlocked and mutually reinforced each other (Blassingame, 1973; Hare, 1969; Robinson, 1969). The first and seemingly most urgent objective was to teach what was called the Black experience in its historical and current unfolding. The category "experience" suggested all that Blacks had encountered, did and endured and sought to reflect the multidimensionality of the process. Moreover, this experience was to be greatly focused on the history and contributions of Blacks who were systematically denied history and contribution to society and humanity or relegated to minor historical significance. Finally, it was advocated that the data and instruction include both the Continental African and Diasporan African experience, the Diasporan focus treating first Afro-Americans and then all other Africans spread across the world. Although this was the projected scope, in practice data and instruction were essentially concentrated on the Continental and Afro-American experience with some curricula offering a few courses on the Caribbean experience.

A second beginning objective of Black Studies was to assemble and create a body of knowledge which was contributive to intellectual and political emancipation. Intellectual freedom was posed as a prerequisite to political freedom. In a word, until the white monopoly on Black minds was broken, it was argued, liberation was not only impossible, but unthinkable. For there would be no categorical referent, no way to conceive it and thus, no way to carry it out. Political emancipation as a social goal, then was dependent on intellectual emancipation as an academic goal. These contentions were reflective of Cruse's (1967) and Frazier's (1973) positions on the crisis and responsibilities of the Black intellectual.

Logically linked to the above objective was a third objective of creating a body of Black intellectuals who were dedicated to community service and development rather than vulgar careerism. Restating DuBois' (1961) argument against Washington's over-stress on vocation at the expense of education for social compe-tence and contribution, Black Studies advocates stressed the need for Black intellectuals who were conscious, capable and committed to Black liberation and a higher level of human life. They argued like DuBois (1969) that the race would be elevated by its best minds, a "Talented Tenth" which did not sell itself for money and machines, but recognized and responded creatively to the fact of the indivisibility of Black freedom and their indispensible role in achieving it.

Fourthly, Black Studies advocates posed as an early objective the cultivation, maintenance and continuous expansion of a mutu-ally beneficial relationship between the campus and the commun-ity. This relationship was best posed in Dr. Hare's statement which became a slogan and call to action of the Black Studies Movement, "We must bring the campus to the community and the community to the campus." The intent here was to serve and elevate the life-conditions and the consciousness of the community and rein-force the student's relationship with the community thru service and interaction. Thus, the classic alienation between the intellectual and the community is thwarted in an ongoing mutually beneficial exchange, where knowledge is shared and applied in the service of liberation and development of the Black community (Hare, 1972:33).

Finally, an early (and continuing) objective of Black Studies advocates was to establish it as a legitimate, respected and permanent discipline. This was and remains both an academic and political problem. The political problem is to win the battle of acceptance with administrations and other departments who are threatened by Black Studies or incorrectly and reductively translate its relevance and viability. The academic problem is to answer the critics of Black Studies with counter arguments, critical research, solid intellectual production and effective teaching. Afterall, there are really only two basic arguments against Black Studies, i.e., a charge of academic insubstantiality and its having a political character.

These arguments, however, do not really hold weight given Black Studies' fourteen-year history of teaching, research, intellectual production and service to students and the university. Moreover, to answer a tired contention, Swahili is no more frivolous or irrelevant to Blacks than Hebrew or Croation is to Jews or Croats who were not born in Israel or Yugoslavia and will never go there. And if white studies or traditional college courses seeks to produce socially competent and committed leaders for the white community, how does one justify calling such an academic and social mission political for Blacks and proper for whites? Afterall, the basic justification for all education is that it enhances our social competence and, therefore, our capacity to make a more significant contribution to society.

Thru the 16 year practical and theoretical struggle to achieve and refine these early objectives, a broad, fundamental and undeniable relevance of Black Studies has been established which clearly defines the academic and social contributions and purpose of Black Studies. The first relevance of Black Studies is that it is a definitive contribution to humanity's understanding itself. As Samir Amin (1974:5) contends, there is only one possible science, the science of human society, of humans in the process of self, social and world construction. But humanity is an abstraction, a mere construction for the convenience of conversation unless it is seen in its diversity and particularity as well as its unity and universality. Black Studies, then, becomes important because it is a study of a particular people which aids in the study of humanity as a whole. In other words, Black Studies (and other Third World Studies) represents in its most definitive sense, a necessary and significant study of a particular form and part of humanity in certain socio-historical conditions. Moreover, Black Studies is an important contribution to humanity's self-understanding because Blacks, i.e., African people, are the fathers and mothers of both humanity and human civilization (Jackson, 1970). Thus, to omit a study of the parent people of humanity is to deprive oneself and humanity of a holistic and effective understanding of itself.

Secondly, the relevance of Black Studies is found in its contribution to U.S. society's understanding of itself. It is not an exaggeration to say that Black and other Ethnic Studies are the most trenchant criticism and most definitive mirror of American society. If it is true that one does not evaluate a society by its public pronouncements but by its social practice, then, the study of the Black experience in the U.S. would obviously give an incisive look at American life, from both a race and class perspective. U.S. society claims freedom, justice and equality for all, but Black Studies poses a more definitive view of social wealth and power in the U.S. Moreover, as Cortada (1974:41) has argued, the curricular reform in American universities is as beneficial to whites as others "if the U.S. is to be socialized in a world where only 21.8 percent of the population is white" and where U.S. and European power is declining and Third World power is on the rise. It is thus to the credit of Black Studies and the social struggles which inform its focus, as I

(Karenga, 1977:50) have argued elsewhere, that they "have provided the U.S. with an essential theoretical and practical self-criticism." Moreover, Black Studies and struggle "have forced the U.S. into a necessary self-knowledge, unmasked its self-indulgent myths and confronted it with internal contradictions so elemental that only a broad and profound social change can resolve them."

Thirdly, and as a logical consequence of the first two contentions, Black Studies has established its relevance as a contribution to the university's realization of its claim and challenge to teach the whole truth, or something as close to it as humanly possible. No university can claim universality, comprehensiveness, objectivity or effectiveness in creating a context for the development of a socially competent and aware student, if it diminishes, denies or deforms the role of African peoples in history and society. Moreover, as has been so often noted:

> Until quite lately higher education in the United States of America has been almost completely under the sway of an illusion shared by nearly everybody of European descent since the Middle Ages — the illusion that the history of the world is the history of Europe and its cultural offshoots; that Western interpretations of that experience are sufficient, if not exhaustive and that the resulting value systems embrace everything that matters (Wright, 1970:366).

Such an academic and cultural provincialism can only discredit the university's claim of inclusiveness, objectivity and rigor for its curriculum. It also reflects an image of irreality in a world where Africans, Asians and Latin Americans have stepped back on the stage of human history in both dramatic and unavoidably significant ways and roles and must be on the educational agenda.

Fourthly, Black Studies has demonstrated its relevance as a contribution to the rescue and reconstruction of Black history and humanity. As both an affirmative and negative academic and social project, Black Studies affirms the truth of our history and humanity and negates the racist myths assembled to deny and deform them. Refusing to answer frivolous racist contentions, it rises to challenge traditional white studies which have intellectualized their biases, omissions and distortions. It realizes the link between history and humanity and is conscious of the fact that Europe denied and deformed Black history in order to deny and diminish Black humanity. Black Studies then begins with rigorous research and critical intellectual production in the key social science, history, which lays the basis for and informs all others and which will affirm the truth of the Black experience and negate the racist myths which have surrounded it.

Fifthly, the relevance of Black Studies is that it is a critical contribution to a new social science which will not only benefit Blacks, but also the U.S. and the world. Joyce Ladner's (1973) announcement of the death of white sociology can only be answered with the creation of an alternative (affirmative and negative) sociology or more accurately, a new social science which sets a model for others by the standards it sets for itself and reflects. Black Studies, as a contribution to that academic project, has already developed along those lines in the light of Cruse's (1967) and Frazier's (1973) criticism and the challenges posed by students, other departments and the demands of the discipline itself (Turner and Perkins, 1976).

As a contribution to a new social science, Black Studies, which is interdisciplinary, becomes a paradigm for the multidimensional approach to social and historical reality. Secondly, it is a model of a holistic social science, not simply focusing on Blacks, but critically including other Third World peoples and whites in appropriate socio-historical periods and places of interaction with Blacks and denying no people its relevance, unlike the case of traditional white studies. Thirdly, as a contribution to a new social science, Black Studies is critical and corrective of the inadequacies, omissions and distortions of traditional white studies. In fact, it is its severe and uncompromising critique that so disturbs its traditional critics who are secure in old assumptions from by-gone eras. Moreover, as a new discipline, Black Studies is not as restricted by old data and methods as white studies. It comes without the burden and baggage of sacred assumptions about society's righteousness and imperviousness to change and thus, it introduces generative ideas which are corrective to social science and stimulate innovation and deeper inquiry (Apter, 1977:36).

Moreover, Black Studies, as both an investigative and applied social science, poses the paradigm of theory and practice merging into active self-knowledge which leads to positive social change. In a word, it is a discipline dedicated not only to understanding self, society and the world but also to changing them in a positive developmental way in the interest of human history and advancement. In this quest, it challenges the false detachment of traditional white studies which contradicts reality and obscures clarity (Ladner, 1973; Hamilton, 1970).

A final expression of the relevance of Black Studies is its contribution to the development of a Black intelligentsia and professional stratum whose knowledge, social competence and commitment translate as a vital contribution to the liberation and development of the Black community and thus as a contribution to society as a whole. It is at this point that the academic and social missions of Black Studies merge most definitively and become an expression of knowledge self-consciously placed in the service of community, society and ultimately humankind. It is also an effective response to DuBois' (1969) call in his seminal essay, "The Talented Tenth," for the academic and social cultivation of a body of conscious, capable and committed men and women who would assume leadership of the Black community, set its ideals, directs its thoughts and aspirations and lead its social movements in the struggle for social change.

This goal of Black Studies, however, is also reflected in the educational philosophy of American universities which have historically structured curricula and instruction to produce the social servants and leaders society needs. Black Studies, then, as both an investigative and applied social science, follows that tradition. It simply focuses more intensely on a particular part of society, the Black community. And in this focus which seeks to create persons capable of critical thought and problem-solving, Black Studies not only benefits the Black community, but society as well. For in essence, the problems of the Black community are the problems of the larger society, and their collective solution is clearly in the larger society's interest.

SCOPE OF THE DISCIPLINE

The scope of Black Studies is expressed in its definition and by the parameters it has set for itself as an interdisciplinary discipline. *Black Studies, is the scientific study of the multidimensional aspects of Black thought and practice in their current and historical unfolding.* Thus, Black Studies is a social science and as all social sciences, it has its own particular focus on human relations and behavior. Whereas the economist is concerned with economic behavior and the political scientist with political behavior, Black Studies focuses its inquiry and analysis on Black thought and behavior. And since Black thought and practice (or behavior) is such an inclusive focus, Black Studies is compelled to be interdisciplinary, i.e., inclusive of and informed by many disciplines.

Black Studies, then, is both a particular and general social science and shares with the other social sciences similar foci of inquiry and analysis. It shares with political science the concern with the problems of gaining, maintaining and using power, especially as it relates to Blacks, and with economics, the concern of the relationship of race and class to economic opportunities and distributive inequalities. Likewise, Black Studies shares with psychology a critical concern with questions of identity, alienation, self-concept and mental health and development from a Black perspective, and with sociology, concern with social problems which range from crime, educational opportunities and race and class relations to interest group organization, family and male/female relations. Also, Black Studies shares with history a profound concern for critical interpretation of events, issues, important personages and social units of the past which illuminate understanding of current thought and practice and its concern for heritage and contribution to human advancement.

Black Studies, then, in sharing similar concerns with other social sciences draws from them and strives at an ongoing synthesis and utilization of the most incisive and productive theories, methods, techniques, models, strategies and research designs. Since it has come into being as a critique of and a corrective for traditional white studies, it is compelled to produce generative ideas to encourage new ways of thinking about and handling theoretical and practical problems. Thus, it is committed to challenging the old and developing new analytical frameworks for the study of the Black experience, new techniques for the continuous acquisition of knowledge and new criteria for the validation of claims both in and outside the discipline.

Black Studies, as an interdisciplinary social science allows for and encourages both a *specialized* and *integrative* approach to subject areas within the discipline. Such approach not only satisfies Kilson's (1973) concern that Black Studies students and teachers have a specialization in a traditional discipline, i.e., economics, political science, but also Daniel's (1981) concern that Black Studies maintain its autonomy as a valid and valuable discipline. It is obvious that Black Studies cannot and should not be subsumed under a traditional discipline. Therefore, both Jackson's (1970) suggestion to subordinate it to sociology and Ijere's (1972) suggestion to subsume it under economics are more discipline preferences than substantive recommendations for the development of the discipline. Likewise, if by "curricular control of an established discipline," Kilson means choosing one at the expense of Black Studies rather than as a subject area for specialization within the discipline of Black Studies, he too is incorrect and non-contributive to the developmental and autonomy demands of Black Studies.

Like all disciplines, Black Studies has subject areas of specialization which do not replace the discipline, but sharpen its focus in the given subject area. Thus, international relations, the study of parties and politics of developing countries do not replace political science as a discipline, but rather sharpen its focus in given subject areas. Moreover, each discipline is integrative as well as specialized. This is necessary to check excessive specialization which can make sublevels of research alien, narrow and even counterproductive to the holistic thrust of a given discipline. Therefore, Black Studies, while allowing and encouraging specialization in one or more subject areas, demands as a coherent discipline the linking of these subject areas within it to the overall principles and fundamental thrusts of the discipline.

Black Studies, then, as an interdisciplinary discipline has seven basic subject areas. These intradisciplinary foci which at first seem to be disciplines themselves are, in fact, separate disciplines when they are outside the discipline of Black Studies, but inside, they become and are essentially subject areas which contribute to a holistic picture and approach to the Black experience. Moreover, the qualifier Black, attached to each area in an explicit or implicit way, suggests a more specialized and delimited focus which of necessity transforms a broad discipline into a particular subject area. The seven basic subject areas of Black Studies then are: Black History; Black Religion; Black Social Organization; Black Politics; Black Economics; Black Creative Production (Black Art, Music and Literature) and Black Psychology.

This volume, then, is structured around these subject areas, for they represent core courses in most Black Studies programs and departments and thus serve as excellent foci for a survey course in Black Studies, i.e., a broad but substantive introduction to the discipline of Black Studies. Moreover, this conceptual framework is taken from *Kawaida* theory, a theory of cultural and social change which has as one of its main propositions, the contention that the solution to the problems of Black life demand critiques and correctives in the seven basic areas of culture (Karenga, 1980). These areas of culture are: mythology (religion), history, social organization, economic organization, political organization, creative motif and ethos. The categories of mythology, creative motif and ethos were changed to coincide with course titles, but the definition and analysis of these subject areas in this volume are essentially the same.

It should also be noted that Kawaida theory "defines culture in the broadest sense to equate it with all the thought and activity of a given people or society" and focuses on the seven areas of culture as core areas of analysis and problem-solving, or in Kawaida terms, of critiques and correctives (Karenga, 1980:16-17). The Kawaida seven-area focus and definition of culture obviously coincides with the core focus of Black Studies on the totality of Black thought and practice. The similarity would not appear as amazing and coincidental, if we remember Cruse's (1969:6-7) contention that the historical "demand for Black Studies...falls under the heading of the movement, tendency (and) ideology of 'Black cultural nationalism.'" This theoretical and practical thrust of Black cultural nationalism emerged among "young Black intelligentsia, young Black students and young Black activists" and was, as Cruse states, "in response to the feeling that at (that time) there (was) no viable intellectual approach to the problems facing both Blacks and whites in American society." Black Studies was then posed as a critical alternative intellectual approach to the development of critiques and correctives necessary to understanding and changing the Black community and the larger society. As the guiding theory of Black cultural nationalism and the Black Cultural Revolution of the 60's, then, Kawaida theory played a key role in the definition and defense of the foci and academic and social mission of Black Studies (Pinkney, 1976:Chapter 7).

In summing up, the scope of Black Studies as a discipline is the totality of historical and current Black thought and practice, but expresses itself most definitively in seven core subject areas: 1) Black History; 2) Black Religion; 3) Black Social Organization; 4) Black Politics; 5) Black Economics; 6) Black Creative Production (Black Art, Black Music and Black Literature); and 7) Black Psychology. As an interdisciplinary discipline concerned with the coherence and unity of its subject areas, Black Studies, of necessity, has core integrative principles and assumptions that serve as thematic glue which holds together these core subject areas. This volume, the survey approach it employs and the subject areas it includes are all given coherence and informed by four of these integrative principles and assumptions.

The first of these is that each subject area of Black Studies is a vital aspect and area of the Black experience and, therefore, contributive to the understanding and appreciation of its wholeness. Secondly, the truth of the Black experience is whole and thus, any partial and compartmentalized approach to it can only yield a partial and incomplete image and understanding of it. Thirdly, effectively integrated into the pattern of the discipline as a whole, each subject area becomes a microcosm of the macrocosm, the Black experience, which not only enriches our knowledge of the Black experience, but also enhances the analytical process and products of the discipline itself. Finally, all the subject areas mesh and intersect not only at the point of their primary focus, i.e., Black people in the process of shaping reality in their own image and interest, but also in their self-conscious commitment and contribution to the definition and solution of the social and discipline problems which serve as the core challenges to Black Studies.

STUDY QUESTIONS

1. What is Black Studies?
2. What were the four thrusts of the Student Movement of the 60's and the focus of each?
3. How was the Black Studies Movement a basic component of the Black liberation struggle?
4. What were the early academic and political concerns of the advocates of Black Studies?
5. What were the early objectives of Black Studies?
6. What are the six major contributions of Black Studies which establish its academic and social relevance?
7. What are some concerns Black Studies share with other social sciences?
8. How does Black Studies handle the question of specialized and integrative approaches to subject areas?
9. What are the seven core subject areas of Black Studies?
10. What are four fundamental integrative principles and assumptions which serve as thematic glue to hold the subject areas together?

REFERENCES

Allen, Robert. (1974) "Politics of the Attack on Black Studies," *The Black Scholar*, Vol. 6, 1 (September) 2-7.

Amin, Samir. (1974) *Accumulation on a World Scale: Critique of The Theory of Underdevelopment,* Vol. 1, New York: Monthly Review Press.

Apter, David. (1977) *Introduction to Political Science,* Cambridge, Mass.: Winthrop Publishers.

Bailey, Ronald. (1970) "Why Black Studies?", *The Education Digest,* 35, 9 (May) 46-48.

Blassingame, John. (1973) *New Perspectives on Black Studies,* Chicago: University of Illinois Press.

Brisbane, Robert. (1974) *Black Activism,* Valley Forge, Pa.: Judson Press.

Carson, Claybourne. (1981) *In Struggle: SNCC and the Black Awakening of the 60's,* Cambridge: Harvard University Press.

Cortada, Rafael. (1974) *Black Studies in Urban and Comparative Curriculum,* Lexington, Mass.: Xerox College Publishing.

Cruse, Harold. (1967) *Crisis of the Negro Intellectual,* New York: William Morrow Publishers.

_____. (1969) *Rebellion or Revolution?,* New York: William Morrow Publishers.

Daniel, Phillip T.K. (1980) "Black Studies: Discipline or Field of Study?", *The Western Journal of Black Studies,* 4, 3 (Fall) 195-199.

_____. (1981) "Theory Building in Black Studies," *The Black Scholar,* 12, 3 (May/June) 29-36.

Draper, Hal. (1965) *Berkeley: The New Student Revolt,* New York: Grove Press.

Dubois, W.E.B. (1961) *The Souls of Black Folk,* New York: Fawcett Publications, Inc.

——————. (1969) "The Talented Tenth" in *The Negro Problem*, (ed.) Ulysses Lee, New York: Arno Press and the New York Times.

Ford, Nick Aaron. (1973) *Black Studies: Threat or Challenge*, New York: Kennikat Press.

Frazier, E. Franklin. (1973) "The Failure of the Negro Intellectual," in *The Death of White Sociology*, (ed.) Joyce A. Ladner, New York: Vintage Books, pp. 52-66.

Frye, Charles A. (1978) *Towards a Philosophy of Black Studies*. San Francisco: R and E Research Associates.

Hamilton, Charles. (1970) "The Question of Black Studies," *Phi Delta Kappan*, 57, 7 (March) 362-364.

Hare, Nathan. (1969) "What Should be the Role of Afro-American Education in the Undergraduate Curriculum?", *Liberal Education*, 55, 1 (March) 42-50.

——————. (1972) "The Battle of Black Studies," *The Black Scholar*, 3, 9 (May) 32-37.

Ijere, Martin. (1972) "Whether Economics in a Black Studies Program?", *Journal of Black Studies*, 3, 2 (December) 149-165.

Jackson, John. (1980) *Introduction to African Civilizations*, Secaucus, N.J.: Citadel Press.

Jackson, Maurice. (1970) "Towards a Sociology of Black Studies," *Journal of Black Studies*, 1, 2 (December) 131-140.

Karenga, Maulana. (1977) "Corrective History: Reconstructing The Black Past," *First World*, 1, 3 (May/June) 50-54.

——————. (1980) *Kawaida Theory: An Introductory Outline*, Inglewood, Ca.: Kawaida Publications.

Kilson, Martin. (1973) "Reflections on Structure and Content in Black Studies," *Journal of Black Studies,* 1, 3 (March) 297-314.

Ladner, Joyce A. (ed.) (1973) *The Death of White Sociology,* New York: Vintage Books.

Lipset, Seymour and S. Wolin (eds.) (1965) *The Berkeley Student Revolt,* New York: Doubleday Anchor.

McEvoy, James and Abraham Miller. (1969) *Black Power and Student Rebellion,* Belmont, Ca.: Wadsworth Publishing, Co.

Pinkney, Alphonso. (1976) *Red, Black and Green: Black Nationalism in the United States,* Cambridge: Cambridge University Press.

Robinson, Armstead, et al. (1969) *Black Studies in the University,* New York: Bantam Books.

Stewart, James B. (1979) "Introducing Black Studies: A Critical Examination of Some Textual Materials," *Umoja,* 3, 1.

Turner, James and Eric W. Perkins. (1976) "Towards a Critique of Social Science," *The Black Scholar,* 7, 1 (April) 2-11.

Wright, Stephen. (1970) "Black Studies and Sound Scholarship," *Phi Delta Kappan,* (March) 365-368.

II
BLACK HISTORY

INTRODUCTION

Black Studies begins with the study of Black History for two basic reasons. First, the core task of Black Studies, which is shared by all the core subject areas, is the rescue and reconstruction of Black history and humanity. This rescue, i.e., freeing both Black history and humanity from alien hands, and reconstruction is a theoretical and practical project. In fact, the work done to achieve this central goal in the academic world is an indispensable requirement for and contribution to its achievement in the social world. For to rescue Black history is not only to free it from denial, deformation and destruction academically, but also to free it socially from the same negatives by freeing the people who are both its producers and products. Likewise, the reconstruction of Black history demands intervention not only in the academic process to redefine and reestablish the truth of Black history, but also intervention in the social process to reshape reality in Black images and interests and thus, self-consciously make history.

Furthermore, the academic and social rescue and reconstruction of Black history is a contribution to and indispensable part of the rescue and reconstruction of Black humanity. For history is the substance and mirror of a people's humanity in others' eyes as well as in their own eyes. It is, then, not only what they have done, but also a reflection of who they are what they can do, and equally important what they can become as a result of the past which reveals their possibilities.

Secondly, Black Studies also begins with Black History because it is relevant, even indispensable to the introduction and development of all the other subject areas. Black History places them in perspective, establishes their origins and development, and thus, aids in critical discussion and understanding of them. Moreover, each of the other subject areas of Black Studies teaches its own particular history which in turn is a part of general Black history. Black history, then, offers not only a broad framework for critically viewing and understanding Black people, but also a necessary background perspective for critical insights into other subject areas of Black Studies.

DEFINITION

The understanding and appreciation of Black History begins with the definition of history itself and then using that definition to define Black history and its relevance. History, then, is the struggle and record of humans in the process of humanizing the world, i.e., shaping it in their own image and interests. To shape the world in a human image is to give it a human form and character and to shape it in human interests is to make it serve humans rather than threaten, deform or destroy them. In a word, shaping the world in human image and interests is to make it a context which reflects and insures human defense, development and ultimate self-realization. African or Black History, then, is the struggle and record of Africans in the process of Africanizing the world, i.e., shaping it in their own image and interests. As a particular people, Africans shape the world in a particular way, i.e., they tend to Africanize it, or shape it in their own image and interests. This adds to the richness and beauty of human diversity and contributes to the overall effort of humans to transform the world from control by nature to control by humanity.

Put another way, then, history reveals itself as human practice directed in its diversity toward self-construction, social construction and world construction. For as a people builds itself, it builds a society it lives and develops in and this effort becomes a contribution to and a vital part of the overall human construction of the world. Thus, as Africans developed agriculture, medicine, science, etc., to defend and develop themselves, they built societies and civilizations which contributed to the overall humanization of the world and to the forward flow of human history (Jackson, 1980; Diop,1974; ben-Jochannan, 1972).

But history does not just happen nor is it the work of unseen forces. On the contrary, it is a process which is defined by five basic characteristics. First, it is human in the fullest and most diverse sense of the word. Secondly, it is social, by and about people in definite social situations, in a definite society in relation to others, themselves and nature. Third, it is conflictual, that is to say, full of contradictions, i.e., conflicts and struggle to solve conflicts. In fact, the motive force of history is struggle against four major oppositions, nature, society, others and self which will be discussed below. Fourthly, history is fluid and changeable, i.e., in constant movement. Finally, history is manageable, i.e., subject to controlled and directed change. Humans make history but not always in their own image. Only thru self-conscious intervention in the social and historical process can history be managed or self-consciously made.

Self-conscious intervention in the social and historical process is intervention in the structure and tendencies of society and the world. The motive force and shaper of history is struggle. Thus to make history, humans must struggle against four major oppositions: (1) nature; (2) society; (3) other humans; and (4) their immediate self. Even a cursory review of African history shows Africans in the process of solving these fundamental contradictions. The very battle to be human, to separate oneself from the animal kingdom is a struggle against nature. As the first humans, Africans began to humanize the world by controlling nature and breaking its hold on them (Clark, 1970). Thus, they discover fire, make tools, clothes, shelter, and devise ways to increase food. They collect seeds, learn the seasons, engage in cultivation, harness the Nile and use it for irrigation and call this science agriculture. They study disease and develop cures and call it medicine; they dig in the earth and discover and extract its resources and call it mining; they move beyond basic structure and build large temples and pyramids and create architecture; and they observe the stars, discover patterns and movements, name them and call this astronomy. As they engage in these activities, they reshape themselves, societies and the world, distinguish and distance themselves from the animal world and make true human history a reality.

The second major opposition humans face and must overcome continuously in making history is society or more precisely the limitations it imposes at various historical periods on the defense and development of human life. It is a fundamental paradox that society which is designed and built as a context for human freedom, defense and development often becomes a context for suppression, exploitation and oppression. In the long march toward human freedom, i.e., the absence of restraint and the capacity for rational self-determination, society has both impeded and aided progress toward this goal. In the constant struggle to shape society in a more human, i.e., freer and more positive image, humans have made bold strokes on the canvas of history. The struggle to break the priests' monopoly on knowledge and make it available to the masses, the struggle against dictatorship and to establish and maintain democracy, the struggle to establish science as superior to sacred and secular superstition and mythologies, are vivid and continuing examples. In Afro-American history, the struggle against society or more precisely society in its various oppressive forms of slavery, racism and capitalism has clearly been its motive force. In fact, the periodization of Black History is foci of struggle against social exploitation and oppression. The European slave trade and American slavery; reversal of Reconstruction and the rise of Jim Crow; lynchings and racism in education, employment and other areas of social life; powerlessness and police brutality are all categories not only of exploitative and oppressive social relations but foci of struggle against them.

But society is only context, other humans are actors who impose, exploit and oppress in that context. Thus at the heart of history is the struggle against others who threaten human life, freedom and development. Slavery is imposed by the slave master, racism by the racist, capitalism and colonialism by the capitalist and colonizer. The ruling ideas and dominant relations in any given society at any historical period are the ideas and relations of those who rule. This social grouping may be a ruling class or a ruling race or as in the USA and Azania (South Africa) a ruling race/class, i.e., made up of and exclusive to the ruling race in a society where race is a category of human worth and social status. Moreover, "others" could be other smaller social units like ethnic groups, political parties or interest groups who challenge and check, or exploit and oppress — or attempt them. And "others" could be other nations, whose nationalism deteriorates into pathological forms such as chauvinism, jingoism, apartheid, fascism, nazism, etc.

However, within this array of "others" who pose challenges contributive to making history, the struggle between classes and between nations (or races) are the most definitive struggles of history. Marxists argue that class struggle is the motive force of history (Bober, 1965). Black nationalists argue that it is the struggle of races and nations, two categories which are often used interchangeably (Williams, 1974). It is important to see however, that class struggle may or may not be the key struggle in every socio-historical setting and the same is true of racial or national struggles. Also, in the panoramic vastness of human history, it is, as argued at the outset, not just social struggle in and against society

which makes history, but four basic struggles, the four major oppositions we are discussing. In a word, it is struggle in its full diversity
which is the motive force of history, although a key struggle (race,
class, etc.) tends to express itself in any given socio-historical setting
(Rodney, 1974:89).

The final major opposition is the struggle of humans against
themselves, against their conception of themselves and their conditions and the possibilities they see in them. That which is seems
permanent and overwhelming. The human personality is often
prone toward submitting to or accepting the immediate. But history
is made when humans collectively and personally break beyond the
current concept of self and distinguish between actuality, that
which is; potentiality, that which can be; and reality, that which
ought to be and becomes when a person, people, society or thing
realizes itself, i.e., fulfills its inherent potential. The Dogon astrono-
mer who discovered Sirius B and C; the Ishongo mathematician
who devised the abacus; the Egyptian physician, Imhotep, who
founded the science of medicine and the Afro-American chemurgist, George Washington Carver, who created over 300 synthetic
and organic products out of the peanut, all reached beyond the
immediate, realized in part the unlimited potential of humankind,
and thus, advanced human history. Fundamental to understanding
this conception, then is to see reality as not being, but as *becoming*
and to see struggle as the motive force of both becoming and
history. For human essence is human possibility and history is the
process thru which that possibility is expressed and realized.

THE RELEVANCE OF HISTORY

History reveals itself as the key social science, the social
science on which all other social sciences depend. But as the mirror
and avenue of human struggle and progress, history has a special

relevance for Blacks which is rooted in its contribution to their intellectual and political emancipation. This contribution takes on its special meaning due to the challenge posed by gross denial, deformation and destruction of Black history as both a *record* and *process*. In a word, not only were records hidden, distorted and destroyed by the slaveholders and their descendants, but also the enslavement and oppression of Africans was an appropriation of their labor and, thus, the effective interruption of their struggle to transform the world in their own image and interests. This appropriation and interruption led to historical amnesia, i.e., loss of self-consciousness based on historical practice and achievement. For we know ourselves by what we have done and do and when our labor is no longer ours and there are no records to reveal our true identity based on historical origin and practice as a people, how do we define and know ourselves?

History, then, becomes the mirror thru which we look to discover and know ourselves and our possibilities. It is in this context that history, as social science, and Black history as a people-specific form of it, contributes to the intellectual and political emancipation of Blacks in five basic ways: (1) as a source of self-understanding; (2) as a source of understanding of society and world; (3) as a measure of a people's humanity; (4) as a corrective for racist self-indulgent myths; and (5) as a source of models to emulate (Karenga, 1980:33-34).

History, therefore, is first of all, a source of self-understanding for Blacks in three basic ways. First, it is a solution to the identity question in terms of historical origin and achievement. That is to say, it eliminates the historical amnesia imposed by slavery and expressed in the myriad of names Blacks in the U.S. call themselves instead of African or Afro-American, i.e., Negro, Colored, Ethiopian, Moors, American, Creole, Bilalian, mixed, or just human. History inevitably points to Africa as the place of origin of Blacks and thus clearly reveals they are African people, heirs of an unsurpassed historical legacy which effectively ends the need to try to identify with others' achievement thru renouncing oneself.

Secondly, history gives Blacks an understanding of themselves by suggesting possibilities of future national and world achievement based on what they have achieved in the past. In other words, history reveals what and who they can become based on what they have been and have done in the past. Finally, Black history is a source of self-understanding in that it reveals the particularity and uniqueness of Black people based on their unique contribution to human history and development. This uniqueness lies not only in the fact of each people's particular way of contributing to the forward flow of human history, but also in the fact that Blacks are the fathers and mothers of human history and human civilization. They, thus, occupy a unique place in human history; and Black history, more than any other history, reveals and affirms this.

A second relevance of history is that it is a source of understanding of society and the world. History which leads to a focus on the origins and development of things demystifies claims of permanence by the established order. It demonstrates clearly that what comes into being goes out of being, that projection of permanence is a characteristic defense mechanism of social orders and that only change is permanent. Thus, history reveals that if Egypt came into being and went out of being, and if Carthage, Zimbabwe, Ghana, Mali, Songhai, the British Empire and the would-be-thousand-year Reich came into being and went out of being, so then can the current American order of things. Moreover, history reveals the contradictions and tendencies and therefore the possibilities of a given context. In the case of the U.S., history shows the development and direction of class, race and sexual contradictions and the struggles these engender and thus suggests their contribution to the possibilities of social change.

Also, history is a source of understanding of society and the world by indicating where a people fit in the social and world scheme of things. In the case of Blacks, history shows their essential role in the progressive liberalization of society. It is they, more than any other ethnic group, who have historically "provided the U.S. with an essential theoretical and practical self-criticism," forced it into self-knowledge and social change thru struggle and pushed it toward the realization of its original claims of freedom and justice to all (Karenga, 1977). Finally, history shows that there are two tides to history, that tide which is rising coming into being and growing stronger and that which is dying, decaying and passing away. History clearly reveals that Third World people, i.e., peoples of color, of which Blacks are an undeniable part, are that rising tide of history, stepping back on the stage of human history as a free, proud and productive people. Likewise, it becomes obvious thru history that the Western order of things is unravelling and will eventually give way.

A third relevance of history is that it is a measure of a people's humanity. History and humanity are inseparably linked. Both a people's perception of itself and others' perception of it are tied to the history they have and make. In fact, Europe declared that the more history you have, the more human you are and then set out to claim all relevant history and deny Blacks any. Thus, Europe moved Egypt, culturally and racially, from Northern Africa to Southern Europe, even though Diop (1974), Williams (1974) and historical evidence argue otherwise. It is a fundamental fact that only humans have history and when Europe could claim without effective challenge during slavery and the colonization of African peoples and lands that Blacks had no history, they could and did also claim Blacks were not human. For to be denied historical achievement is to be placed outside of humanity, for only humans make history. The need, then, became one of rescuing and reconstructing Black history as a basis for and contribution to the rescue and reconstruction of Black humanity. For our historical and social practice identifies us, declares or denies our greatness and establishes our capacity to make progress and contribute to the forward flow of human history. This is why Egypt, whose greatness and contribution to human history is undeniable, becomes a point of struggle between African and European historians. Therefore, Diop (1974:xiv, xvi) states that the history of Africa "will remain suspended in air and cannot be written correctly until African historians dare to connect it with the history of Egypt." Once Egypt then is recognized as a Black civilization and united with the rest of African history, then and only then "The history of humanity will become clear and the (true) history of Africa can be written."

A fourth relevance of history is that it is an obvious corrective for the self-indulgent myths of racism. History is corrective in that it "a) challenges and disproves racist myths of Black non-achievement; b) imposes a racial modesty on whites, especially racists, by doing this; and c) gives fullness and thus truth to world history by identifying the real fathers and mothers of humanity and human civilization" and their continuing contributions (Karenga, 1980:33-34). Europe and her descendants who have claimed to have "discovered" all major knowledge and everyone outside Europe are clearly forced into a sense of racial modesty upon reading Diop's (1974) treatise on the African origin of civilization, or James' (1976) well-documented revelation that the Africans (Egyptians), not Greeks, were the authors of "Greek" philosophy. It is in this spirit that Diop (1974:xiv) states that a reading of Black history will show that "Instead of presenting itself to history as an insolvent debtor, (the) Black world is the very initiator of 'western' civilization."

Finally, history's relevance rests also in its serving as a source of models to emulate. This expresses itself in three basic ways. First, "it offers a subversive content, i.e., ideas, images and events that overturn our current concept of self, society and the world and gives examples which are necessary alternatives" to the established state of things (Karenga, 1980:34). In a word, history is an alternative view of reality imposed by immediate circumstances. For example, the racist and reductive image of Black women on TV is challenged and overturned by the historical images of Mary McLeod Bethune (NEA, 1974), Fannie Lou Hamer (Kling, 1979) and Harriet Tubman (Petry, 1955; Conrad, 1943) who dared to shape social reality into the image and interests of Black people. Likewise, the equally racist and reductive images of Black men on TV are countered and subverted by historical images of Black men from Martin Delaney and David Walker thru Garvey and Malcolm X (Bracey, et al, 1970).

As a logical consequence of the above, history also serves as a source of models to emulate in that it teaches possibilities. As Garvey (1977) argued, what humans have done humans can do. Thus, alternative images of daring, social construction and struggle demonstrate the concrete possibilities of such positive and proactive practice. Finally, history in offering models to emulate, not only presents images which subvert the immediate and teaches alternatives to it, but also inspires. "For to witness greatness and daring is to be aware of its possibility and desirability and be infused with its spirit." (Karenga, 1980:34).

AFRICAN BACKGROUND
INTRODUCTION

The history of Blacks, humans and human civilization began in Africa (Clark, 1970; Jackson, 1980; Williams, 1974; DuBois, 1965). Three major factors, however, have combined to obscure this fact and make the study and writing of African history problematic. The first factor is the vastness of the subject. African history is the history of a continent in flux and in contact and exchange with the world, and one can easily assume, especially given the Eurocentric thrust and character of most histories of Africa, that others rather than Africans gave rise to Africa's many contributions to the forward flow of human history. As Williams (1974:33) remarked, "African history is complex and many-sided, and would be so (even) if we were discussing just one nation and not an entire continent." Thus, without the time or inclination to do the necessary research one ends up repeating what was written before in the image and interests of Europeans. An example of this is the tendency to pass along the French and English translations which call the founders of Ghana "white" (Gailey, 1970) although further investigation shows they were referred to as "red" or "reddish brown" by the people of the region (Fage, 1969:8).

Secondly, the study of African history is complicated by the predominance of oral history in many places as the most definitive African perspective on the subject. The hieroglyphic, heractic and Demotic scripts of Egypt, the Meroitic scripts of Kush, the Sabean and Ge'ez scripts of Ethiopia, the Coptic script of Nubia, and Arabic scripts of Western Sudan and North Africa tend to be exceptions rather than the rule in terms of the existence of scripts providing a basis for a written history. Although Europeans most likely duplicated destructions of documents in other parts of Africa, as in the burning of the library at Alexandria, Egypt by the Romans in 48 B.C.E. (before the Christian Era) and by the Christians in 389 C.E. (in the Christian Era), in most parts of Africa, sources of history were essentially griots, a class of professional oral historians. It was their task to act as the collective memory of a ethnic group, nation or empire and pass on from generation to generation the history of its people. But whereas it is intellectually impressive to remember hundreds of years of key figures, phenomena and processes, it is also a vulnerable form of record keeping. For this "Heritage of the Ears," as the Hova of Madagascar call it, is subject not only to the problems of retention and repetition, but also to the unexpected deaths of the keepers (McCall, 1969:38-62).

Thirdly, and perhaps the most important of the problems of studying African history, is the European conquest of Africa and all that it meant to African history as both record and process. As suggested above, one cannot deny that Europeans destroyed many documents in Africa as well as other evidences of African presence and achievement (Williams, 1974; ben-Jochannan, 1971). Moreover, European scholars often denied the value and authenticity of documents and/or their data, if it did not coincide with what they believed or wanted others and themselves to believe. The record of so-called egyptologists in this matter has been documented by Diop (1974). As Diop (1974:168) states, they operated on this principle, "Given what I've been taught about (Blacks), even if the evidence proves objectively that civilization was created by the said Blacks...it must be wrong."

Finally, with the conquest of Africa by Europe came the attempt also to Europeanize or "Caucasize" all important achievements and deny African presence and accomplishments. James (1976) points this out in his book on the stolen legacy of Egyptian philosophy for which the Greeks are given credit. Diop (1974) shows how Egypt's entire civilization is claimed by whites thru falsification of history, discounting contrary evidence, and arguing racial and racist theories inapplicable to the ancient world. Also, Jackson (1980) shows how the Moors who aided in the civilizing of Europe are Caucasized and Arabized to deny their Blackness. And then there are the useful mythical "Hamites" who are trotted out, whenever others are unavailable, to serve as founders of any civilization when it is important to deny its African origins (Fage, 1969:6-10). However, inspite of these obstacles, significant evidence of African genius and creativity still shine thru and provide us with strong foundation for the rescue and reconstruction of Black history and humanity. Given the vastness of the subject, however, this text can in no way be exhaustive or comprehensive. What it will seek to do then is offer some of the many significant models of

African political formations and achievements which tend to counter the racist lies and affirm the world historical achievement and
significance of African civilization. More detailed and comprehensive treatment of African history can be found in the books cited as
references. The student is thus encouraged to explore them, for the
exploration will be most informative and engaging.

THE ORIGINS IN EAST AFRICA

Inspite of religious and secular myths which attempt to place
human origins at five to six thousands years ago in Mesopotamia,
anthropology cites it as about 2,000,000 years ago in East Africa.
Archeologist, L.S.B. Leakey, discovered remains of *homo habilis*
whom he classified as the direct ancestor of true humans, based on
his body structure, toolmaking ability, brain capacity and erect
carriage. Another hominid, Zinjanthropus, lived concurrently with
homo habilis, but there is question about whether he is in the direct
line of descent to humans.

It was about 35,000 years ago, however, that homo sapiens or
modern humans appeared and began to lay the basis for true
human civilization. It is at this point that humans began to diversify
activities from the early total preoccupation with survival and
engage in art and religious reflection. At about 10,000 years ago,
humans began to establish cultivation as an alternative to hunting
and gathering, thus allowing even more time to lay a basis for
expanded cultural development. It is estimated that about this
time, 8,000 B.C.E, that Egypt rose from the waters of the Nile and its
lakes and marshes; and thus the basis of habitation and cultivation
was established.

THE RISE OF ETHIOPIA AND EGYPT

Jackson (1980), Diop (1974) and Williams (1974) all argue
cogently that Egypt's origin is in Ethiopia. DuBois (1965:117ff)

agrees stating that "In Ethiopia the sunrise of human culture took place, spreading down into the Nile Valley. Ethiopia, the land of the Blacks, was thus the cradle of Egyptian civilization." In the earliest times, DuBois continues, "the Ethiopians looked upon themselves as the source of Egypt and declared according to Diodorus Siculus that Egyptian laws and custom were of Ethiopian origin." In fact, "The Egyptians themselves in later days affirmed that their civilization came out of the south."

Moreover, DuBois (1965:101) states that "the civilization of Egypt began with their invention of the fixing of a calendar, 4241 B.C.E. Jackson (1980:95), however, suggests that it started about eight to ten thousand years B.C.E. Although there are questions surrounding the exact dates of Egypt's origin, the date of 3200 B.C.E. is generally accepted as the date of the unification of the two kingdoms, Upper and Lower Egypt by Aha Mena (Menes, Narmer), a king from Upper Egypt, i.e., the South. This again shows the African origin and cultural thrust of Ancient Egypt. Aha Mena's unification of Egypt marked the beginning of a dynastic era that lasted over 3,000 years during which about three hundred and thirty Pharoahs reigned. Egypt's first and most impressive golden age was initiated by an Ethiopian Pharoah Zoser, who founded the Third Dynasty in 2980 B.C.E. and it culminated in the building of the Great Pyramid at Gizeh by Pharoah Khufu (Cheops). This golden age stretched from 2980 to about 2475 in the Sixth Dynasty, a period of about five hundred years and was the period of the Old Kingdom. It was during the reign of Zoser that great achievements were initiated. and that Imhotep, his prime minister, built him the first of the Great Pyramids. Imhotep was an intellectual giant, whose expertise was in the areas of architecture, political administration, priesthood, astronomy, literature, philosophy and medicine. In addition to prime minister, he held the post of Chief Physician to the Pharoah, and can be rightly called the father of medicine. In his time, Egyptians had diagnosed, treated and cata-

logued over 200 diseases, were conducting surgery and ausculta-
tion and knew of the circulation of the blood. (Rogers, 1972:38-42).

Also during the Old Kingdom, Egypt left other legacies to
humankind. Egypt brought the world, among other things a
calendar, mathematics, astronomy, the alphabet, paper, ink, pen,
geography, literature, art, surgery and magnificent and monumental architecture, represented in the pyramids, which have astronomical, mathematic and scientific value (Jackson, 1980). Yet in
considering all these achievements, it is important to remember
DuBois' (1965:103) contention that the "first great experiment in
human civilization" rose out of African problem-solving, out of the
need to shape their world in their own image and interest. "The
history of civilization which began in Egypt was not so much a
matter of dynasties and dates," DuBois states. Rather, "It was an
attempt to settle the problems of living together-of government,
defense, religion, family, property, science and art." Therefore, to
meet the challenges of nature and society, "African Egypt...made
the beginning and set the pace...in these seven lines of human
endeavor."

WESTERN SUDANIC CIVILIZATION

GHANA. Ghana emerged as a state in approximately 300 C.E. It
reached its height in the eleventh century and came to an effective
political end in 1240. As early as 773-4 C.E., the Muslim author
Al-Fazari wrote of Ghana, calling it the Land of Gold. Also, other
Muslim writers wrote of Ghana and its wealth and importance to
the trans-Saharan trade. Among these were al-Yaqubi in the ninth
century, al-Mas'udin and Ibn Hawqal in the tenth century. But the
most definitive report of the early Muslim writers was *The Description of North Africa* (1067) written by al-Bakri, a Moor who lived in
the Moorish empire in Spain and was also a geographer. However,

two West African Muslims, Mahmud Kati who wrote Tarikh al-Fattach (*History of the Seeker After Knowledge*) and Abdal Rahaman who wrote Tarikh as-Sudan (*History of the Sudan*) also wrote on Ghana, as well as on the other Sudanic civilizations.

From al-Bakri's report and other sources, we know that Ghana's wealth was a result of the control of trade in two key items —salt and gold. Strategically located along routes of the trans-Saharan trade, Ghana controlled the flow of trade and levied import and export taxes on the traders. Ghana controlled two main routes which stretched north to Morocco and Libya and West to the Bornu region near Lake Chad which tied in with the Nile Valley trade (Harris, 1972:51). Moreover, the report reveals that Ghana's capital city, Kumbi Saleh, had two sections to it —one for the King or Tunka and Ghanaian people and the other for the Muslim traders.

Tunka Menin, the king at the time, circa 1065, was an absolute monarch with an elaborate court of counselors, ministers, interpreters and a treasurer. Much revered, he held court with impressive splendor often ruling on great and small matters. Moreover, he maintained a large standing army of 200,000 and more than 40,000 were bowmen. To gauge how impressive and politically powerful this was, one can remember that about this time, the Norman army which conquered England in 1066 was only 15,000 strong. Recognizing the rise of Islam and Muslim popularity in his empire, Tunka Menin showed political and economic wisdom by appointing several Muslims as ministers, treating the rest justly and allowing them to practice their religion freely. This not only contributed to peace in the empire, but received the economic benefit of good relations and increased trade with the North.

The trans-Saharan trade was brisk and varied passing thru towns like Walata, Kumbi Saleh, Tichitl and Awdaghost. From the North, traders brought salt, daggers, silk, jewelry, time pieces and fine cloth and from other parts of the Sudan, they brought bars of iron, gold, leather, cotton, kola nuts, shea butter, millet and sorghum. At the peak of its empire, Ghana contained a population of several million and territory of about 250,000 square miles. Its imperial might rested on the 200,000 man army, its control of trade and the revenues from it, as well as good political administration which was able to keep revolts at a minimum and put them down when and if they occurred. In 1076, religious reformers called the Almoravids led a Berber army which captured Kumbi Saleh. By 1087, however, they had lost control of the empire and Ghana disintegrated into smaller states, laying the basis for the rise of Mali.

MALI. The empire of Mali has its roots in the state of Kangaba, a small state which was part of the Ghana Empire. The first Malian emperor was Sundiata, who defeated his rivals, established his rule approximately 1230 and reigned until his death in 1255. During this time, he took control of the trans-Saharan trade and set up Niani, his capital as a key trading and financial center. He also turned his attention to agriculture, transforming many of his soldiers who now had no wars to fight into farmers. This attention to agriculture paid off in a few years and Mali established itself as one of the richest farming areas in West Africa.

Mali's most illustrious and well-known emperor was Mansa (emperor) Musa who came to the throne in 1312 and ruled until 1332. In his brief reign, he built Mali into one of the world's largest empires and his fame spread thruout the Muslim world and Europe. Conquering most of the major Berber cities of the western desert, Musa extended Mali into what is now Mauritania and southern Algeria in the north, and as far south as northern Nigeria to establish contact with the Hausa states. By the time of his death, he had made Mali twice the size of Ghana with a population of approximately ten million.

Mansa Musa is best known, however, for his famous *hajj* or pilgrimage to Mecca in 1324. With him he took 60,000 persons, many of them soldiers, baggage men, and royal secretaries to record this momentous trip. Also included were friends, doctors, teachers and local political leaders. To finance the trip, Musa took 80-100 camel loads of gold dust. Passing thru Cairo, he was honored and given royal assistance from the Sultan of Cairo for the remainder of his trip. In Mecca and Medina, he gave gifts generously and on his return trip he passed thru Cairo again giving out so much gold, he depressed the price of gold in Egypt. One writer in the service of the Sultan stated that it took twelve years for the Egyptian economy to recover from Musa's generosity with gold.

Musa went thru Cairo, Mecca, Medina and Tripoli and brought back many Muslim scholars, jurists, architects and other skilled men among them African scholars from the University of Fez, Morocco. This had a tremendous impact on the development of African civilization. Among the master architects who returned with Musa was as-Saheli, a Moor from Granada who was also a poet. As-Saheli built many buildings in Mali, especially mosques and a palace for Musa. Most importantly, however, he built the University of Sankore at Timbuktu that became an intellectual center which attracted students and professors from all over the Muslim world. Also Musa encouraged learning, building many Koranic schools which taught reading and writing especially of the Quran. In addition, he sent ambassadors to Egypt and Morocco and representatives to many North African and Sudanic cities and the forest kingdoms near the Coast.

Mansa Musa laid the basis for European recognition and respect of Africa below the Sahara during that time. European scholars and traders were aware of his empire and in 1375 Charles V of France had an atlas drawn showing "Rex Melli" or "Musa Mali" in the area of West Africa wearing robes and a crown and holding a gold nugget in one hand and a scepter in the other.

Mansa Musa left a strong impression on the African, Muslim and European world and a strong empire so that even when Mali was in decline in 1494, the Portuguese sought and established diplomatic relations and exchanged ambassadors with Mali. Mali began to decline in 1400 and in 1468, Songhai began its rise.

SONGHAI. The largest and greatest of the Western Sudanic civilizations was Songhai. Songhai's foundation was laid by Sunni (Sonni) Ali Ber who came to the throne in 1464 and recaptured Timbuktu in 1468 from Mali, the year usually fixed as the beginning of the Empire. Sunni Ali was described by as-Sadi, author of Tarikh al-Sudan, *(History of the Sudan),* as a brutal and fierce tyrant. "Sunni" was the title of Ali's dynasty and "Ber" means "the Great," a name established thru fierce and uncompromising conquest by this warrior-king. During the twenty-eight years of his reign, he was always at war and on the march, defeating all challengers and strengthening his army thru a systematic build up of his calvary. He even drafted soldiers from vassal states and built a navy of war canoes which sailed the Niger. By the time of his death, he had consolidated and greatly expanded his empire and laid the basis for the renowned glories of Songhai.

The most illustrious emperor of Songhai was Muhammad Toure, a distinguished general who served in Sunni Ali's army. Muhammad, who bore the title Askia (general), showed himself an able administrator as well as general. Ruling from 1493-1529, he built an effective army out of POW's and ex-slaves whom he freed and put into service to the empire. He based his administration on Islamic law, built a support system among the learned and the wealthy urbanites of Gao, Jenne and Timbuktu and surrounded himself with professionals in law and administration to insure uniform justice in the empire.

It is Askia Muhammad, also called Askia the Great, who built the largest empire in the history of West and Central Africa. DuBois

(1975:47-48) states that Askia Muhammad "during his reign conquered and consolidated an empire two thousand miles long by one thousand miles wide at its greatest extent — a territory as large as all Europe." He divided this great empire into a series of provinces and appointed professional administrators as governors. Emulating Mansa Musa of Mali, Askia Muhammad made a spectacular hajj to Mecca in 1495. With him he took 300,000 pieces of gold which he used for expenses, gifts and purchases. At Mecca, he was appointed as Caliph of the Western Sudan by the Sharif of Mecca, who was the spiritual ruler of all Islam. This had both political and religious ramifications, for it gave him claim to allegiance of all Muslims westward to the Atlantic. It also put him in a united front against the encroaching Christians and cemented his conquests and economic relations with the Muslim world.

Askia Muhammad is also responsible for a flowering of intellectual achievement. In Gao, Jenne and Timbuktu, many universities and schools were established. In the universities were taught philosophy, medicine, law, government, astronomy, math, literature, ethnography, hygience, logic, rhetoric, grammar, geography, music and poetry writing. Scholars and students from other parts of Africa, Asia, the Muslim world and Europe visited the universities for study and exchange. One of the famous scholars at the University of Sankore at Timbuktu was professor Ahmad Baba, who was a faculty member, an author of forty books on such diverse fields as astronomy, ethnography, biography and theology, Islamic law, and owner of a library of 1600 volumes (Jackson, 1980:217). So enduring are his works that thirteen of them are still used in parts of West Africa. This was also the time of the famous *Tarikhs* (Histories) of Western Sudanic civilization by Mahmud Kati and Abdul-Rahman as-Sadi.

In 1528, Askia the Great, who was now blind, was deposed by his son Musa, ending a brilliant and enlightened reign. The empire saw few dramatic developments after this reign and due to weak leadership, revolts sprang up and continuously increased. Finally, in 1591 a Moroccan army, led by a Spanish Christian and composed of captured Christians, Spanish Muslims and Moroccans, set out to attack and sack Songhai. The fire power of the army, which had lost many of its members crossing the Sahara, prevailed and the Songhai troops retreated down the Niger. Although the Moroccans held the main cities, they could not hold the empire, for Songhai troops continuously harrassed them with guerilla warfare. Eventually, the empire disintegrated into city states and the Moroccans were assimilated in the indigenous populace. Songhai, the greatest and largest empire of the Western Sudanic civilization had thus come to an end.

THE MOORISH EMPIRE IN SPAIN

In his *Introduction to African Civilizations,* John Jackson (1980) devotes a chapter to "Africa and the Civilizing of Europe." In it he builds a strong case for Europe's debt to Africans, namely Moors, who pulled the Spaniards out of the Bleak Ages (500-1000 C.E.) which they call the "Dark Ages" and gave them a civilization no other country in Europe had at the time, but from which all Europe would eventually borrow. The Moorish conquest and civilizing of Spain began in 711. In that year, Tarik, a Moorish general, landed in Spain near a cliff later named Jebel Tarik, the Rock or Mountain of Tarik, i.e., Gibraltar, in his honor. After conquering some towns near Gibraltar, Tarik met and defeated Roderick, King of the Visigoths in Spain at the Battle of Xeres. This marked the beginning of Spain's golden age which she has never since duplicated (McCabe, 1935; Lane-Poole, 1886). The Moors brought Spain and thus Europe several gifts from African creativity and inventiveness, including agriculture, engineering, mining, industry, manufacturing, expanded commerce, beautiful skilled architecture and education and scholarship.

In agriculture, the Moors brought new products, but also skill and literature in the field. They introduced rice, strawberries, cotton, sugar cane, ginger, lemons and dates. Ibn-al-Awam and Abu Zacaria produced scholarly works on agriculture and husbandry. As late as 1802, Ibn-al-Awam's treatise on agriculture was being translated and used in Spain. As first-rate engineers, the Moors built Spain its aqueduct system for irrigation, its reservoirs for water, underground silos for grain, tunnels thru mountains, raised sidewalks, lighted paved streets and dams. They also built a sewer system and artificial lakes to beautify cities. In the areas of mining and manufacturing, they mined gold, silver, copper, tin, lead, iron and alum and made luxury and utilitarian items out of these and brass. In addition, the Moors were respected for their fine jewelry, mosaics, pottery and glass work, tile and fine silk and cotton products. It is, in fact, the Moors who introduced cotton manufacture to Europe. Finally, Jackson (1980:188) states that also "the Moors introduced the manufacture of gunpowder into Europe." Given this economic boom, the Moors also engaged in shipbuilding and expanded trade. This maritime commerce on the Mediterranean by the Moors and other Muslims was greater than that of the Christians and maintained its dominance up to the 12th century.

In terms of architecture, the Moors built structures not simply for use, but equally for aesthetic value. Their arches, courtyards and gardens are reflected in the architecture of California and the Southwest with its so-called Spanish motif. Actually, its Moorish motif passed on thru the Spanish to the Mexicans from whom the white Americans borrowed it. In Cordova alone in the 10th century, there were 200,000 homes, 10,000 palaces of the wealthy and many royal palaces with exquisitely designed gardens. Also, there were 900 beautiful public baths and many private ones at a time when the rest of Europe considered bathing self-indulgent and a sin.

Finally, in terms of education and scholarship, the Moors were equally impressive in stature and contribution. At a time when even European kings could not read or write, and 99% of Christian Europe was illiterate, the Moors made education universal. And in the 10th and 11th centuries when Europe had no public libraries and only two significant universities, the Moors gave Spain more than 70 public libraries, built Spain seventeen famous universities and established an observatory at Seville. According to Rocker (1937:412), astronomy, physics, chemistry, geometry, philology, geography and math were taught at these universities. Also, artists and scholars formed professional associations and held regular conferences "where the latest achievements of research were announced and discussed which naturally contributed greatly to the spread of scientific thought."

In addition to the subjects listed above, trigonometry, botany and history were taught in the university where students from Africa, the Middle East and Europe flocked. Lane-Poole (1886) reports that even women were encouraged to engage in serious study and that there were women doctors. Jackson (1980:181) states that Moroccan science and scholarship were an integral part of the overall Muslim cultural achievement which produced advances in math, algebra, physics and astronomy. He points out that approximately 400 years before Magellan's trip in 1519 established for Europe that the world was round, Moors taught it in geography classes using a globe. In fact, El Idrisi, a Moor, wrote a book in the mid-twelfth century observing that according to astronomers and other learned men and philosophers, "the world is round as a sphere." He also suggested a concept of gravity, stating in his book that the earth draws "to itself all that is heavy in the same way as a magnet attracts iron."

By 1492, the Moorish empire in Spain came to an end with the fall of Granada. This was almost an 800 year Moorish reign of culture and science which developed Spain as no other European country. For a brief while Spain tried to maintain her cultural standards and progress. Isabella and Ferdinand had used the wealth from Granada to finance Columbus' voyage to America where he found Blacks had already preceded him (Van Sertima, 1976:11). And then there was a push for trade and exploration in the New World which was no doubt aided by Moorish and other Muslim navigational experience and knowledge (Parry, 1966: Chapter 1). But as Lane-Poole (1886:vii-ix) observed, "this was but a last halo about the dying moments of a (once) mighty state." What followed was the vulgarity and unbridled violence of the Christian Inquisition, a condemnation of science, closing of universities and libraries with not one public library in Madrid in the 18th century, the decrease by four-fifths of the number of looms in Seville, destruction of the baths in the hysterical drive against imagined sin, deterioration of the irrigation and decline of agricultural production and decay in general. It is important that this assessment was made by Europeans, not Africans so that no claim of "sour grapes" or non-objectivity can be seriously made. And it's interesting to note that after all the commentaries on and claims about the tragedy that would descend on Africans if and when Europeans left Africa, it was a major European state, Spain, that deteriorated after Africans left. Such is the irony and severe instruction of history.

OTHER STATES AND EMPIRES

There are numerous other states, empires and ethnic-nations which need to be studied by serious students of African history. Among these are the ancient empires of Ethiopia Kush, Nubia and Axum in the North East (El Madhi, 1965; Pankhurst, 1967; Shinnie, 1967). Secondly, there are the Hausa states and the Kanem-Bornu empire in the Western Sudan (Ajayi and Epsie, 1972; Trimingham, 1962). Thirdly, there are the West African states and empires — Ife, Oyo, Benin, Dahomey and the Akan states and empires of Ashanti and Fante (Murdock, 1959; Davidson, 1966). Fourthly, there are Central African states — Kongo, Luba and Lunda (Collins, 1968; Vansina, 1968); and the lake states of Bunyoro and Buganda (Oliver, 1963; Beattie, 1960). Finally, there are the southeastern and southern states and empires, the Omani Sultanate, the civilization of Zimbabwe (The Mutapa Empire) and the Zulu Empire (Davidson, 1959, 1967; Oliver and Mathews, 1963; Vilakazi, 1962; Omer-Cooper, 1966). These, however, are but selective examples of the rich variousness of African history and the struggle for self, social and world construction it represents.

THE FALL OF AFRICAN SOCIETIES

Invariably students of Black Studies raise the question of why did Africa with all its glory and achievement fall to the European advance. There are several reasons, but before we treat them, we should put the question in historical perspective with three fundamental observations. First of all, one should know that all civilizations, regardless of how great they are or seem, eventually decline for various internal and external reasons. Egypt, Ethiopia, Rome, Greece, Ghana, Mali, Songhai, and of late the British, French and American empires all suffered this tendency. So it should not be seen as a special weakness or oddity that the civilizations of Africa eventually declined and fell to the onslaught of Europe. Secondly, it should be noted that the conquest and colonization of Africa took over 400 hundred years, from mid 1400's to the end of the 1800's which culminated in the partition of Africa. Thruout this time, Africans continuously resisted and won many battles and wars against the Europeans. Queen Nzingha of Angola's long war with the Portuguese; Samory Toure of the Western Sudan's ongoing war with the French, the Zulu nation's defeat of the British at the Battle of Isandlwana, 1896; Menelik's defeat of the Italians at the Battle of

Adua, 1898; the Asante's long wars with the British and the Mahdi of Eastern Sudan's victories in the Sudan are but a few examples of African resistance and victories (Ajayi and Epsie, 1972; Rogers, 1972 Vol. I). In fact, as suggested above, Europe first came to Africa as an equal and sometimes as an inferior on the cultural and political power level. The exchange of ambassadors between Portugal and Mali, the Moorish domination of Spain and superiority in science and scholarship to all Europe and the tribute and tax paid to kings and local rulers, all show an early deference and often higher level of culture of Africans at that time.

As July (1970:168) points out, the city-states of the Niger Delta offer another strong example of resistance to European penetration and of control of exchange by Africans. Although the Europeans built forts for stability, defense and as a launching base, "at first they gained no more than a minimum foothold for their garrisons remained by sufferance, unable to either exert political authority outside their walls or to enforce their desired trade monopoly." In fact, local leaders "characteristically extracted payment of tariffs, fines and rents while refusing traders access to the interior-,...maintaining control over the inland trade." July argues that a typical situation was related by a European agent who reported the authority and power of the Fante who neither the English or Dutch "dare oppose...for fear of being ruined themselves." Finally, July states that perhaps "the degree of tenacity in opposition to European penetration was best exemplified by John Conny," a political leader of the then Gold Coast (Ghana) of the early 18th century. He fought off the Dutch for seven years when they attacked to take his fort and negotiated a settlement "only after seven years of combined diplomatic and military pressure."

Finally, to discuss critically the fall of Africa one must realize that Africa did not fall; separate empires, states, nations and ethnic groups were eventually conquered and colonized. To talk of Africa as if it were a self-conscious political unit rather than mostly a geographical fact with various cultural similarities is to obscure the reality and damage clarity. Africa did not fall with the defeat of the Asante and Zulu empires nor with the conquest of the Hausa states or the Sudan. There was no capital or central government for Africa. Africa was a continent in itself, but not self-consciously for itself. Only with the rise of Pan-Africanism did the peoples of Africa begin to see and define themselves as one. This was to Europe's advantage, but still the conquest and colonization of Africa proved to be a 400 year project which ended in great part in less than seventy-years as a result of the African independence struggles. Thus, it might be better to rephrase the question and ask, not why Africa fell, but rather what factors led to Europe's temporary conquest and colonization of African societies?

With these observations in mind, one can begin to answer the question by citing Europe's technological advantage. It is important to note here that Europe at first did not have a serious technological advantage over Africa, especially during the Moorish occupation of Spain and up to the end of the 1400s. As Rodney (1974:10) states: "in the fifteenth century European technology was not totally superior to that of other parts of the world." In fact, Europeans imported African and Asian cloths and other consumer goods during this period. However, there were three things which Europe possessed which would eventually give them the technological advantage: 1) guns; 2) long distance ships; and 3) capitalism as a system of production. Both Rodney and Parry (1966) agree with these, but Parry adds maps as a significant factor in the rise of European hegemony. Also, both give Africans and/or Muslims (Africans and Arabs) credit for most of the basics which led to maritime science and capability.

The gun and the monopoly on it gave Europeans the capacity to impose; ships gave them the capacity to collect and synthesize technique and other knowledge from around the world, as well as control, block or bombard the African coast, and capitalism gave them the capacity to mass produce, monopolize and expand technology in great strides. Thus, by the colonial era in the 1800s, Europe was able to: 1) conquer cities, states and empires thru force of arms; 2) dictate political developments in Africa; 3) force abandonment of productive processes like clothing manufacture and iron-smelting, and therefore encourage loss of technique and scientific inquiry necessary for technological advancement; and 4) refuse to share its borrowed and synthesized technology with Africans inspite of request. This process not only increased Europe's technological advantage, it also contributed to technological arrest in Africa.

A second factor which increased Europe's ability to conquer and impose its will on Africa was its economic advantage. In fact, the technological advantage and economic advantage are linked. Europe's ships which gave them capacity for long-distance travel and trade and valuable military capability, its guns which gave them the capacity to conquer and impose, and capitalism which gave them the capacity to mass produce and outproduce others clearly had both a technological and economic dimension. Therefore, with this combined power, they were able to: 1) graft African economies into the capitalist system; 2) disrupt African trade routes and relations as the Portuguese did in Upper Guinea with the cotton trade, in Angola with salt and in Kongo with cowries; 3) reduce African economies to a one-product or low number product economy, i.e., slaves, kola nuts, etc. to satisfy European demands; 4) force consumption of European goods; and 5) continue the European stranglehold on African consumer markets. Moreover, as Rodney (1974:106) points out, "the lines of economic activity attached to foreign trade were either destructive as slavery was, or at best extractive like ivory hunting and cutting comwood trees." This too produced developmental arrest and vulnerability.

Directly related to the economic and technological advantages was the slave trade which deprived Africa of conditions for development and made security a priority over development. Furthermore, this trade deprived Africa of her youth, the major source of inventiveness and inquiry. Caught in a vicious cycle of needing to give Europeans what they demanded in order to get the guns Europeans had given their enemies, African rulers more and more got bogged down in the slave trade which not only cost Africans many millions, but also created a context for insecurity, fear and lowered internal productivity. As July (1970:170) states, "no doubt an economy based on slaving was based insecurely, while nations devoted to slave mongering became brutalized and unproductive."

A fourth factor which led to the decline of African societies and their eventual conquest was internal and external problems of the various societies at given times of European penetration. Often they were too small for effective resistance to large well-armed European armies or contingents. Certainly, small ethnic groups were little match for states. And in fact the African states and empires put up a more effective resistance. Secondly, they might have been at war with various neighboring states or peoples, thus making them and their neighbors more vulnerable to European manipulation thru arms supplies. Thirdly, the class divisions and antagonisms in African societies were often played on where they existed and created where they did not. In this regard an example is the rise of mulatto strata or classes thruout Africa which acted as buffers, agents and middlemen for Europeans. Also with the rise of the European slave trade, an indigenous slave class was developed by the late 18th century in parts of West Africa where once there were none. This further divided African societies in terms of class and color given Europe's fixation on race.

Finally, African societies found themselves culturally vulnerable to European penetration and conquest on several levels. First, except for Islamic societies, they lacked a unifying ideology which cut across the various socio-political formations to which they belonged. The Europeans had Christianity, capitalism and racism and though they often rivalled each other, these ideological focuses were also points of unity against the so-called Black heathen. Thus, "Pope Alexander VI issued a papal bull in 1493 giving, by the grace of an understanding god, the people of color of the world (all considered heathen) and especially their resources to Portugal and Spain" (Karenga, 1978:55). This had the effect of turning their immediate attention from killing each other to killing, enslaving and exploiting the so-called swarthy heathen.

Moreover, African vulnerability was increased by the communalistic character of African societies where this obtained. This included a tendency toward xenophilia rather than xenophobia as with the European, the non-aggressive approach toward nature and thus, the likelihood of being technologically unable to meet the challenges of a society literally out to conquer and fully exploit nature. Such a people dedicated to the conquest of nature and others is more likely to be prepared for war than those deeply spiritual and deferential to nature and concerned with living in harmony with it rather than conquering it.

Even now such a cultural emphasis remains a problem for the development and defense of African and other Third World peoples. For the needed thrust to control and utilize nature often clashes with cultural values which are more spiritual than material. The question is raised here of how to synthesize the need and growth of science and technology with the need for human sensitivity and morality or how to humanize nature without denaturalizing and dehumanizing humans? Europe by its own admission has failed in this project. It now falls on Africans and other Third World peoples to demonstrate its possibility.

CONCLUSION

As stated in the Introduction, a comprehensive and detailed treatment of African history is not possible in this work. What was attempted was some definitive examples of African genius, creativity and historical struggles to shape the world in their own image and interests. Egypt was chosen because it was the oldest, contested and high achieving; the Western Sudanic civilization because of its undeniable Africanoid character, level of achievement and its being the source of many Africans brought to the New World; and the Moorish empire in Spain because, it like Egypt, shows Europe's immense debt to African and African peoples whom they, thru racial or racist immodesty, like to think owe them everything real and worth mentioning.

AFRICANS IN AMERICA

INTRODUCTION

It is important to restate here some of the basic concerns listed in the section on African Background. First, this section, as the one on Continental African history, will not seek to be an exhaustive treatment of Afro-American history. The intention is rather to acquaint the student with major issues, processes, events and historical figures which have shaped the course and character of Black history. Secondly, in achieving this, focus will be placed more on modal experiences than on establishing neat chronological periods in which these experiences took place. By modal experience, I mean major experiences which defined Black life with Blacks in the roles of both producers and products of history, those who make and are made by these historical experiences.

Thirdly, stress will be placed on Blacks as historical actors rather than the object of historical action, on them struggling to define, defend and develop their interests rather than their being imposed on by others. The interest here is in the rich diversity of proactive responses Black had to life in a new and hostile land. It, thus, will not be a litany of lost battles, a dirge of endless defeats or a chronical of simple survival. Rather this section will seek to show Blacks as they were and are, meeting major challenges with impressive adaptive vitality, durability and achievement. It will show them then, not simply surviving, but more importantly, self-consciously developing, a process which carries with it both the assumption and insurance of survival.

Finally, this section will seek to present concise, critical summaries of major issues, events and processes so that the student can grasp the essence of each rather than get bogged down in insubstantial or less relevant data. The attempt here is to isolate and present the core and kernel of major phenomena and processes in Black History. The detailed presentations are in the general and specific works in the field. This, in a word, is a critical and concise introduction.

EGYPT, MALI AND THE OLMECS

There is strong evidence that Africans did not come to America first on slave ships or as crew members and pilots on white ships, but on their own ships as early as 800-700 B.C.E. A mind plagued by the white paradigm would obviously be unable to believe or accept the validity of evidence presented to support such a contention, but the critical mind is compelled to consider it. Afterall, if whites could reach America by accident, why couldn't Africans reach it by design and skill? Easily the seminal and most definitive work on African presence in ancient America is Ivan Van Sertima's (1976), *They Came Before Columbus*. In this major and controversial work,

Van Sertima argues not only that Africans were here before Columbus but that they helped build the Olmec civilization, the parent
civilization for all subsequent ones in Mesoamerica (Coe, 1962).

The Olmec civilization, Bernal (1979:9) informs us, "marks the
dawn of civilization and the formation of the cultural area of
Mesoamerica." It is a civilization known for its magnificent temples
and pyramids, ceremonial plazas, colonnaded courts for religious
rituals, its reverence for the jaguar, its elegant and exquisitely
carved figures in jade and other stones. It is also known for its
hieroglyphic writing and calendar "which was used throughout
early Mesoamerican history and represents an advanced knowledge of astronomy and mathematics, including knowledge of
zero." But the most extraordinary and discussed monuments to and
of Olmec artistic and technical skill are a series of eleven colossal
heads in Southwest Mexico carved out of basalt, each standing
nine feet tall and weighing about fifteen tons. Emmerich (1963:53)
points out that these heads "portray men with characteristic Olmec
features: thick, heavy lips, full cheeks, broad nostrils, almost
swollen eyelids and a peculiar close-fitting headress or helmet."

This helmet is not "peculiar" to Van Sertima. For he sees them
as typical helmets used by Nubian soldiers of the 25th Dynasty of
Egypt whom he argues came here and contributed to the building
of the Olmec civilization. Moreover, nor are the bold features   an
unsolvable mystery, for they too show an unmistakable Africanoid
character and *origin*.

Van Sertima offers and documents two main contentions to
develop his thesis that Blacks did in fact come to ancient America.
First, he argues that they came as Nubians from the 25th Dynasty of
Egypt (751-656 B.C.E.) to the Olmec Heartland between 800-700
B.C.E. This, he states, would put them here in time to be at the
founding of Olmec civilization which began to establish itself
around 800 B.C.E. and lasted until 400 B.C.E.

Secondly, he posits that Africans also came to America from the Mali empire. In 1310, Malian Emperor Abubakari II sent a fleet of 200 master ships and 200 supply ships into the Atlantic Ocean toward America. Only one ship returned, but could not report the fate of the others which seemed to be swept away by ocean currents which drive anything in them inevitably to America. In 1311 Abubakari, undeterred from exploring the possibilities of a trans-Atlantic voyage, led a fleet of 2,000 ships to America, and never returned, leaving his brother Mansa Musa in authority.

Some of the major evidence supporting African presence, influence and achievement before the coming of Columbus, especially in Olmec civilization, which Van Sertima cites is as follows. First, he shows cultural and artistic influence, providing over thirty plates to show Africanoid heads, masks, symbols, shields and similarity in phallic cults in Egypt and Mexico. Secondly, Van Sertima demonstrates similarity in socio-religious beliefs and practices showing the Egyptian Gods Sokar and Aken in Mexico, similar burial customs such as mummification, the Horus burial jar, golden mummy masks, and the bird-serpent motif in coats of arms and royal diadems. Thirdly, he (1976:155-156) contends that the step-pyramid or ziggurat is a distinctive religious structure and that it is significant that "the very first American pyramid or stepped temple appears at La Venta, the site of the collosal (Africanoid) heads...." Moreover, he continues, not "only are the shape and religious function the same" for the Olmec pyramid and its presumed Egyptian prototype, "but also the astronomical and spatial relationships."

A fourth kind of proof, Van Sertima offers, is the similarities of plants in Africa and Mexico. Among those listed which appear to have been transplanted, he lists the banana, bottle gourd, cotton, Jackbean, yams and tobacco. Fifthly, linguistic evidence is offered in the form of similarities in Egyptian and Mexican words respectively like *Ra* for sun in both, and *kuphi* and *copal* for sacred incense. Moreover, Van Sertima also shows West African and Mexican word similarities. A sixth form of evidence offered for African presence and influence is observation and reports by European travellers as well as documents of East and West Africa reporting voyages to the West.

Also, Van Sertima presents a further proof, skeletal evidence, from studies by craniologist Andrzej Weircinski which reveal a clear presence of Africanoid skulls among skulls from Olmec B.C.E. sites. He also notes that 13.5% were evident in the pre-classic period and only 4.5% in the classic period indicating the fusion of Africans in the native population. Finally, Van Sertima, argues the technological possibility in support of his thesis. He cites Thor Heyerdal's Atlantic crossings to prove the possibility of Egyptians' crossing the Atlantic, argues that both East and West Africans had the capacity for trans-Atlantic travel and makes the point that Africans navigated the Atlantic before the Christian era and conquered a part of Ireland in an early period.

Van Sertima has clearly shown the African presence and legacy in Ancient America and thus, given an alternative image and period of our arrival here. In a word, he has demonstrated the Africans came first to America, not as slaves, but as explorers, traders, visitors and built with the Indians a great civilization that fortunately could not be erased by Europeans' wholesale book burning and vandalism in Mexico. In doing this, he has made a significant contribution to the rescue and reconstruction of Black history and humanity.

THE EUROPEAN SLAVE TRADE

It is clear from all historical evidence that the European slave trade and its accompanying violence, destruction and enslavement was one of the most catastrophic events in the history of humankind. If one objectively calculates the costs to Africa and

Africans in terms of the 50 to 100 million lives lost thru mass murder, war, the forceable transfer of populations, and the brutal rigors of the Middle Passage and of slavery as well as the attendant dehumanization and cultural destruction, one cannot help but conclude that of all the holocausts of history, none surpasses or equals this one. To discuss the basis for this contention we can begin by clearing up some of the basic misconceptions about th slave trade. Secondly, we will discuss its impact in more detail to demonstrate the toll it took on Africa and African peoples.

MISCONCEPTIONS. First, as Rodney (1974:95) contends, the category "trade" does not reveal the reality of the process and practice. In fact, although there were transactions between Europeans and Africans which would be called trade of slaves, "on the whole the process by which captives were obtained on African soil was not trade at all." On the contrary, "it was through warfare, trickery, banditry and kidnapping." Thus Rodney concludes, "when one tries to measure the effect of European slave trading on the African continent, it is essential to realize that one is measuring the effect of social violence rather than trade in the normal sense."

Secondly, Europeans do not escape moral indictment by blaming Arabs and Africans for participation in the trade. In terms of the Arabs, when the so-called Arab slave trade in East Africa was at its height in the 18th century and early 19th century, it was still tied to and controlled by Europeans (Rodney, 1974:97). For the destination of most of those captured by the Arabs "was the European-owned plantation economies of Mauritius, Reunion and Seychelles - as well as the Americas, via Cape of Good Hope." Moreover, in the same centuries Africans who were slaves in certain Arab countries "were all ultimately serving the European capitalist system which set up the demand for slave grown products such as the cloves grown in Zanzibar under the supervision of Arab Masters."

Furthermore, "as European political and economic influence in North Africa increased from the 1870's, the northern slave entrepots of the trans-Saharan and Nile Valley were drawn into the European orbit..." (Harris, 1972:78). Thus, one discovers that what looked like an Arab-controlled trade was in fact a European dominated trade with Europeans using Arabs as middle men. None of this is to deny Arab involvement or even the involvement of some East Indians, but rather to focus the bulk of responsibility for the ultimate and greatest demand, and the wholesale destruction and depopulation of Africa where it belongs - squarely on the shoulders of Europeans. Moreover, granted Arabs had slaves before Europeans demanded them for their labor systems, but Arab slavery was domestic and escapable. In fact, there were many incidents of Arab slaves or servants who rose to power and social and political achievement in the world of Islam.

In terms of African involvement, it is true also that Africans had slaves before the coming and demands of the Europeans. But three other facts must be added to this statement to give a holistic picture. First, African slavery was in no way like European slavery. It was servitude which usually occurred "through conquest, capture in war or punishment for a crime" (Davidson, 1968:181). It could also resemble serfdom as in Medieval Europe where peasants were tied to the land and a lord for protection. They were thus obligated to provide certain goods and services. Moreover, they "were not outcasts in the body politics" as in European chattel slavery. They often lived as members of the family, married their masters' daughters and rose to political and economic prominence and did not face the brutalization and dehumanization which defined European chattel slavery.

Secondly, it is the European demand which forced Africans into a system whose implications few Africans realized at first. This forcing came from among other methods: 1) using their knowledge of local African politics to foment factionalism, launch war and thus get captives; 2) supplying arms to kings or local leaders to raid enemies cities or villages in exchange for war prisoners; 3) demanding captives for guns from a king who needed them to counter an armed rival king; 4) hiring and launching raiding parties; 5) demanding captives in order to continue providing military supplies to given societies; 6) obtaining some African laborers under false pretenses and enslaving them afterwards; and 7) beginning in one kind of commerce and then demanding slaves at a point at which failure to comply would destroy a merchant's business.

Thirdly, it must be remembered that Africans resisted the slave trade also. In fact as Harris (1972:79) points out, "Resistance marked the whole endeavor from initial raid to sale abroad." Queen Nzinga of the Angolan state of Matamba fought fiercely for approximately thirty years against the Portuguese and their slaving until isolated and overwhelmed and forced back into the European economic orbit. The same is true of the political leader, Tomba, of the Baga people who lived in what is present-day Guinea. About 1720, he tried to build an alliance against the slave trade but was defeated by an alliance of Europeans, Mulattos and Africans involved in slave trading and forced also back into the system. King Nzenga Meremba (Alfonso) of the Congo also resisted Portuguese slaving vigorously, and is often cited as a strong example of African opposition to slavery. Even King Agaja Trudo of Dahomey, a state known for slavery later, sent armies to capture and destroy slave-trading centers on the coast in 1724, but was also forced into the system by superior arms and economic pressures. But as Harris notes, "Agaja, like Alfonso and other Kings in Futa Toro, Benin and elsewhere, all lacked local and international power to change the situation." Thus, they were forced into a system imposed from outside and the tragedy and loss were incalculable.

IMPACT OF THE TRADE. The impact of the European slave trade expressed itself in various tragic ways. First and most easily perceived is the depopulation thru murder, societal disruption and destruction, and forced transfer of populations, especially in Angola and other parts of West Africa. Estimates run as high as 50 to 100 million persons lost to Africa. Secondly, the slave trade caused the loss of youth and skilled personnel, thus affecting the scientific, technological and cultural progress of Africa. The youth were key, for it is among them that the thrust toward scientific inquiry and inventiveness is greatest. And loss of skilled people could only blunt and in some cases eliminate development and induce technical arrest.

Thirdly, the slave trade affected economic activity. It not only interrupted and destroyed markets and industries, but grafted the African economies on and subordinated them to the slave trade leaving other branches of the economic activity underattended or unattended. This meant Africans entered into a vicious cycle of dependence and severely diminished ability to produce and provide for themselves and to continue the battle to control and utilize nature. Fourthly, it created war raids and other violence, and then destruction of life and material achievements as well as conditions of uncertainty and insecurity which accompanied them. Finally, the European slave trade led directly to the underdevelopment of Africa and overdevelopment of Europe. In fact, as Rodney (1974) points out, underdevelopment in Africa is dialectically linked to overdevelopment in the West. Williams (1966) systematically shows how the slave trade and slavery led to vast capital formation and expanded industries in shipbuilding, textiles, sugar refining, metal, insurance and banking in Europe. This exploitation, oppression and appropriation of the vast human and material resources of Africa for their use in the West, unavoidably led to an interruption and deformation of Africa's development.

Moreover, it represented the combination of these two economic processes, underdevelopment and development, into a single system, capitalist imperialism. This system was/is characterized by the tendency to concentrate wealth at the Western center and impose poverty in the so-called marginal areas, i.e., the Third World. It is further defined by an internal logic of competitiveness which pushes it to seek control of markets, raw materials and profitable fields of investment in less developed countries. Colonization grew to secure these necessary factors for capitalist growth and was possible because of the precolonial power and wealth Europe had amassed at the expense of Africa and the rest of the Third World.

Thus, when one raises the question of why Africa is not where she was in relation to Europe during the Egyptian or Mali Empire, one must focus on the period of the European slave trade which interrupted African history and development, drained it of its human and material resources and thus, imposed the pattern of underdevelopment we witness in Africa today. Of course, the reasons Europe was able to do this which are explained in the above section entitled "The Fall of African Societies" can be argued. But it is impossible to deny that European exploitation and oppression of Africa, beginning in the 1400s, marks a clear turning point in African and world history at the expense of Africa and its peoples.

SLAVERY: BASIS AND SYSTEM

THE BASIS OF SLAVERY. American slavery had its basis in three major sets of factors: 1) its profitability; 2) its practicality; and 3) its justifiability in European racist thought. The profitability of slavery and the slave trade was alluded to above. Williams (1966) in his often quoted work, *Capitalism and Slavery,* has shown clearly the contribution of the system and the trade to capital accumulation and economic development by England. Some of these areas were: 1) shipbuilding, 2) rise of seaport towns and connected manufacturing centers, 3) banking and insurance houses like Barclay's and Lloyds; 4) the textile industry; 5) sugar refineries; and 6) metal industries. This was true for other European countries as well.

The USA profited from the slave trade and slavery both as a colony and as a free interdependent part of the world capitalist system. In the USA, the slave was profitable on three basic levels: 1) as a commodity to be sold; 2) as an object of labor to be rented; and 3) as a producer of cash products such as cotton, sugar, tobacco and rice. Around this economic process, commercial and industrial areas grew up, first in New England and New York and then the South. This growth led DuBois (1969) to conclude in his seminal work that this economic process, involving merchants and planters, became "the very life of the colonies." In fact, up to the mid-19th century, American economic development rested mainly on foreign commerce with slavery and slave-grown products at the center of the process.

Slavery also had its basis in the practicality of the process. As Bennett (1975) states, forced labor was first tried on the Indian and then on indentured whites. But several factors made the enslavement of these groups unattractive and the enslavement of Africans more practical. First was Africa's closeness to the Caribbean where plantations were set up early and where Africans were "seasoned", i.e., made manageable, and then re-exported. Secondly, Africans already had experience in large-scale agriculture with their own fields and European plantations in Africa, unlike the Indians who mainly hunted and gathered their food. Thirdly, Africans had relative immunity to European diseases due to long-term contact, whereas the Indians did not and were decimated at first by this.

Fourthly, the practicality of African enslavement rested in their low escape possibilities as opposed to Indians and whites due to unfamiliarity with the land, high social visability and lack of a nearby home base. Fifthly, there were no major political repercussions for the enslavement of Africans, unlike the Indians who had people here to retaliate and the whites whose enslavement would challenge the tenets of Christianity and the age of enlightenment and reason on which Europe prided itself (Bennett, 1975:65).

Finally, the basis of American slavery was in its justifiability in European racist thought. Although the enslavement of Africans was based in economic reasons, it also rested in racism as an ideology. Racism as an ideology became a justification and encouragement for African enslavement. It expresses itself in religious absurdities, biological absurdities and cultural absurdities. Thus, religiously, it was argued God ordained whites to conquer, civilize and christianize the African "heathen" and of course, take his/her wealth in the process. Moreover, the biological absurdities included redefinition of Africans out of the human race, denying their history and humanity and giving them animal characteristics to suit their bestial treatment by whites. And finally, the cultural absurdities revolved around claims of white cultural superiority and social darwinist claims of having both the natural right and responsibility to conquer and use the human and material resources of "lesser" peoples for the advancement of the more "noble and advanced" ones. Although Rodney (1974:88-89) at first argues that Africans were enslaved for economic rather than racist reasons, he later concedes the dialectical relation between the two. He correctly concludes that "oppression of African people on purely racial grounds accompanied, strengthened and became indistinguishable from oppression for economic reasons." Moreover, he maintained that "by the nineteenth century white racism had become so institutionalized in the capitalist world (and notably in the USA) that it sometimes ranked above the maximization of profit as a motive for oppressing Black people."

THE SYSTEM OF SLAVERY. The American system of slavery has been classified in several ways. Phillips (1963) a major apologist for slavery, called it benign and civilizing. Stampp (1965) classifies it as peculiar, cruel and brutal. Genovese (1974) describes it as paternalistic. Elkins (1966) sees it as infantilizing. And cliometricians,

Fogel and Engerman (1974) think it was simply efficient. It is obvious that the first of the above descriptions are more apologetic than critical and that regardless of the various other descriptions, the system was brutal and defined by the domination, exploitation and oppression which permeate all systems of slavery.

American slavery as a system, then, can be defined by: 1) the extent of its brutality; 2) its cultural genocide; and 3) its machinery of control. The brutality of slavery expressed itself on the physical, psychological and sexual level. It included violence in various forms - whippings, mutilations, torture, murder, overworking and deprivation of food, clothing and shelter. Psychological brutality included daily humiliation, denial and deformation of African history and humanity.

It was, in fact, an objectification of the slave, reducing him/her to an object of labor, and using his "race" as proof and assignment of human worth and social status. Sexual brutality was imposed on slave women, men and children. Each was subjected to the sexual lust and exploitation of the master and his family. "Breeding" and rape became the two principal forms of sexual abuse and brutality which they all suffered, but especially the women.

The second major aspect of American slavery as a system was its cultural genocide against Africans. By cultural genocide is meant, the wholesale intentional destruction of a people's culture and cultural identity and their capacity to produce, reproduce and expand themselves. It includes the destruction of: 1) political identities and ethnic units and identities; 2) families; and 3) cultural leaders. These were all units of the preservation and transmission of African culture. But they were also units of real and potential resistance - on the cultural and physical level and thus, the slave master sought to destroy them.

Finally, American slavery can be defined and discussed in terms of its machinery of control. This machinery of control was one of the most brutal and extensive in the history of slavery. Basically, it involved five mechanisms of control: 1) laws; 2) coercive bodies; 3) the church; 4) politically divisive strategies; and 5) plantation punishments. The slave laws were directed toward defining Africans as property and depriving them of any legal or human right or personality. Under these laws or Slave Codes, the African slave could not make a contract, could not testify against anyone except another African, could not strike a white man even in self-defense; could not leave a plantation without authorization; could not possess firearms; could not visit whites or free Africans or entertain them in their quarters; could not assemble without whites; could not learn or be taught to read or write; and could not even beat drums or blow horns (Franklin, 1974:140-141).

The coercive bodies included first, local, county, state and federal armed bodies, soldiers and militias, patrols and vigilante committees dedicated to enforcing the laws even against whites who dared defy them, as in the case of teaching or allowing Africans to learn to read and write or fraternizing with them.

Also the Church, as Bennett (1975:73) states was "an integral part of the governing mechanism" and thus, a part of the machinery of control. It was directly involved in upholding the law, buying and selling slaves, and teaching doctrines supportive of the subordination and dehumanization of Africans.

A fourth aspect of the machinery of control was the use of politically divisive strategies to split consciousness and disrupt and deny unity among African slaves. These included strategies to develop "class" or rather stratum divisions among Africans, i.e., the house, yard and field slaves and to develop a collaborator corps that spanned all strata and was used to stifle dissent, spread disinformation and mostly nip revolts in the bud.

Finally, the machinery of control included plantation punishments. Stampp (1965:171-191) in his chapter "To Make Them Stand In Fear," lists some of the viciously ingenious ways whites punished Africans who would not accept or broke the laws and rules of the slave systems. Those included: demotions for the house Africans, foremen or drivers to field work; denials of food, clothing, shelter or recreation; splitting up families; imprisonment in private plantation jails; placing in stocks; brandings; whippings; torture; mutilation; and murder. Some of the most heinous and savage punishments were washing wounds in salt, purposely allowing dogs to maul rebels and forcing a person "to eat worms he failed to pick off the tobacco leaves."

None of this is said to shock or indulge in victimization history, but to clearly depict the system as it was. It is also presented to lay the basis for discussing slave resistance. For in depicting in stark detail the obstacles slavery posed to initiative and resistance, one can better appreciate the strength and depth of human will and spirit which led Africans to resist even in the most brutal and controlled situations.

RESISTANCE TO SLAVERY

African resistance to slavery began in Africa, as argued above, and continued in America thruout the period of slavery. Inspite of works which question the quality or extent of African resistance to slavery, there is ample evidence to demonstrate real and unrelenting resistance to slavery by both enslaved and free Africans. Given that slavery threatened and affected even free Africans and that they were thus constantly defending themselves as well as trying to liberate enslaved Africans, African resistance will be treated as a single process, even though more stress will be placed on the resistance activities of the enslaved. There are many works which discuss and analyze various forms of resistance, but no single volume deals thoroughly or extensively with all the ones listed below (Aptheker, 1968, 1943; Mullin, 1975; Price, 1973; Sorin, 1973; Quarles, 1969; Genovese, 1981). But the problem and truth are not that Afro-Americans resisted less, but rather that interpretations of their resistance were less critical and often failed to take into consideration the different circumstances and variables involved. Thus, their comparative analyses were deficient and could not but make Black resistance in the U.S. look likewise.

Variables to take in account when comparing African resistance in the U.S. with African resistance in other societies in the Western Hemisphere are: 1) the smaller population size; 2) the existence of less nearby unsettled regions for maroon societies; 3) the isolated character of the U.S. plantations which hampered organized unified efforts; 4) the harsh winters which made survival of maroon societies more difficult to maintain as opposed to tropical areas where food and shelter were less a problem; 5) the drastic decline of importation of large numbers of new Africans after 1807 with the federal prohibition of the slave trade, thus depriving enslaved Africans of a vital source of revitalization and rebellion; 6) the greater balance between the sexes and division into family units in the U.S. which often dampened male rebellion and flight in consideration for their family; and finally 7) the pervasive severity of the system which was not content to dominate physically but engaged in the most brutal and racist deculturalization process in the Western Hemisphere. This process, as shown above, did not destroy all culture or cultural resistance, but joined to the fact of reduced and halted revitalization from newly imported Africans, the toll it took was significant.

Still, evidence reveals that resistance among Afro-Americans was strong and continuous. But given the arguments surrounding resistance, it is necessary to define it as a preface to discussion of its forms. Resistance here then can be defined as any and all personal and collective acts designed to: 1) deny support to, challenge or overturn the established order; 2) deny, diminish or eliminate its hold; 3) force changes in its structure and functioning and/or; 4) escape its control and jurisdiction. From this definition and available evidence, free and enslaved Africans engaged in five basic forms of resistance to slavery: 1) cultural; 2) day-to-day; 3) abolitionism; 4) emigrationism; and 5) armed struggle.

CULTURAL RESISTANCE. Undoubtedly the most impressive and inclusive book on cultural resistance by enslaved Africans is Blassingame's *The Slave Community*. In this work Blassingame (1979:6) argues that the personality and initiative of the African in slavery was determined not simply by the impositions of the slave-holder, "but rather the interaction between certain universal elements of West African culture, the institutionalized demands of plantation life, the process of enslavement and (the African's) creative response to enslavement."

Among the forms of cultural resistance, Blassingame lists the following: 1) cultural retention and synthesis; 2) cultural creation; 3) maintenance and development of a family against all odds. Blassingame observes that most distinctive survivals or retentions are dances, folktales, music, magic and language patterns. Synthesis took place in these same areas especially in religion and music where, as Blassingame (1979:20-21) notes, "in the process of acculturation, the slaves made European forms serve African functions."

Cultural creation was a form of cultural resistance in that the European sought not only to destroy the African's past but to limit and control his/her future. But the Africans carved out space for themselves wherever and whenever they could and proved that "however oppressive or dehumanizing the plantation was, the struggle for survival was not severe enough to crush the slave's creative instincts" (Blassingame, 1979:105).

A third form of cultural resistance was building and maintaining the African family against all odds. The slavemaster's sexual abuse of African women, his division and selling of family members, his breeding practices, and the denial and restriction of the African man's ability to protect, provide for and exercise authority in his family, all militated against a viable and durable Black family. Yet not only did the Black family survive, but it developed and performed the basic functions of socialization and care all families provide. However, it was not only "an important buffer (and) refuge from the rigors of slavery," but also a space where values of resistance were taught, where the trust needed for successful resistance was found and where active support for resistance was often available (Blassingame, 1979:191).

DAY-TO-DAY RESISTANCE. Most literature on resistance to slavery focuses on day-to-day resistance as the definitive form but as this section shows, there were equally important other forms which deserve critical study. Day-to-day resistance was, however, very important to the resistance process (Bauer and Bauer, 1942). Its regularity and pervasiveness are suggested by the category used to define it, i.e., "day-to-day." This form of resistance reflects the daily refusal and challenge with which Africans confronted the slave system and include sabotage, i.e., breaking tools and destroying crops, shamming illness or ignorance, taking property, spontaneous and planned strikes, work slow-downs, self-mutilation, arson, attacks on whites and poisoning of slaveholders and their families. Also, this form included suicide and infanticide which was designed to prevent life in slavery of both parents and children and thus deny the slaveholder both the profit and the perverse pleasure of domination and slavery. Finally, although many writers list flight as distinct from day-to-day resistance, I included it because of its regularity and the daily preoccupation with it (Mullin, 1975). All these forms, however, not only prove the real and unrelenting daily presence of resistance, but also disprove the image of the docile slave that Phillips (1963) and Elkins (1966) contrived.

ABOLITIONISM. This form of resistance includes all efforts dedicated to abolishing slavery conducted by both free Africans and formerly enslaved Africans like Harriet Tubman, Frederick Douglass and Sojourner Truth (Quarles, 1969). As early as 1797, African fugitives from slavery petitioned Congress to consider "our relief as a people." And in 1800, a group of Philadelphian Africans peti-

tioned Congress to revise federal laws concerning the slave trade
and fugitive slaves and adopt measures for eventual emancipation.
By 1830 free Africans had organized fifty antislavery societies
dedicated to abolition of slavery and aid to slaves in escaping and
to those who escaped or were freed by purchase or other means.
They also were founding members of multi-racial anti-slavery
societies, such as the American Anti-Slavery Society and the New
England Anti-Slavery Society and were 400 of the 450 original
subscribers to William Garrison's famous anti-slavery paper the
Liberator (Quarles, 1969).

The diversity and intensity of the activities of the Black abolitionists are extremely impressive. Among these activities were: 1)
fundraising efforts for purchase, aid and legal defense of slaves
and anti-slavery literature; 2) provision of security forces for
defense and anti-slavery rallies and to prevent kidnappings of
fugitive and free Africans by former holders and slave catchers; 3) a
massive publications effort including at its height major slave narratives, anti-slavery books and 17 newspapers, including the first
Black paper in the U.S., *Freedom's Journal*, 1827; 4) establishment
of a distinguished speakers bureau of former slaves and free Blacks
to disseminate information and call for support in the struggle in
the U.S., Canada and throughout Europe; 5) boycott efforts against
slave-made products which though largely unsuccessful were significant as an expression of exhausting all avenues; 6) establishment of legal committees to defend free and enslaved Africans
against enslavement and return; 7) establishment of vigilance committees and self-help and mutual aid societies to aid ex-slaves in
adjusting to freedom; and 8) the building and maintenance of the
Underground Railroad, a system of freeing, transporting and placing ex-slaves in the North or Canada.

It is important to stress two of the activities above. First, the
publication efforts also included such decisive works as *David
Walker's Appeal* (1820) which was a severe and famous criticism of

slavery, a call for revolt by the slaves and for aid by the free; George Moses Horton's *Hope of Liberty* (1829), and Robert Young's *Ethiopian Manifesto* as stringent as Walker's criticism, Henry Highland Garnett's *Address* (1843), and Frederick Douglass' *Narrative of My Life* (1845) among others. Secondly, the Underground Railroad represented in "a most dramatic way the determination of the abolitionists to destroy slavery" (Franklin, 1974:198). For it was a direct act against the slave system, depriving it of its key units, its objects of labor and inspiring in them thoughts of freedom and a sense of possibility. Both the fear and effectiveness of this underground effort to free slaves are expressed in a governor of Mississippi's claim that "between 1810 and 1850 the South lost 100,000 slaves valued at more than $30 million" (Franklin, 1974:203). Although, it had many distinguished "conductors" or group leaders, none was as outstanding in legend and reality as Harriet Tubman. Freeing herself, she also freed her children, sister and mother and father as well as hundreds of others. With the largest bounty ever on the head of a slave, she went South at least 19 times, defying death and capture, and refusing to let any slave turn back under penalty of death. She was also an excellent lecturer and raised funds for the cause, setting an example of the determination of slaves to be free and their dedication to freeing others they had left behind.

EMIGRATIONISM. Another key form of African resistance to slavery was emigrationism, the push to emigrate back to Africa or go elsewhere where Africans could be free and self-determining. As early as 1773, a group of slaves in Massachusetts petitioned colonial officials for permission to work in order to earn money for transportation to "some part of the coast of Africa where we propose a settlement" (Aptheker, 1951:8). Also, in 1787, "a group of eighty Boston Blacks "petitioned the state legislature to assist them in getting to Africa, providing them money to pay passage and buy land" (Quarles, 1976:96). These Africans were members of the African Society which was dedicated to encouraging emigration to establish a self-determining, self-reliant African nation on the West Coast of Africa. Paul Cuffee, a Black Quaker, was also one of the early advocates of emigrationism and used his own money to repatriate 38 Africans to Sierra Leone in 1815. He also petitioned the U.S. President and Congress for aid in this project in 1814 but to no avail. It is in light of this that he used his own money and urged others to help to repatriate as many Africans as he could before he died in 1817.

In 1817 the Negro Convention Movement was organized in Philadelphia and became in time a source for the ardent advocacy of emigrationism. The Convention Movement was abolitionist and emigrationist and though it focused on sending Blacks to Canada, at an 1854 convention, it met to consider emigration to other areas including Africa, the Caribbean and Central America. Some of its best known members were Martin Delaney, who argued for the indispensability of Black nationhood; James Holly, who stressed the need to go to Haiti and develop it; and Daniel Payne and Alexander Crummell, giants of the African Methodist Episcopal Church.

Although only some members of the Convention Movement advocated emigrationism, all of them opposed the colonization schemes of the American Colonization Society. This was an essentially a white initiated and dominated organization which had supported the founding of Liberia and advocated that all Blacks including free Blacks return to Africa. The free Africans opposed this wholesale immigration for four basic reasons: 1) they saw it as a way to get rid of free Blacks to better secure slavery; 2) they considered it their duty to stay and fight for emancipation; 3) they assumed it would give weight to the arguments of Black inferiority and inability to cope with "civilization"; and 4) they reasoned that they were as much Americans as whites in terms of their contribution and birth. Given these strong positions and fear of emigration-ist sentiments being manipulated by racists wanting to get rid of all Blacks, emigrationism lost much of its appeal and appeared strongest at times of extreme oppression and anti-Black agitation.

ARMED RESISTANCE. Obviously, the ultimate criticism of and resistance to a society is armed action against it. And enslaved Africans engaged in this form of resistance not only in the U.S. but also on the disease-ridden death ships on which they were being transported here. Although much of the literature on armed resist-ance focuses on revolts, there were other forms (Aptheker, 1943; Carroll, 1938; Genovese, 1981). In addition to revolts, four other basic forms stand out: ship mutinies; guerilla warfare, Afro-Mexican alliance and struggle, and Afro-Indian alliance and struggle.

Over 250 revolts are recorded in the U.S., but only a few have been researched and written on at length. Among the most notable and most written on are: 1) the New York City revolt in 1712; 2) the Stono, South Carolina revolt in 1739; 3) the southern Louisiana revolt in 1811; 4) the Nat Turner revolt in 1831. In addition, two planned revolts or conspiracies are also well-written about and well-discussed, i.e., the Gabriel Prosser conspiracy in 1800 and the Denmark Vesey conspiracy in 1822.

The importance of these and other revolts or attempted revolts lies not so much in their military effectiveness, for a revolt by defini-tion is an unsuccessful revolution, i.e., an unsuccessful armed upris-ing which does not end in seizure of state power. Rather their significance lies in: 1) what it revealed about the rebels, especially their leaders; 2) the chilling effect they had on the slaveholders; and 3) the effect they had on the other enslaved Africans and eventually their descendents.

The major revolts reveal rebel leaders conscious of and prone toward use of religion as an instrument of unity and struggle. Both traditional African religion and Africanized Christianity were used to call the rebels to arms, to justify the moral right to rebellion and freedom, and steel them against overwhelming odds. Moreover, the rebel leaders, especially Prosser, Vesey and Turner were aware of and sought to use current political realities to their advantage. Prosser expected French help in its war with the U.S.; Vesey looked to Haiti for inspiration and support, and Turner saw in the internal debates on slavery a good omen reinforced by the religio-political visions he had of war and liberation. Each having taught himself to read and write, kept up with the news and used the concepts and arguments for freedom and rights in the Declaration of Independence, the Constitution and the Rights of Man, demonstrating a grasp of the ideologies of the Age of Revolution. Finally, one is struck by the dedication, determination and audaciousness of these rebels, risking all to be free even though being as knowledgeable as they were, they knew the overwhelming odds. Given these odds, as Genovese (1981:50) notes, "only the most heroic souls, even as measured by the highest standards of revolutionary self sacrifice could contemplate such a course..."

The effect those rebels and revolts had on whites is clear from the record. The reactions of the slaveholders and other whites were invariably reflective of bloodthirsty hysteria. The bloodletting they engaged in and the stringent laws they passed after each revolt showed their fear and tended to erode their contrived image of invincibility. Often they even imagined revolts and conspiracies where there was none, showing a respect for Blacks they would never admit and even many historians fail to observe. Thus, inspite of their writings about the docile, happy slave, they could not easily deny their own deaths at the hands of African rebels. They could and did often hide these realities, but they knew them and were thus forced to face the constant fact and threat of revolt throughout slavery. What Franklin (1974:160) noted about the result of the Prosser conspiracy can be said of other conspiracies and revolts, "The large numbers (at least a thousand), together with the disre-

gard the slaves seemed to have for their own lives caused the whites
to shudder." Moreover, "the 'high ground' they took in maintaining
silence added to the *stark terror of the situation*" (emphasis mine).

The effect these rebels and revolts had on the other enslaved
Africans was strong and positive. Although some may argue that
their capture, death and lack of success discouraged other slaves,
this is only partly true. For as some were discouraged as in the case
of slave revolts throughout the world and throughout history, many
were also encouraged by the audaciousness and determination
shown by the rebels and the exposed vulnerability of the slaveholder. One cannot but be impressed by the slave rebels' willing-
ness to risk their lives and those of their loved ones against such
overwhelming odds. One is also unavoidably impressed by the
political commitment and political awareness of an enslaved African in 1800 slaveholding America, informing his captors who asked
what he had to say during his "trial" that:

> I have nothing more to offer than what General Washington would have
> had to offer, had he been taken by the British officers and put to trial by them.
> I have ventured my life in endeavoring to obtain the liberty of my countrymen,
> and am a willing sacrifice to their cause; and I ask as a favour, that I may be
> immediately led to execution. I know that you have predetermined to shed my
> blood. Why, then all this mockery of a trial?"

The witnesses to this bold and well-presented statement and stand
were not only the captors but other enslaved Africans who
undoubtedly felt admiration and respect.

Nat Turner reports an exchange between himself and a newcomer to his group of rebels which indicates a similar political
commitment to the freedom struggle. He reports that he:

> ...asked Will (the newcomer) how he came there? He answered (that) his life
> was worth no more than others, and his liberty as dear to him. I asked him if he
> meant to obtain it? He said he would or lose his life.

Again, this commitment was recognized and respected by other enslaved Africans. A strong evidence of this recognition and respect is found in the following popular song praising Nat Turner and noting the vulnerability of the slaveholder and slave system:

> You mought be rich as cream
> And drive you coach and four-horse team.
> But you can't keep de world from moverin' round
> Nor Nat Turner from gainin ground.
> And your name it mought be Caesar sure.
> And got you cannon can shoot a mile or more,
> But you can't keep de world from moverin' round
> Nor Nat Turner from gainin ground.
> (Quoted in Stuckey: 1973:141).

It is this legacy also which has inspired the descendants of the once enslaved Africans, negated the lies their oppressors have told them about their foreparents' resistance, taught posibilities of struggle and the strength to endure and prevail based on historical precedence and models, and demonstrated to the slaveholders, the enslaved Africans and their descendants, and the world the impossibility of destroying the will and thrust of African peoples to resist and be free.

Ship mutinies constituted a second form of armed resistance to slavery. (Harding, 1981: Chapter 1). These struggles also stand out for overcoming the obstacles placed in their way to prevent them. Greene (1944:347) reports that "every possible precaution was taken to prevent the slaves from revolting." Not only were the crews well armed with canons, guns and knives, but guards stood on constant watch. Also the enslaved Africans - men, women and children - were chained in compartments only three feet three inches and sometimes no more than 18 inches high to prevent their sitting erect. Forced to lie spoon fashion to increase carrying capacity and prevent any defiance, the enslaved Africans often were rubbed raw by rolling ships, caught all kinds of diseases and died of suffocation.

But inspite of this oppressive and restrictive Middle Passage ride, the enslaved Africans although weakened by confinement and ship- contracted disease, often rebelled and attempted to seize the ship and return to Africa. From evidence, ship mutinies seemed to have been more successful than revolts on land. Among the many successful mutinies were those on the Little George (1730), the Jolly Bachelor (1740) and the Amistad (1839). In the case of the Little George, the ship had sailed from the Guinea Coast in 1730 with ninety-six enslaved Africans. Freeing themselves from shackles, they put the crew to flight in the cabin below. They guided the ship into Sierra Leone River, removed all the women and children and left the ship. The Jolly Bachelor which was carrying captives down the Sierra Leone River in 1740 was attacked and captured by other Africans who freed the enslaved Africans and stripped the ship of its sails and rigging and then left ship.

Perhaps the most famous ship mutiny in Afro-American history, however, is the Amistad mutiny in 1839. In this mutiny, a group of Africans, led by Joseph Cinque, an African prince, seized the ship, killed their captors and attempted to return to Africa. Intercepted by a U.S. naval vessel, they were captured and brought to trial. Abolitionists hired John Quincy Adams to defend them and they were freed and allowed to return to Africa. Again, this form of armed resistance proves the will and spirit to be free among enslaved Africans and contributes definitively to an important legacy.

A third form of armed resistance to slavery was guerrilla warfare conducted by members of maroon or runaway communities. Although attention and credit have been given to maroon societies and struggles in other part of the Western Hemisphere, comparatively little has been written on Maroon societies and warfare in the U.S. (Price, 1973; Aptheker, 1968; Mullin, 1975).

There is evidence of the establishment of at least fifty Maroon communities between 1672-1864 with varying life-spans. These communities existed in the forest, mountain and swampy regions of several states, i.e., Virginia, North Carolina, South Carolina, Georgia, Louisiana, Mississippi, Alabama and Florida. However, the most notable and largest communities existed in the Dismal Swamp, along the Virginia-North Carolina border and in Florida in union with the Seminole Indians which will be discussed under Afro-Indian alliance and struggle. These Maroons sought in varying ways to duplicate the African societies from which they came. They built communal agricultural societies, raised crops and animals and fowl, maintained families with African kinship patterns and even engaged in trade with whites in certain areas.

The significance of these Maroon communities as a source of resistance, express itself on five basic levels. First, they represented a reality and possibility of self-determination and power to other enslaved Africans. Both their existence and their victories against search-and-destroy expeditions and successful attacks on plantations reaffirmed this reality and possibility. Secondly, they were sources of asylum for fugitives daring enough to escape and reach them. Thirdly, they were bases from which to launch attacks on plantations for supplies or in retaliation and thus, on the slave system itself, even if only in a minor and isolated way. Fourthly, they often raided plantations to free enslaved Africans. Fifthly, they often provided leadership and inspiration for revolts among the enslaved. Thus, although isolated, limited means of subsistence and regular search-and-destroy measures reduced the Maroon communities' capacity to expand and consolidate and wage a more effective guerrilla warfare, the contribution they did make to the overall process and legacy of resistance stands out and must be recognized and respected.

Afro-Mexican alliance and struggle offers a fourth form of armed resistance by Africans against slavery. Enslaved Africans began to come to Mexico early in the 1800's to seek freedom. This was due to three basic reasons. First, Mexico was close to the South, especially close to Texas, Louisiana and Florida from which most came. Secondly, local Mexicans would often protect them from pursuing Anglos whom they resented or hated. Thirdly, the Mexican government was favorable toward enslaved Africans, having abolished slavery in 1824 and put it in the Constitution in 1857, the same year, the U.S. Supreme Court ruled in the Dred Scott decision that Blacks had no rights whites were bound to respect (Schwartz, 1975).

Mexico's antislavery position was both humanitarian and political. In its war with Spain, it had raised the cry of freedom for all and took it seriously. In terms of its political position, it saw Africans as barriers against Anglo invasion and encroachment on their lands. Thus, they offered Africans and Indians land on the border in states such as Tamaulipas and Coahuila where Blacks who have not totally merged still live today. In the early 1850's hundreds of Seminoles (Afro-Indians) migrated from Oklahoma to Coahuila forming military colonies and buffers against Anglo soldiers and slave-raiders. Other Blacks received land in the state of Vera Cruz for development and were exempted from all taxes and from military service, barring foreign invasions.

A fifth and final form of armed resistance by enslaved Africans to slavery was Afro-Indian alliances and struggle. (Foster, 1935; Littlefield, 1977; Bennett, 1975). One of the earliest known examples of Africans and Indians allied in resistance and war was in an uprising of Africans and Indians in Hartford, Connecticut in 1657 (Bennett, 1975:89). From 1657 on Bennett reports a continuous series of plots, insurrections and armed actions against Europeans by Afro-Indian joint action. In fact, in the New York City rebellion of 1712, Indians fought jointly with Africans. These alliances and joint actions were rooted in their association as fellow slaves, their common mistreatment by the European, their intermixture and need to defend themselves from the threat of conquest and enslavement.

Easily, the most clear and impressive example of Afro-Indian alliance is the Afro-Seminole Alliance in Florida. In no other Indian nation or ethnic group were Africans treated with such deference and did they rise to such leadership roles in politics and war. As early as 1738, enslaved Africans began to regularly escape from South Carolina taking refuge among the Creeks or Seminoles in Florida.

The Seminoles were a group of Creeks whose name in Creek means runaways and who in 1750 seceded from the Creek Nation and went to a territory in Florida. There they settled near African maroons and began to build a strong bond. In fact, it can be argued that the Seminole Nation developed early into an Afro-Indian nation controlled and run by Africans. Even though Porter (1932:326) refers to slavery among the Seminoles, he has to admit that "not only were the Seminole slaves not slaves in the usual sense of the word; they might even lay claim to being *the true rulers of the nation*" (emphasis mine). Porter attributes this rise to political leadership by Africans among the Seminole to four basic factors: 1) Africans' knowledge of the European and his culture and thus their value in war and peace exchanges; 2) their indispensibility as negotiators, guides and interpreters, often speaking French, Spanish and English; 3) their agricultural skills and thus value in creating and sustaining agricultural economies; and 4) their courage and skill in war. Therefore, he concludes, the Africans were valued as allies and associates and accepted as equals and later, leaders in war and politics.

Moreover, in the Seminole wars, Africans were both generals and often most of the soldiers. They fought fiercely, won many victories and would not often surrender because of the certainty of re-enslavement. They also used their key political and military positions in the Seminole Nation to refuse emigration to Oklahoma

Territory suggested by the U.S. Government and prolonged the struggle to avoid reenslavement and maintain self-determination. This is why Gen. Jessup, a U.S. commander in the war, argued that Seminole wars were "an (African) not an Indian war which if not quickly put down would affect the enslaved African population."

CIVIL WAR AND RECONSTRUCTION

The road to Civil War was most definitively laid in the stormy 1850's (Franklin, 1974:208ff). In this decade, a series of events made war almost inevitable. First was the passage of the 1850 Fugitive Slave Law which made the fugitive guilty until proven innocent, denied his/her testimony and was retroactive. It gave the abolitionists another opportunity to expose the viciousness and recalcitrance of slaveholders and slavery advocates. Secondly, in 1854 Congress passed the Kansas-Nebraska Act which repealed the Missouri Compromise of 1850 which prohibited slavery in the Kansas-Nebraska Territory. This increased the bloody struggle in the territory and foreshadowed larger battles. Thirdly, the U.S. Supreme Court ruled in the Dred Scott case (1857) that neither free nor enslaved Africans were citizens and had no right whites were bound to respect. Fourthly, John Brown, a white radical abolitionist attacked Harper's Ferry in 1859 to gain arms for at least 500 slaves and wage a war in the South. Although Black abolitionists like Frederick Douglass and Harriet Tubman thought correctly that his move was premature and unwise, he became a martyr of the abolionist movement and foreshadowed the coming war. The final straw came with the election of Lincoln whom the South hated and whose election they saw as an abolitionist vote.

CIVIL WAR. The Civil War began with the Confederate attack on Fort Sumner, S.C. in April 1861. Although many factors can be cited as causes of the Civil War, the question of slavery and by extension the question of the future of Africans in America stand at the core of its causes. The Civil War is important in Afro-American history not only because it led to their emancipation, but even more important, because they fought heroically and in great numbers in the war and played other significant roles in it. As Quarles (1969:296) states, African Americans "took stock in the adage that they who would be free must themselves strike the blow." Thus, they took up arms and became self-conscious agents of their own liberation.

At first the whites resisted, feeling that: 1) to call and depend on Blacks implied their inadequacies; 2) arming Blacks meant arming potential rebels; 3) serving in the armed forces would change the social attitude and status of Blacks and thus pose a problem for white rule and power. They also pretended to doubt the fighting qualities of Blacks, but this was irrational and based more on racist ego-needs than evidence as the war would prove. By the summer of 1862, after a series of military defeats by Union forces, Congress passed the Confiscation Act and the Militia Act which opened the way for Afro-Americans - free and freed - to aid the war effort. Moreover, Lincoln, seeing the indispensibility of Afro-American participation in the war, if it were to be won, issued in the same year The Emancipation Proclamation.

The Proclamation was not a blanket declaration of freedom for all enslaved Africans, *only* for enslaved Africans in states and parts of states in rebellion against the U.S. government. Loyal slave states like Missouri, Kentucky, Maryland and Delaware were exempt. Moreover, it did not grant freedom, only "declared" it, a declaration totally unenforceable. For the Proclamation was declaring freedom for enslaved Africans in the Confederacy, a land which had already rejected U.S. jurisdiction and was at war with it to defend its decision. Its value was as a propaganda document to appease abolitionists and Radical Republicans, give the war the moral character it lacked and contribute further to the rebellion and flight among enslaved Africans which had already reached a high level (Quarles, 1953:117).

Africans, anxious to fight for freedom, respect and better status and role in society, enlisted in large numbers and served in various capacities. In addition to serving as regular soldiers and sailors, they served as guides, scouts, intelligence agents, engineers, nurses, surgeons, chaplains, construction workers, teamsters, cooks, carpenters, miners, farmers, commandos and recruiters. An estimated 186,000 Africans participated as soldiers and 29,000 as sailors accounting for 25% of U.S. sailors. The real number of participants is probably much higher but was disguised by many mulattos being registered as whites. Moreover, Blacks served in every theatre of operations, fought in 449 engagements, thirty-nine of which were major battles and won seventeen Congressional Medals of Honor on land and four on sea. These achievements were made inspite of vicious racism exhibited in treatment, pay and time differentials, poor equipment, bad medical care, excess fatigue details, wreckless and hasty assignments and the no-quarter policy of the South against Black soldiers.

The Civil War ended April 9, 1865 with the surrender of Gen. Robert E. Lee to Gen. Ulysses S. Grant. The end of the war and the Union victory was important to both Afro-Americans and the nation as a whole. For Afro-Americans, it was an end to slavery which had lasted almost 250 years. Secondly, it represented a victory won only as a result of their entry and heroic participation in the struggle which was not only to free them but win respect and a new status in society. Thirdly, it meant the beginning of a new struggle to secure economic and political rights which did not automatically come with emancipation. For the nation, the victory meant the federal government had clearly established its sovereignty over the states, freed the South from a morally indefensible and politically and economically backward system and thus opened for the South and the nation a new era of economic growth and political change - as well as the problems which accompanied this process.

RECONSTRUCTION. The period of Reconstruction (1865-1877) represented for Afro-Americans "the best of times and the worst of times." It was a time of great leaps forward and hope and great disappointment and betrayal (Logan, 1954). For the U.S., it represented a time of great possibility to realize its ideals of freedom, justice and equality for all. But after a strong start it betrayed its own ideals and failed in solving the problems the post-war period posed, i.e., the problems of Reconstruction. These problems were essentially: 1) rebuilding the South's economy on the basis of free labor and its industrialization and reintegration in the national economy; 2) politically subduing and transforming the South; and 3) integration of the freed Africans into the social fabric, especially in the South and protecting them from reenslavement, exploitation and abuse. Out of these problems, only the reintegration of the South economically and politically was really achieved. This took place on the South's own terms and included the betrayal and sacrifice of the Afro-American (Harding, 1981).

However, early events seemed to suggest an alternative outcome. The Freedman's Bureau was established by Congress in 1865 to guide and protect the freed Africans. It was to: 1) set up schools for them; 2) provide medical services, 3) write, supervise and enforce their contracts; 4) manage, lease and sell them confiscated and abandoned lands; 5) resettle them; and 6) provide them legal assistance and protection. Moreover, Congress passed three cornerstone Amendments directed toward integration of Blacks in the social fabric on the basis of equality, i.e., the Thirteenth, Fourteenth and Fifteenth Amendments. Essentially, the Thirteenth freed them; the Fourteenth made them citizens, and the Fifteenth gave them the right to vote. Also, Congress passed the 1866 Civil Rights Act (CRA) declaring Blacks citizens again; the 1870 Civil Rights Act to expand and strengthen the 1866 CRA; and the 1871 CRA which sought to establish equal rights in public facilities and also passed the 1871 Enforcement Act which outlawed white terrorist societies like the Ku Klux Klan.

However, economically, Congress did not give Blacks the support they needed and they were essentially reintegrated back into the southern economy under semi-slave conditions as sharecroppers. Whites, never accepting the freedom and equality of Afro-Americans, passed Black Codes, patterned after the antebellum slaves codes which made "the control of Blacks by white employers...about as great as that which slaveholders exercised" (Franklin, 1974:241). Inspite of the general assumption among Blacks that the federal government would give them lots of forty acres, and the tacit encouragement given this assumption by the bill which created the Freedman's Bureau, the government never did, thus posing one of the main problems of Black economic adjustment. For with no land of their own, the majority of freed Africans slowly but inevitably returned to the plantation more or less at the mercy of the employers.

Moreover, those who did go to urban areas were met with crippling discrimination and severe exploitation. Black carpenters, bricklayers, painters, blacksmiths and other skilled workers were strongly opposed by white artisans in their employment efforts. Skilled and unskilled workers were denied union membership and white employers often used Blacks to break union strikes thus, splitting the labor movement and casting Blacks as essentially strikebreakers and ones who would work for the lowest wages. In 1869 Afro-Americans created two unions, the National Labor Convention of Colored Men and the National Negro Labor Union, and sought affiliation with white labor, but to no avail. By 1874, due to this exclusion and other factors, these Black labor union thrusts were effectively finished.

The Reconstruction period, however, did provide some political gains for Afro-Americans although they were short-lived. During this period 22 Afro-Americans served in Congress. Two served in the Senate, Hiram Revels and Blanche K. Bruce, both from Mississippi and 20 served in the House. Inspite of the racist claims that they were uneducated, 10 had gone to college and five had degrees. Moreover, most had some political experience before going to Congress as delegates to constitutional conventions and as local and state officials and state senators and representatives. Although Afro-American legislators were unable to pass much legislation in Congress, at the state and local levels they were able to achieve much more. They expanded suffrage, instituted free public education, improved the tax system, reorganized the judicial system and repealed imprisonment for debt laws as well as negative labor laws of 1865 and 1866 which were part of the Black Codes.

Eventually, however, the efforts to reconstruct the life of the Afro-American and the South on the basis of freedom, justice and equality, failed for several reasons. (Harding, 1981:Chapter 16). These included: 1) the failure of the federal government to give Blacks land and equipment, thus forcing them into semi-slaves status; 2) the return of Southerners to a status of respect represented by the repeal of the loyalty oath requirement for reentering national political life; 3) the rise of white terrorist societies like the KKK and the Camelias inspite of the 1870 and 1871 laws against such socieites; 4) the Supreme Court's eroding constitutional and legislative Black gains thru rulings favorable to the South; 5) the disintegration of the old coalition of abolitionists, Radical Republicans and northern industrialists thru fatigue, retirement, disenchantment and the push for social peace in the South which would allow economic growth; and finally, 6) the Hayes-Tilden Compromise in 1877 which saw Hayes grant the South federal troop withdrawal, assistance in internal improvements and better representation in Congress for its electoral votes. In 1878, federal troops were withdrawn leaving Blacks at the mercy of racist governments and terrorist societies. In 1894 federal marshals were withdrawn and in

1896 the Supreme Court issued its Plessy s. Ferguson decision, the "separate but equal" doctrine that lasted until 1954 with the Brown Decision.

THE GREAT MIGRATIONS AND URBANIZATIONS

The end of the Civil War brought migrations in three basic directions, i.e., to the southern cities, southwestward to Arkansas, Oklahoma, Texas and Kansas and to the northen cities. The Kansas migration in 1879 was the largest southwest movement and included over 7,000 Blacks going to Kansas with lesser numbers to Missouri, Iowa and Nebraska. But the greatest migrations were to the northern and southern cities - and between 1890-1910, the urbanization of Blacks moved from 20 to 27 percent. At first the southern cities received the majority of Black migrants, but by the 1900's the tide was turning in favor of the northern cities. Thus by 1903 DuBois noted that "the most significant economic change among (Blacks) in the last ten or twenty years had been their influx into northern cities."

The Great Migration of the World War I era was due to several factors. First, it was due to the dissatisfaction with and determination to escape the oppressive and exploitative race relations in the South. Secondly, it was prompted by the depressed economic situation in the South which included crop failures, the ravage of the boll weevil and natural disasters like the 1915 floods in Alabama and Mississippi which had disastrous results on the agricultural economies. A third factor was the growth of industry in the North, especially with increased semi-skilled and unskilled labor demands due to World War I. Fourthly, the world war had cut off immigration from Europe and with it its pool of unskilled laborers and domestic servants. And finally, there were intense efforts by manufacturing companies who sent recruiting agents in the South to solicit Black labor as well as by Black newspapers who induced Blacks to come North for greater opportunities (Quarles, 1969:193-194).

But the North was not the heaven promised. On the contrary, racial violence, discrimination and abuse continued in the North. As Drake and Cayton (1962, Vol. I:174) noted, the migration led to the rise of the ghetto or "Black Belt," a segregated residential area "whose inhabitants can neither scatter as individuals nor expand as a group..." Moreover, it was defined by its dilapidated houses, overcrowdedness, poor health, high mortality rate, police brutality and other social ills. Secondly, Blacks encountered continued white terrorism and violence evidenced in lynchings and racial riots by whites. In the summer of 1919, often called the "Red Summer," there were twenty incidents of white mob violence of riots, against Blacks in the North and South. Also, in the first year of the century, there were a hundred lynchings and by 1914, there were more than 1,100. Athough most occurred in the South, as with the riots, the North had its share. Finally, the Black migrant met worsening conditions of the labor market. After the war, employment declined rapidly due to the dry-up of government contracts with industry, the return of 4,500,000 soldiers and traditional discrimination which made Blacks the "last hired and first fired."

To aid in readjustment and fight discrimination, the Niagara Movment, the NAACP and the Urban League were formed. The Niagara Movement was formed in 1905 by W.E.B. DuBois and others to fight against injustice. It demanded the right to justice, the vote, education, the abolition of Jim Crow, equal treatment in the armed forces and enforcement of the 13th, 14th and 15th Amendments. This militant organization gave way to the National Association for the Advancement of Colored People which was formed by 1909 by Afro-Americans and white liberals. The NAACP, which absorbed many of the Niagara Movement's members including W.E.B. DuBois adopted much of the Movement's philosophy but was not as militant, due to the whites that controlled its executive

board. In fact, DuBois was the only Afro-American among its original executive officers. However, the NAACP went on to launch and
win effective campaigns against lynching and Jim Crowism, and to
secure the vote. Finally, the Urban League was founded in 1911 and
dedicated itself to social welfare programs. Like the NAACP, white
liberals controlled it and it devoted itself to social service programs
for jobs, housing, recreation facilities and health clinics, etc., shun-
ning politics and the social struggles of Afro-Americans.

ACCOMMODATIONISM, CONFRONTATION AND BLACK NATIONALISM

In the wake of the failure of Reconstruction, Afro-Americans
were confronted more and more with discrimination and mob
violence. By the end of the century, Jim Crowism, the racist system
based on the separate-but-equal doctrine and the political, economic and social subordination of Blacks, was firmly in place. Most
of the Southern states had passed such discriminatory laws and in
1896 in the *Plessy v. Ferguson* case, the Supreme Court had upheld
and enshrined such practices, a ruling that would last until the 1954
Brown Decision. In the areas of politics, economics and justice,
Afro-Americans were excluded from voting, jobs and union, and
jury duty. And white terrorist societies rose to ensure such exclusion
and subordination.

Moreover, Southern patterns of race relations and racist ideology were shaping public opinion in the North and West. The
doctrine of African inferiority was supported by most white anthro-
pologists, and historians and political scientists reinterpreted
Reconstruction in the interest of the whites. Social Darwinism,
which advocated the right and responsibility of the assumed strong
to conquer and use the assumed weak for their own more noble

ends, not only served as a justification for Black subjugation in the U.S., but also for American imperialism against other Third World peoples. In this precarious context, two major leaders rose and were later followed by a third. Separately and through their ideological struggles with each other they established political tendencies which even today serve as models and points of debate concerning the future and struggle of Blacks in the U.S. These leaders were Booker T. Washington, W.E.B. DuBois and The Hon. Marcus Garvey.

BOOKER T. WASHINGTON. The career of Booker T. Washington was indisputably an impressive one. Having been born in slavery in Virginia, he rose to national and international fame and was accepted in the North and South as the major Black leader of his time. In 1903, even DuBois (1969:79), his major opposition, was compelled to state that "Easily the most striking thing in the history of the American (Black) since 1876 is the ascendency of Mr. Booker T. Washington." Washington's base was at Tuskegee where he arrived in 1881 to found a school which would serve as a model of the vocational education he saw as the way for Blacks to raise themselves and gain the respect and tolerance of whites.

Washington's thought and practice were moulded and informed by four major factors: 1) his experience in slavery; 2) his education at Hampton Institute; 3) the tasks before him at Tuskegee; and 4) his reading of the socio-historical setting in which he operated. Slavery taught him the viciousness, violence and power of whites; Hampton taught him the value and intense appreciation of hard work; Tuskegee taught him the need to conciliate whites in order to get necessary resources and stay operating; and his reading of the times brutally suggested that protest in the South was counterproductive and extremely dangerous (Washington, 1968).

The core contentions of Washington's philosophy were advanced in his famous Atlanta Exposition Speech in 1895

(Washington, 1968:218-224). In it he advanced propositions which he would repeat and expand on throughout his life. First, he argued that vocational education was the key to Black economic success and urged Blacks to get into practical occupations such as agriculture, mechanics, commerce, domestic service and the professions. Secondly, he advanced the concept of social separation with economic integration in his famous statement "In all things that are purely social we can be as separate as the fingers, yet one as the hand in all things essential to mutual progress."

Thirdly, Washington suggested Black accommodation to social inequality and disenfranchisement, arguing that "agitation of questions of social equality is the extremest folly" and that not "artificial forcing" but productive labor and business would end discrimination. "No race that has anything to contribute to the markets of the world," he stated, "is long in any degree ostracized." Fourthly, he asserted the essentiality of Black-white cooperation in social progress with whites as superior benefactors and Blacks as a subordinate pliant work force and the "most patient, faithful, law-abiding and unresentful people."

In later interviews, speeches and writings, Washington expanded on these themes (Thornbrough, 1969). He also argued that economic progress was both a way to and substitute for equality and political rights. Moreover, he stated that economic progress could not only raise Blacks but make "the white man partly dependent on (Blacks) instead of all the dependence being on the other side." Stressing economic self-help and racial solidarity, he urged Blacks to pull themselves up by their own bootstraps and not let grievances blind them to opportunities. Finally, he emphasized the need for moral regeneration of Blacks, i.e., the cultivation of virtues and values which would destroy the slave legacy of laziness, immorality and wastefulness and other vices.

However, Washington's policy of accommodation was contradicted by his private efforts against racism (Meier, 1957). He was deeply involved in the struggle against disenfranchisement and other forms of discrimination. He not only lobbied in the background against disenfranchisement and other forms of discrimination, he also raised money to pay lobbyists and fight court cases against racism. Moreover, he was for Black economic power and built the National Negro Business League to advance Black economic interests. Furthermore, he was an expert politician himself, and inspite of his talk against political participation, ran the Black Republican campaign for Roosevelt and was instrumental in both the appointment and rejection of Blacks in high office and employment throughout the country.

Although Black leaders like DuBois and Monroe Trotter strenuously opposed Washington for his open accommodationism, he nevertheless maintained his power until his death in 1915. Washington's success was obviously rooted in his mastery and manipulation of three major socio-political and economic tendencies, i.e., capitalism, racism and Christianity. His stress on vocational education, pliant industrial and agricultural workers and social peace provided capitalism with its supply of cheap, nonstriking and apolitical workers. His stress on separateness, his disinterest in political and civil rights and his promise to be loyal to whites, not compete with them, and start at the bottom, satisfied the demands of racism.

Finally, his emphasis on the need for Black moral regeneration and putting behind the assumed moral negatives developed in slavery appealed to the Christian mentality. Thus, he spoke to the spirit and motion of the times, much of which was accepted by Blacks as well as whites. For many middle class Blacks had recognized the problems of political participation, accepted literacy and property qualification if equally applied to both races, saw the economic realm as the key area of advancement and advocated self-help, racial solidarity and the cultivation of middle class virtues.

W.E.B. DUBOIS. Washington's foremost critic was W.E.B. DuBois, an impressive leader in his own right whose rise to national and international fame was based not on white patronage, but on his own intellectual genius and role as an activist-scholar. DuBois studied at Fisk University and the University of Berlin, received three degrees from Harvard and became in 1895 the first African American to receive a Ph.D. A historian and sociologist, DuBois' doctoral dissertation, *The Suppression of the African Slave Trade*, was the first published work in the Harvard Historical Studies and his *Black Reconstruction,* a monumental and voluminous work, as well as his *Philadelphia Negro* became classic studies of Blacks.

Washington had been understandably impressed with DuBois' scholarly achievement and at first tried to enlist him as an aide, but DuBois obviously could not work in Washington's shadow. His intellectual achievement, self-conception as a leader and his opposite political approach to social struggle all militated against such a relationship. In 1903 in his classic work, *Souls of Black Folk,* DuBois (1969) wrote an essay "Of Mr. Booker T. Washington and Others" in which he offered the core points of his opposition to Washington. Throughout his ideological struggle with Washington, he repeated and expanded on these with the severe and incisive criticism which so characterized his writings.

DuBois saw Washington's leadership as not so original as it was reflective of the times. He called Washington's Atlanta Exposition speech the "Atlanta Compromise," criticized him for silencing his critics in unprincipled ways and trying to maintain a monopoly on Black leadership. He defined three basic kinds of historical Black leadership and response to oppression - revolt, accommodation, and self-realization and self-development. Nat Turner and David Walker represented the first kind; Washington represented the second; and Frederick Douglass whom he called "the greatest of American (Black) leaders" represented the third.

Washington, DuBois argued, had not only assumed and advocated "the old attitude of adjustment and submission," but in catering to the times, had introduced "a gospel of Work and Money to such an extent as apparently almost completely to over-shadow the higher aims of life." Moreover, he criticized Washing-ton for not only catering to triumphant capitalism, but also to Southern racism which demand Black subordination. He cited three basic paradoxes of Washington's program: 1) advocacy of Black business and ownership of property and denunciation of struggles for political rights to defend them; 2) insistence on thrift and self-respect yet counselling "a silent submission to civic inferi-ority...bound to sap the manhood of any race...;" and 3) advocacy of common schools and industrial training and disappreciation of institutions of higher learning from which teachers for his industrial and common schools came.

DuBois rejected Washington's demand that Blacks give up "political power, insistence on civil rights and higher education." He noted he did not oppose industrial training, only the exclusive emphasis on it.; he did not oppose reconciliation in the South, only "the industrial slavery and civic death" of Blacks which it demanded. And he complimented Washington's practical achievement in open and behind-the-scenes efforts against racism and oppression, but he opposed his apologies for injustice, support of the caste system and opposition to higher education.

DuBois, however, did not simply oppose Washington, he offered his own form of confrontation and agitational leadership (Broderick, 1969; Moon, 1972; Weinberg, 1970). First, he argued for a "Talented Tenth," an intellectual and political vanguard which would lead Black people to freedom and a higher level of human life. Secondly, he advocated a multidimensional education which would enable Blacks to grasp, confront and be effective in society and the world. He abhorred the vulgar careerism which reduced education to money-making at the expense of an effective social competence and social commitment. Thirdly, he advocated a cultural nationalism and pluralism, which stressed pride in Black heritage and unity yet a full and effective membership in American society.

Fourthly, Dubois insisted on confrontational activities in the struggle for social, political and economic rights and gains. He also saw political rights as the basis for economic opportunities and defense of economic gains. Moreover, he too argued for self-help and racial solidarity. Fifthly, DuBois advocated Pan-Africanism and called and presided over four of the five pre-independence Congresses from 1919 to 1945. He recognized and advocated the unity and common interests and struggle of all Africans and the world historical importance of Africa. In his later years, he went to live in Africa and died in 1963 at 95 in Ghana working on the *Encyclopedia Africana*. Finally, DuBois advanced socialism as a viable and necessary alternative to capitalism. He argued cooperative economics for the Black community at first and later advocated socialism for the country. In this, he saw socialism as an alternative to capitalism's unequal distribution of wealth, enslavement of labor and reduction of human aspiration to material pursuits.

HON. MARCUS GARVEY.   Born in Jamaica, Marcus Garvey arrived in Harlem in 1916, an ardent Pan-Africanist dedicated to the liberation of Africa and building a nation-state in Africa that would demand the rights and respect of Africans everywhere. He had admired and written to Booker T. Washington and expected to see him when he arrived, but Washington died a year earlier. It might seem strange to some that Garvey, the father of modern Black Nationalism, would admire Washington, the assumed paradigm of Tomism. But, as argued earlier, a one-dimensional portrait of Washington is not an accurate one. Garvey admired Washington's stress on social separateness, racial solidarity, economic self-help and self-sufficiency and institution-building.

Moreover, Garvey, while condemning whites' denial of Black

rights, did not see Blacks' political salvation in the U.S., but in Africa and thus, like Washington, put no real emphasis on political struggles in the U.S. However, he did not reject politics as Washington and he argued that "If Washington had lived he would have had to change his program." For the problem of Black power "must be solved not by the industrial leader only, but by the political and military leaders as well." In a word, the new leader must recognize that the New African "does not seek industrial opportunity alone, but a political voice" (Garvey, 1977, Vol. I:56).

Garvey and DuBois clashed openly in their struggle for leadership preeminence. Garvey criticized DuBois for a year in his paper *The Negro World* before DuBois responded. He accused DuBois of being equivocal and unvigorous in his criticism of imperialism. Agreeing with A. Phillip Randolph, he argued that DuBois was controlled by the white capitalists on the NAACP's board. Also, he criticized DuBois' elitism, his theorizing while Garvey was acting and his focus on integration.

DuBois' first public response to Garvey was in the *Crisis*, his NAACP organ, in December 1920. He called Garvey an "extraordinary leader of men" and acknowledged that Garvey was "essentially an honest and sincere man with a tremendous vision, great dynamic force, stubborn determination and unselfish desire to serve." But he also thought him a "dictatorial, domineering man" and without any real business sense. He also criticized him for introducing the Jamaican Black-Mulatto division, alienating the British whom he needed for his international trade, alienating Liberia where he hoped to establish his base and unnecessarily antagonizing and attacking other Black leaders. Eventually, they both began to argue ad hominem, questioning each other's sanity and sincerity.

The source of their conflict was both their different philosophies and their struggle for leadership preeminence. Garvey was a global Pan-Africanist engaged in the practical redemption of Africans everywhere, posing a liberated Africa as a base. DuBois focused on continental Pan-Africanism and stressed continental self-determination. Garvey was an effective mass leader, organizing over six million Blacks - working class and petty-bourgeoisie-in the Universal Negro Improvement Association (UNIA), whereas DuBois was elitist and by his own analysis unable to reach the masses. His concept of the Talented Tenth was both positive and problematic. Garvey was a man of action, an institution builder; DuBois was more the theoretician and scholar. Garvey argued for race purity and race first; DuBois was for integration. Finally, Garvey advocated statehood and state power for Blacks while DuBois stressed political participation within the U.S. system.

Garvey, however, advanced a larger strategy for liberation and a higher level of life for Blacks. As the father of modern Black Nationalism, he wrote and spoke extensively on all four emphasis of nationalism - economics, politics, religion and culture, and thus laid the theoretical bases for all subsequent nationalist assertions. Likewise, his practice - politics, organization and institution-building - has served as models for all subsequent practical nationalist thrusts (Garvey, 1977, Vols. I & II).

Economically, he advocated economic autonomy, arguing that "A race that is solely dependent upon others for its economic existence sooner or later dies." Thus, there is a need for factories, businesses and commerce based on self-help and self-reliance. Moreover, he saw class struggles and revolution as a fundamental feature in the rise and fall of nations, and argued for checks on corporate ownership to prevent monopoly and the rule of the few at the expense of the masses.

Politically, Garvey posited "Race First" as a principle of theory and practice, i.e., an Afro-centric approach to the definition, defense and development of Black interests. He used nation and race interchangeably and thus argued for a global Pan-Africanism which sought to free "Africa for the Africans at home and abroad."

His Pan-Africanism stressed anti-imperialism, global unity of Blacks and continental liberation and reconstruction. He sought to establish a national power base to defend African interests all over the world, to raise the level of the African masses and return an effective number of Diasporan African pioneers to start and sustain the project. Garvey also advocated armed struggle in the liberation of Africa stating that "any sane man, race or nation that desires freedom must first of all think in terms of blood," i.e. costly struggle.

On the question of religion, Garvey advocated a race-specific God. It is only human, he stated, to see God through one's own eyes, thus Black people must see God in their own image and interests. He criticized the bankruptcy and hypocrisy of white Christianity, attacking white Christian control of Africa through mass murder and brutality and Christians preaching brotherhood and everywhere killing Third World people. A forerunner of Black Liberational theology, he posited the need for religion to be socially rooted and socially relevant. Thus, he posed Jesus as a social reformer, organized and used ceremonies to reinforce nation-building, painted Jesus and Mary Black and posed God as a warrior God whose assertive defense of his rights humans should emulate. Moreover, he gave humans the central role after creation in building the world. "Man is supreme lord of creation," he contended, and in him "lies the power of mastery of all creation."

Finally, Garvey advocated cultural nationalism, a bold redefinition of reality in Black images and interests. This thrust, he contended, should begin with a rescue and reconstruction of Black history, for little can be expected from whites who "have tried to rob the Black man of his proud past." Blacks, he said, "have a beautiful history of their own and none of any other race can truly write it but themselves." Moreover, he urged encouragement of Black authors "who are loyal to the race" and exhibit race pride and severe criticism for those who prostitute their skills for white patrons and allies. Also, he urged an education that was socially relevant, i.e., applicable and inspirational in the struggle of Blacks to free themselves and rebuild the world in their own image and interests. To do this, Garvey called for a Black Vanguard, "men and women who are able to create, originate and improve, and thus make an independent racial contribution to the world and civilization."

BLACK SCIENCE AND INVENTIONS

One of the most important factors contributing to the rapid industrialization of the U.S. was the increase in inventions. Between the period of 1860 and 1890 which transformed the U.S. from an agricultural to an industrial nation, hundreds of thousands of patents were registered. Among some of the most important inventions contributing to this industrialization process were some of those by African Americans (Diggs, 1975; Adams, 1979; Carwell, 1977; Hayden, 1972; Haber, 1970; Klein, 1971). By 1913, Blacks had patented an estimated one thousand inventions, especially in the fields of electricity, transportation and industrial machinery, and the records showed that more than twenty of the approximately 190 Black inventors were Black women.

Before the Civil War, Black inventions were hardly recognized or known due to the fact that enslaved Africans could not patent their inventions. In fact in 1858, the U.S. Attorney General ruled that since a slave was not a citizen and a patent was a contract between the government and a citizen inventor, a slave could not make a contract with the government or assign the invention to his slaveholder. Nevertheless, reports are numerous of enslaved Africans inventing useful devices. At first the inventions centered on household and agricultural devices, but eventually the field of Black inventions widened to include achievements in nearly all branches of industrial inventions.

The first African American to receive a U.S. patent was Henry Blair who in 1834 registered a seed planter and in 1836 registered a corn harvester. In 1846, one of the most important inventions by an African American was patented. In that year, Norbert Rillieux patented the revolutionary multiple-effect vacuum evaporation process for refining sugar. Today, his basic technique is not only used in manufacturing sugar, but also condensed milk, gelatin, glue, soap, etc.

After the Civil War, the most significant inventors near the turn of the century were Lewis Latimer, Jan Matzeliger, Elijah McCoy, Garret Morgan and Granville T. Woods. Lewis Latimer invented the first electric lamp with a carbon filament, an inexpensive production technique for making carbon filaments for lamps, and the cotton thread filament which made electric light bulbs practical and inexpensive. Thus, although Edison is credited with inventing the bulb, it is important to note that his bulb continuously burnt out quickly, and it was Latimer's inventions which made it last and become a useable item. Latimer also drew designs for Alexander Bell's telephone patent, worked for Thomas Edison, General Electric and Westinghouse and in 1890 wrote the first book of the electrical lighting system.

Jan Matzeliger, revolutionized the shoe industry with his invention of the shoe lasting machine in 1891. Within the first twenty years of Matzeliger's invention, the shoe industry doubled its production in dollars from $220,000,000 to $442,631,000 and shoes became 50% cheaper and of much better quality. Elijah McCoy's most important invention was the automatic lubricator for use on locomotive engines in 1872. This drip cup eliminated the need to stop and restart engines in order to lubricate them. His product was so respected the phrase "the real McCoy" was used to question or confirm the genuineness of his and other products.

Garret Morgan invented a belt fastener for sewing machines in 1921, the smoke inhalator in 1914 and the automatic traffic light in

1923. His smoke inhalator was a life-saver used by fire departments and was transformed into a gas mask in World War I to protect soldiers. His automatic traffic light was sold to General Electric for $40,000. The most productive inventor was Granville T. Woods who patented over one hundred inventions. His first patent was in 1884 for an improved steam boiler furnace. In 1887, he patented his most important invention, the Induction Telegraphy System which permitted communications between moving trains and between them and the stations, and thus made rail travel safer. Thomas Edison attempted twice to claim priority in this invention but Woods won in both cases and was certified by the U.S. patent office as the real inventor. His other inventions include a telephone transmitter (1884); an apparatus for transmission of telephone and electric messages (1885) which was bought by the American Bell Telephone; an electro-mechanical brake and appratus (1904-1905) both of which were sold to Westinghouse Electric Company, and an electric railway (1901) which was sold to the General Electric Company of Thomas Edison. Edison tried to hire him, but he remained independent forming his own company, Woods Electric Company.

There were, of course, other significant inventors and inventions during this period among which were John Parker, a screw for tobacco presses, 1884; William Purvis, over a dozen inventions in machinery for making paperbags; J.A. Burr, a lawn mower, 1899; G. Grant, the golf tee, 1899; J. Winters, a fire escape ladder, 1878; J. Standard, a refrigerator, 1891; and A. Miles, an elevator, 1887. The importance of these inventions lies not only in their value to industrial growth, but also in their being a model of achievement under the most severe discrimination and oppression.

Finally, it is important to mention the significant contributions of Afro-America's most distinguished scientist, George Washington Carver, even though most of his work was done after the major period of industrialization. Carver was a chemurgist, i.e., a chemist pioneer in the field before it became a recognized science. Determined to free the South from overdependence on cotton, he encouraged farmers to grow peanuts, sweet potatoes and soybeans and developed hundreds of products from them. In his small ill-equipped laboratory at Tuskeegee, he made over 300 synthetic products from the peanut, over 100 from the sweet potato and over 75 from the pecan. Some of his synthetic products were adhesives, axle grease, bleach, facial cream, dyes, fuel briquettes, ink, insulating board, linoleum, metal polish mucilage paper, rubbing oils, soil conditioner, shampoo, shoe polish, shaving cream, synthetic rubber, woodstain, wood filler, buttermilk, cheese, flour, instant coffee, mayonnaise, meal, meat tenderizer, milk flakes, sugar and worchester sauce.

He also developed dehydrated foods and the U.S. army used his sweet potato flour during WWI. Although Thomas Edison and Henry Ford offered him large sums to come to their laboratories, he stayed at Tuskeegee. He never patented any of his discoveries, refuse to profit from them and instead donated them all to humanity.

CRISIS AND THE NEW DEAL

The decade of the great depression was especially difficult for African Americans. The New Deal, under President Franklin Roosevelt, held out hope and relief for Blacks through its focus on social welfare and public work programs. Blacks recognizing the importance of this new focus shifted dramatically from their traditional Republican voting to support Roosevelt and the Democratic Party by 1936. Also, the New Deal marked a significant turning point in Black-white relations for the better. This was due to the continuous struggle of Blacks for equality and the end of discrimination as well as to the humanitarian focus of the Administration.

Through the initiative of the NAACP and Urban League, several social activist organizations established the Joint Committee on National Recovery (CNR) to oversee federal government policy and oppose discriminatory aspects of it. The JCNR exposed unequal wage rates, lobbied for race relation advisors in major federal departments and generally fought for federal respect and defense of Black rights. Blacks were also successful in getting the Public Works Administration to stipulate numerical goals for Blacks in slum clearance projects. The Civilian Conservation Corps, and the Works Progress Administration (WPA) were valuable to the employment of Blacks during this period. The Federal Arts Project which was a branch of the WPA employed many Black actors and writers. In addition, the National Youth Administration had a Black division headed by Mary McLeod Bethune.

The new Deal passed two major Acts which were of great importance to Blacks. The first was the Social Security Act of 1935 which not only guaranteed old-age and unemployment insurance for workers, but also provided federal monies for social welfare. Secondly, the Wagner Labor Relations Act of 1935 guaranteed the right of collective bargaining and outlawed company unions. In the same year, the CIO was formed, began to organize workers and opened up to Blacks. At first, distrustful based on past discrimination, Blacks, urged by the Urban League and other Black organizations, joined and were very instrumental in organizing the steel workers in the Steel Workers Organizing Committee. Moreover, they joined and helped build the Ladies' Garment Workers Union and the Amalgamated Clothing Workers Union, the International Longshoreman's Union and the United Auto Workers. Through these struggles and gains, Black workers penetrated organized labor and thus gained a strong base from which to wage even larger struggles.

Finally, Blacks achieved an increased respectability in the Roosevelt Administration as specialists and advisors in various

governmental departments. This marked a change in the Washington model of unofficial advisor whose relationship with the president, more than his skill, fitted him/her for the job. These were
highly respected specialists and advisors who were civil servants.
They were called the "Black Cabinet" and the "Black Brain Trust"
due to their academic and professional achievements.

Among the most notable of this brain trust were Robert
Weaver, an economist who served in the Department of Interior
and several federal agencies; Mary McLeod Bethune, founder-
president of Bethune-Cookman College, National Youth Administration; Eugene Jones, Executive Secretary of the Urban League,
Department of Commerce; Ralph Bunche, Department of State;
Rayford Logan, Coordinator of Inter-American Affairs, and Abram
Harris, economist, National Recovery Administration. Although
these positions were not cabinet level, they were a breakthrough in
appointment by merit and paved the way for advances in the 60's
and 70's.

CIVIL RIGHTS AND REVOLTS

*This slightly revised summary of the 60's, appeared first in the
Black Collegian, February/March, 1980, under the title "From Civil
Rights to Human Rights: Social Struggles in the 60's."*
Inspite of reductive translations by liberals, Marxists and
established historians, the Sixties marks one of the most definitive
and significant decades in the history of Black people in the U.S. It is
in this decade that major civil rights and nationalist organizations
and personalities reached their height. This is also the decade in
which Blacks made the most severe and successful theoretical and
practical criticism of the structure and content of U.S. society. And
it has become through its achievements and often exaggerated
"failures" the unavoidable historical referent - both for analyses of
the 70's and the projections for the 80's.

To discuss the Sixties as a unified process is not to deny that there were varying tendencies and interpretations of what was to be done. There were, in fact, two main tendencies, the integrationist and the nationalist. Chronologically speaking the integrationist tendency reached its height first and through its failures laid the historical groundwork for the resurgence of nationalism. The logic of the process seems to suggest that only after the integrationist thrust had proven itself unworkable and historically exhausted, was the nationalist alternative able to challenge it successfully and eventually overshadow it (Brisbane, 1974). Thus, in 1963 and most definitively in the period 1965-1968 the strategy of non-violence was challenged by the urban revolts and in 1966 SNCC led the move from integrated groups and aspirations to Black groups and Black Power. It was also in the mid-Sixties that the "Back to Black" thrust expanded to reach beyond the U.S. to Africa for models and inspiration. Thus, though we speak of the 60's as a unified process on one hand, it is instructive on the other hand to recognize the two basic tendencies which shaped and informed this critical decade.

The Civil Rights Movement, which was essentially integrationist, gave Black people in the U.S. their first major accomplishments of the decade. The integrationist thrust, in its political sense, was an effort to break down barriers to full participation in U.S. society and remove the penalties and other negative consequences of racial distinctions. Thus, a major accomplishment of this period and tendency was not only major civil right executive orders and legislation to overcome these negatives, but also the building of a mass movement which mobilized and politically educated millions of Black people. It is a significant number of these mobilized and politically educated people who would go beyond the vision and aspirations of civil rights to demand human rights and Black Power. Therefore, it can be said that the Civil Rights Movement produced activists and organizations which would prove effective in transforming it into its Black nationalist alternative.

The Civil Rights struggle was led by major groups such as SNCC, CORE and SCLC, although countless smaller groups played fundamental and indeed indispensible roles in the civil rights struggle. Likewise, major personalities like Fannie Lou Hammer, Bob Moses and Martin Luther King, Jr. were key to the civil rights struggle, but there were countless "unknown soldiers" without whom the struggle could not have begun or been sustained (Lomax, 1962; Clark, 1963).

The turning point in the Black civil rights struggle is usually considered to be the winning by the NAACP of the 1954 Supreme Court Decision *Brown v. The Board of Education*. The decision put a legal end to the "separate but equal" doctrine established in the 1896 Supreme Court decision of *Plessy v. Ferguson*. Even though the decision was hampered in implementation, it gave a necessary psychological boost to the Black struggle and gave legal support to the struggle against segregation.

The beginning of the Montgomery Bus Boycott in 1956 marked another key event in the civil rights struggle. On Dec. 1, 1955, Rosa Parks, having decided that she was not going to give up her bus seat in servile deference to whites, became the catalyst to a struggle which not only catapulted Martin Luther King to national fame, but also built a model that Blacks in other Southern cities were soon to emulate. The economic boycott was thus established as an effective instrument of breaking down segregation barriers (King, 1958).

On February 1, 1960, four students from North Carolina Agricultural and Technical college in Greensboro, N.C., decided they would no longer accept segregation of public facilities and moved to protest and challenge the state of things by sitting down at lunch counters in a variety store and ordering coffee (Wolffe, 1972; Proudfoot, 1962). This marked the beginning of the sit-in movement and a sustained period of Black activism and societal confrontation that would last a decade, only declining with police suppression in the late Sixties and defection in the early Seventies.

In May, 1961, the Congress of Racial Equality developed another strategy to force the civil rights issue - the Freedom Rides (Farmer, 1965; Peck, 1962). CORE, an essentially integrationist group, developed the Freedom Rides to challenge segregationist laws and practices in interstate transportation which forced seating by race. However, the strategy had the spinoff effect of forcing the federal government to take a more vigorous stand on protection of the civil rights guaranteed by the Constitution. The Kennedys (John and Robert, who were in power at the time as President and U.S. Attorney General respectively) were disturbed by the assertiveness of these activists and asked for a cooling-off period. But the activists continued their thrust and forced the Attorney General to dispatch a force of 600 marshals and other federal officers to intervene in a freedom ride confrontation in Montgomery.

In 1963, the centennial year of the Emancipation Proclamation, Black people launched a series of massive demonstrations to expose the contradictions in U.S. society and demand serious social change. One of the most notable of these was the Birmingham Demonstration of April 3 under the leadership of Martin Luther King and the Southern Christian Leadership Conference (King, 1962). Again, racist violence flared, but the marchers were adamant in their push for fair employment, desegregation of public facilities and dropping of politically motivated charges against the thousands of demonstrators arrested. Easily the largest and most dramatic was "The March on Washington for Jobs and Freedom," August 28, 1963, which involved over 200,000 participants.

It is important to note here that throughout this period, the Student Non-Violent Coordinating Committee (SNCC) from its inception had been the most effective and largest contributor of freedom fighters to the struggle (Carson, 1981; Forman, 1972; Zinn, 1964). It had participated in great numbers in the major strategies of the civil rights - including boycotts, sit-ins, voter registration campaigns, cooperative projects and even political party building. It was SNCC who, along with Fannie Lou Hamer and Bob Moses, built the Mississippi Freedom Democratic Party and the Lowndes County Freedom Organization which was popularly called the Black Panther Party. Later, Huey Newton and Bobby Seale of Oakland would use both the symbol and inspiration of the Black Panther Party of Lowndes County to launch their group. It was also SNCC, as mentioned above, who would lead the movement discussion and organizational move away from one of integration to one of Black Power (Carmichael and Hamilton, 1967).

A critical analysis of the civil rights struggle, then would reveal a series of major accomplishments. As mentioned above, its first and perhaps most important achievement was the increased liberalization of the U.S. system. Through legal, economic and political challenges, Blacks were able to achieve among other things: 1) the 1954 Brown Decision; 2) the Civil Rights Act of 1957; 3) the 1960 Civil Rights Bill; 4) the Interstate Commerce Commission ruling September, 1961, against racial segregation on interstate carriers and terminals; 5) the Civil Rights Act of 1964 which was the most far-reaching and comprehensive civil rights law passed by Congress; 6) mass voter registration; 7) the 1965 Voting Act; and 8) widespread desegregation of public facilities.

Secondly, as mentioned above, the Civil Rights Movement severely exposed the contradictions of the American dream in both the eyes of the U.S. society and the world. This uncompromising and fierce exposure contributed to the internationalization of the Black struggle which was another gain for the Movement. It brought world attention to the struggle and won it moral and political allies around the world. The U.S. was thus, forced to operate under the attentive world eye and, therefore, sought to check its excesses against Blacks in a way it was not compelled to do before.

Thirdly, the Movement mobilized and politically educated people who before were, in fact, outside the political process. It is significant to note here that King was able to do with religion in the South during the late 50's and early 60's what Iranian leaders would do with religion in Iran in the late 70's, i.e., turn religion into a political force for massive social change. King, stressing the social aspect of religion, taught civil disobedience against unjust practices as a moral imperative, gave Blacks boldness by stressing that they were God's soldiers in an unjust world and thus, enabled an otherwise reluctant people to dare take control of their destiny and daily life.

Fourthly, the Civil Rights Movement laid the organizational and political-educational basis for continued struggle in other areas. The mobilized and organized masses did not simply disband and the end of the Civil Rights Movement, but went on to win elections, build co-ops and unions and in general build institutions that housed, defended and expanded their interests. Finally, the Civil Rights Movement, by its uncompleted tasks, the non-attainment of its core social objectives, the timidity of its methods and its eventual historical exhaustion, laid the historical basis for the rise of its nationalist alternative.

The Civil Rights Movement was thus, limited in its goals and methods for their achievements. Moreover, its Black leadership was unnecessarily concerned with and deferential to the wishes and support of white allies. Whites, through financial contributions and organizational positions, limited the Movement's possibilities and ultimately had to be confronted and rejected from leadership positions. And it is in the process of reassessment of the goals, methods and leadership of the Black Civil Rights Movement that the nationalist alternative appeared, grew and eventually checked and surpassed the thrust toward integration.

It is important at this point, however, to stress that all the gains made during the 60's, both of the Civil Rights and Nationalist

Movements, were not the gifts of presidents, Congress or liberal allies, but the result of a people's self-conscious struggle to free and realize themselves. As evident in the case of the liberal Kennedys, Black needs and the political concerns of liberals easily clash. But, through the self-conscious collective struggle of Blacks to control their destiny and daily lives, presidents, Congress and shaky allies were time and time again forced to act even against their will.

The painful process of reassessment which occurred in the middle 60's produced, perhaps, the most definitive aspect and achievement of the Sixties - the self-conscious decision of Africans in the U.S. to initiate a theoretical and practical thrust to redefine and restructure society in Black images and interests. Even the integrationists wanted Black interests to be recognized and respected. Even they fought for a society which did not penalize Blacks for their color and which would concede to affirmative action to end and compensate for such behavior. But it was the nationalist tendency which redefined both society and the world in Black images and interests.

The thrust for self-determination, self-respect and self-defense, as the Black Power Movement was defined by Us Organization, gave the Black Power Movement a new vitality and dynamics. it was this thrust which began to solve the Crusian-posed crisis of the Black intellectual, raised the political and cultural consciousness of the Black masses, linked our struggle with African and other Third World peoples and introduced the concept and practice of armed struggle in urban centers among other things. The nationalist struggle can be, for analytical purposes, divided into three basic tendencies or thrusts: 1) the religious thrust; 2) the cultural thrust; and 3) the political thrust.

The religious thrust was both Islamic and Christian. The Islamic section was personified by the Nation of Islam (NOI) under the leadership of the Honorable Elijah Muhammad (Muhammad, 1965;1973). Muhammad posed Islam as a necessary alternative to

Christianity, which he saw as the oppressor's religion. Secondly, he argued that Blacks were the chosen people of God, and that God was Black and the devil was white. This reversal of the world order was a bold redefinition of reality and was instrumental in reinforcing the concept of the beauty and creative genius of Blacks. Thirdly, Muhammad contended that separation of Blacks was a divine imperative. This was central in order to escape the degenerative effect of white society and the wrath of Allah who would destroy the U.S., a modern-day Babylon. Muhammad also argued for economic self-help and national racial solidarity in a Black United Front. Finally, he stressed the need for racial and Islamic solidarity throughout the world.

Although the Nation had its beginning in 1930, it reached its height in the early Sixties. Muhammad's achievements, as leader of the NOI, lie in both the area of theory and practice. He broke the monopoly whites had on good and God by revealing an alternative truth and reconstructing reality in Black images and interests. Moreover, he likewise broke the traditional monopoly Arabs and other Asian Muslims had on the doctrinal interpretation of Islam in the U.S. Thirdly, in doing this, he established a socio-historically specific form of Islam for Blacks. And fourthly, through this theological achievement and the building of its practical, organizational and institutional complement, he placed himself in the ranks of the most significant Black men in the history of the Afro-American people.

The Christian nationalist focus was best personified by Albert Cleage, the minister of the Shrine of the Black Madonna (Cleage, 1968; 1972). Cleage began his thrust by arguing that the Judeo-Christian heritage was, in fact, Black and needed to be redefined and reappropriated. He portrayed Jesus as a Black revolutionary who led a national liberation struggle against a white power, Rome. Moreover, he argued God is Black and partisan and demands social struggle, not submission. Power, he contended, is a basic aspect of group existence and blacks can only demand and establish respect and end oppression through unity and power. Cleage finally argues that the church must assume its historical revolutionary role and lead "God's Chosen People," Blacks, to liberation and social reconstruction.

The cultural thrust during the 60's was most definitively represented by Us Organization under the leadership of this author (Karenga, 1980; 1978). Us, established in 1965, was organized around the ideology and practice of *Kawaida*. The basic concepts of Kawaida centered around the contention that the key crisis in Black life is the cultural crisis, i.e., a crisis in views and, especially, values. The need, thus, is for a cultural revolution which would break the monopoly the oppressor has on Black minds and begin to rescue and reconstruct Black history and humanity in their own image and interests.

The ideology of Kawaida, which is essentially a theory of cultural and social change and which seeks to draw from and synthesize the best in nationalist, Pan-Africanist and socialist thought, became the most structured and widespread body of Black nationalist thought in the country. It is Kawaida out of which this author developed *Kwanzaa* and the *Nguzo Saba* and which, as a system of thought, affected in varying degrees the early political development of people like Angela Davis, Amiri Baraka, Haki Madhubuti, Kalamu ya Salaam, and Jitu Weusi. It is Kawaida which laid the ideological and organizational basis out of which grew Black United Fronts like the Black Congress in Los Angeles, the Black Federation in San Diego, Committee for A Unified Newark, the Congress of African Peoples and the National Black Assembly, and in whose theoretical framework was shaped the three national Black Power Conferences in the 60's.

Another definitive cultural achievement of the Sixties was the widespread positive turn toward Africa for revitalization and roots which was fostered by all Black nationalist groups. It was a logical outgrowth of the rejection of white values. It represented a defiant acceptance of Blackness and the search for an Afro-centric perspective and national program. This turn toward Africa was not simply symbolic in terms of dress and hairstyle, but was both cultural and political. It expressed a Pan-Africanism which culminated in the African Liberation Support Committee, the Congress of African Peoples, the Sixth Pan-African Congress and FESTAC in the Seventies.

Finally, the cultural thrust was defined by its stress on a new education for Blacks. From this came the Black Students' and Black Studies Movements. SNCC had been at the center and head of the student movement during the Civil Rights Movement and during the Nationalist Movement, it remained vital. It was joined by Us, the Panthers, CORE and small groups in building both Black Student Unions and a climate and structure for the demand and achievement of Black Studies.

It was, thus, during the Sixties that the Black Student Movement came into being, won Black Studies programs and challenged the traditional wisdom and structure of white academia (Robinson, et al, 1969; Edwards, 1970; Hare, 1972). The Black Student Movement stressed the need to bring the campus to the community and the community to the campus. Thus, inherent in its assumptions and aspirations was the thrust toward a new educational process which would be focused not only in established academia, but also in alternative institutions in the community. Some definitive examples were the School of Afro-American Culture of Us, the Ahidiana Work/Study Center, Uhuru Sasa of the East, and the Institute of Positive Education. (Kawaida served as the ideological base for these institutions.) These structures sought to define, introduce and reinforce new Afro-centric values and visions of self, society and the world and their impact on the Movement was central and continuing.

The political thrust of the Nationalist Movement was best exemplified by Malcolm X who served as a model, ideologically and personally, for countless nationalist groups and leaders (Malcolm X, 1965; 1966; 1970). Malcolm X was schooled and reached his height in the Nation of Islam. There, he laid the organizational basis for its national expansion and introduced it to the country and world. Malcolm, however, came into conflict with a changed direction and character of the NOI. He was first suspended in 1963, and then, left to set up his own organizations, Muslim Mosque, Inc. and the Organization of Afro-American Unity, in 1964.

Malcolm advocated several concepts which informed and inspired the Movement (Karenga, 1979). Thus, although he was a Muslim, he reached beyond the religious and had a profound effect on the entire movement. Malcolm, like his former teacher Muhammad, argued that Blacks needed a moral and spiritual regeneration and that it was best achieved through Islam. He stressed also the need for a Black United Front and built the Organization of Afro-American Unity modeled after the OAU on the continent. Moreover, Malcolm taught the need for Pan-Africanism and Third World solidarity. He emphasized the values of breaking the "minority mentality" by seeing ourselves as part of the majority in the world - Third World peoples as opposed to a minority in the U.S. He, thus, urged a linking of struggles and a worldview of our problem using the spirit and movement of Bandung as a model.

Closely linked with this concept was Malcolm's contention that blacks need to redefine our struggle from one of civil rights to human rights. This, he argued, would break the UN and international prohibition against interference in domestic affairs. He reasoned that the domestic character of issues prohibit world intervention, but issues of human concern demanded humanity's intervention both morally and politically in terms of the UN Charter.

Finally, Malcolm stressed the right and responsibility of self-defense. Joined to this was the logical extension of the right and responsibility to struggle for freedom by any means necessary. He argued that it was criminal to teach Blacks not to defend themselves and to leave them defenseless in the face of violence. Moreover, he contended, that it was equally criminal and dispiriting to teach Blacks that they do not have the right to win their freedom by struggle - armed and otherwise - like all other peoples in the world. To the end of his life, Malcolm served as a model of audaciousness, defying threats from the system, and travelling to world capitals to gain support for the Black liberation struggle.

That the Sixties witnessed Black people becoming less convinced about the viability of non-violence and daring to explore armed struggle and self-defense against racist violence was not due entirely to Malcolm. Robert Williams, who had been the President of the NAACP in Monroe, North Carolina, had argued in the late Fifties that self-defense was a natural and constitutional right (Williams, 1973). Moreover, he contended that the capacity for self-defense often limited the need to use it. For the attackers would be less likely to attack if they knew swift and effective penalties would follow. To illustrate this in practice, Williams organized a defense group which successfully protected the Black community against Klan attacks and intimidation and, thus gave Blacks a new method and model of struggle. His model produced the Deacons for Defense in Louisiana, which protected civil rights workers, and it served as inspiration to urban nationalist groups in the North.

Moreover, Williams deserves much credit for helping to internationalize the Black struggle. Fleeing a trumped-up charge (which he later beat) and death threats, he travelled to Canada, Cuba, China and Tanzania, where he wrote extensively on the Afro-American struggle. In China, he succeeded in getting Mao to issue a statement in support of the Afro-American liberation struggle in 1963 and was asked for comments on a subsequent support statement in 1968.

The Sixties also saw the rise and transformation of the Black Panther Party from a nationalist community defense structure to a Marxist-integrationist structure (Marine, 1969; Seale, 1970; Newton, 1972). Its early history is marked with bold, physical challenges to police structures in the name of self-defense of the Black community. In 1968 with Huey Newton in jail, Eldridge Cleaver made alliances with white radicals and denounced nationalism and other Panther leaders followed suit. What followed was a transformation of the Panther Party into a "revolutionary" surrogate for the left. This forced them into "custer stands" with the police they were ill-prepared to deal with, put them at odds with nationalist groups, helped contribute to their violent internecine struggle with Us and their effective reduction to essentially a legal defense committee. In fact, their legal cases consumed the bulk of their efforts. Their contribution to the Movement was essentially in their early period and must be seen, then, as a contribution of the Williams-Malcolm legacy.

Finally, the Sixties saw the rise of and focus on the land question. Although the Muslims had stressed the question during the Malcolm period, after '64 it was stressed less. Carmichael also raised it in the end of the 60's and stressed it in the 70's. However, it was the Republic of New Africa which, under the leadership of Imari Obadele, pressed it in a political and practical way (Obadele, 1975). Borrowing a lot from Malcolm and Muhammad, Obadele argued that Blacks were not citizens of the U.S. and were due a referendum to choose among three options: 1) U.S. citizenship; 2) nationality in Africa or a country of choice; or 3) building of a nation on this soil. Obadele and the RNA chose this land, declared independence from the U.S. in 1968 and demanded five Southern states (South Carolina, Georgia, Alabama, Louisiana and Mississippi) to construct a Republic of New Africa. Moreover, the RNA demanded reparations from the U.S. to build the nation and solicited world support. The question is still a burning one and is not solved by non-believers dismissing it as utopian.

The nationalist thrust, thus, contributed greatly to the character, course and achievements of the 60's. It included: 1) the building of economic institutions mainly through the NOI; 2) alternative educational institutional constructions; 3) the building of Black Student Unions and a Black Student Movement; 4) the construction of Black Studies programs, centers and departments; 5) the necessary relinking with the African people on the Continent and in the Diaspora; 6) the exploration of armed struggle and self-defense as a right and responsibility; 7) the redefinition of the world in Black images and interests; and 8) laying of the foundations for any and all benefits enjoyed in the 70's.

In conclusion, it is important to note that the Sixties left a fundamental lesson both in the process of its development, as well as in its comparison with the 70's. It is a lesson written in life struggles all over the world, i.e., the liberation of a people depends primarily on its own strength and struggle - regardless of the sincerity or support of its allies. In the final analysis, the Sixties taught Black people that a people that cannot save itself is lost forever. It was in opposition to their erstwhile allies, that Blacks charted a new course and made the new gains listed above. And if one reviews the 70's and the lull and losses they reflect, one cannot help but see the dismantling and weakening of Black structures as a significant factor in that development.

Bakke, Weber, the rise of the vulgar right and the cutback in social welfare gains in the 70's and 80's point to the structural incapacity of Afro-Americans to check these assaults on previous gains. It was Black structural capacity and struggle which brought Black gains and it was the absence of these which emboldened their adversaries. To paraphrase Frederick Douglass, if you want to know how much a tyrant will impose on a people, find out how much they will take. The misinterpretation of Black history and gains in the Sixties led to faulty reassessments and wholesale defections from the Afro-centric ideological and practical thrust. This led to the structural incapacity to respond to assaults on previous gains and reduced petty bourgeois leadership to making moral denunciations rather than taking concrete political steps to challenge and check such assaults.

Finally, it might be of use to note that if a people are assaulted in their identity, they have no alternative but to organize in defense and development of it. This, perhaps, was the most significant and provable legacy and lesson of the Sixties.

POST-SIXTIES

THE SEVENTIES. The decade began with recovery from the massive suppression and havoc wreaked on the Black Movement by the Cointelpro or counterintelligence program launched by the FBI in 1968. Hoover in a November 1968 memo asked 41 field offices for hard-hitting ideas to disrupt, discredit and destroy all real and potentially threatening Black leadership. This included groups such as the Black Panthers, Us, CORE, SNCC, the Nation of Islam and leaders as moderate as Martin Luther King. From this, violent internecine struggles were provoked and sustained as between the Panthers and Us, activists shot and murdered, put in captivity on trumped-up charges or driven into exile, and families as well as organizations disrupted and destroyed.

Hoover feared the unity of the Movement and rise of a Messiah who could unify it and create the basis for a real Black revolution. Cautioning the media never to advertise Black activists, expecially nationalists, except to discredit them, he created and fed disinformation to them. Using agent-provocateurs, he penetrated organizations, provoked them into internal struggles and violence and adventuristic acts which led to their arrests and deaths. This and other information was obtained through the Senate Select Committee Hearings on Intelligence and the Freedom of Information

Act which allowed citizens to get copies of files kept on them by intelligence agencies.

The violence and shock of the suppression destroyed morale, provoked both critical and uncritical reassessment and made many wonder whether organized activism was any longer a valid strategy for social change. Much which passed as critical assessment of the Sixties was in fact Black self-condemnation and reflected both a loss of heart and vision of what the 60's were all about and certainly what was achieved. As I have argued, the 60's was the most important decade in Black history and their achievement was substantial. And even though Blacks lost ground during the Seventies, they made gains also.

Easily the greatest gains of African Americans during the Seventies were their penetration and victories in electoral politics. Taking advantage of the Voting Rights Act of 1965, Blacks went to the polls in great numbers, especially in the South. Whereas in 1966, there were only six Blacks in Congress, ninety-seven in state legislatures and no mayors, by 1976, Blacks had elected eighteen Blacks to Congress, several hundred to state legislatures, two lieutenant-governors in California and Colorado and several mayors of major cities, including Los Angeles, Atlanta, Washington, D.C., Newark and Cleveland. Moreover, thousands had been elected to other state and local offices (Conyers and Wallace, 1976).

Also, Blacks sought to build national independent power structures throughout the decade, beginning with the first National Black Political Convention in Gary, Indiana, March 1972. Here over 3,000 delegates and approximately 5,000 alternates and observers passed resolutions, produced an historic document titled The Black Political Agenda and created a structure, the Black Assembly, that was posed as both a national body for collective planning and an organizing structure for independent electoral participation. The Black Political Agenda called for a new vision and bold and independent politics to meet the challenge of a clear social crisis in the U.S. (Gilliam, 1976: Chapter 6). Although the Agenda criticized the Democratic and Republican parties, it did not call for an independent Black one. Not until August 1980 at the Fourth National Black Assembly Convention in New Orleans was the decision made to form an independent Black party. In November, over 1,300 delegates from various organizations and political tendencies met to form the National Black Independent Political Party (NBIPP) "to advance a new Black politics of social transformation and self-determination" including, organizing, party-building, mobilization and "lobbying around private and public policy" and effectively and independently participating in electoral politics.

The Seventies also brought a resurgence of Pan-Africanism and the formation of two key organizations to advance its principles and practice. The first was the African Liberation Support Committee, a united front of Nationalist, Pan-Africanist and Marxist tendencies, dedicated to supporting liberation struggles on the continent of Africa through yearly massive African Liberation Day rallies in May, political education, and raising material and financial resources for the struggles. ALSC was eventually split by the Nationalist/Marxist ideological struggle for hegemony within it and lost the massive support it once had (Salaam, 1974). Still, however, various Pan-Africanist and nationalist groups continue to support the Continental liberation struggle and celebration of African Liberation Day, May 25. The second major organization was TransAfrica, an Afro-American lobby for Africa and the Caribbean. It has grown through the years and still monitors legislation and policy concerning Africa and the Caribbean and conducts political education through lectures, conferences and its bulletin. Also, it has recently developed a journal on U.S. policy toward Africa and the Caribbean.

Affirmative Action was another major issue and struggle in the Seventies. Growing out of Title VII of the 1964 Civil Rights Act, it was extended and reinforced by Executive Orders and the Equal Employment Opportunities Act of 1972. Although there were other cases as the DeFundis and Weber court cases which challenged affirmative action terming it "reverse discrimination," none was so argued and followed as the Bakke case. The Bakke case which originated in California over the special admissions policy of U.C. Davis' medical school, brought to head the struggle over the questions of numerical goals vs. quotas, preferential treatment vs. corrective measures for historical injustices and racially-weighted criteria vs. race-conscious criteria for school admission as well as employment.

Blacks parted company with many of their traditional allies among Jews, liberals and labor who felt threatened by the implications of affirmative action. Although moral and philosophical arguments were understandably raised, the basic problem centered around the fact that Black entrance into law, medical and other professional schools and areas of employment meant increased competition and struggle for critical social space with those who traditionally held a monopoly of them. The Supreme Court seemed to straddle and ruled in 1978 that reservation of places for minorities (Third World people) and uncompetitive evaluation was prohibited, but that consideration of race and ethnic origin as one criteria for selection as well as consciously seeking diversity were permissible. (Sindler, 1978: Chapter 4).

Key also to the Seventies was the emergence of an open and ongoing discussion among Black men and women on the quality, forms and future of their relationships and the transformation this produced. Major Black journals and magazines like Black Scholar and Black Books Bulletin, Essence and Ebony, regularly carried articles and sometimes dedicated whole issues to the question of Black Male/Female relationships. Books, poems and plays self-consciously concerned themselves with this pressing issue, and debates and discussions on campuses, in the community and on TV and radio were regular occurrences. Moreover, psychologists, Nathan and Julia Hare started a new journal, *Black Male/Female Relationships,* dedicated entirely to critically discussing, understanding and improving them. The impetus for this reassessment was rooted in three basic factors: 1) the general reassessment of the thought and practices of the Sixties; 2) the collective agreement of its urgency; and 3) the influence of the general social struggle of women for social equality. Although Black women did not join the Women's Liberation Movement in great numbers, they raised many of its questions, influenced and were influenced by much of its literature and were thus part of the overall struggle to end sexism in social and personal relations.

Finally, Vincent Harding (1980, Chapter 30) lists in addition to the above key issues and events of the Seventies, the prison revolts as at Soledad and Attica, the transformation of the Nation of Islam, and the awesome tragedy of Jonestown. The prison revolts reflected a continuing relationship with the struggles of the Sixties and the transformation of the NOI represented the loss of an important Black "religiously based challenge to the structures of White American life" and a symbol of defiant Blackness. And Jonestown represented the great dangers of unguided and uncritical searches for spiritual community in the context of cynicism, hedonism, materialism, individualism and alienation which marked the Seventies. It also underlined the absence of a Black mass movement which historically served as a base of meaningful relationships, community and hope. As Blacks moved into the 80's, they were keenly aware of the value and urgency of the need to rebuild a self-conscious united and active community which characterized the 60's.

THE EIGHTIES. The decade began with three major challenges to African Americans: 1) the continuing crisis of U.S. society; 2) the rise of the vulgar and respectable right; and 3) the continuing struggle to rebuild a Black mass movement and appropriate alliances and coalitions in order to defend Black gains, win new ones and minimize losses. The continuing crisis in U.S. society is marked most definitively by severe economic problems including high level inflation and unemployment, especially among Blacks, a perennially unbalanced budget, an aging productive structure, resource shortages, large military spending and massive cutbacks and cutoffs of government spending in other areas, especially in social welfare. And it is clearly complicated by self-confessed confusion at the highest levels of government as to how exactly to address these problems (Greider, 1981).

The rise of the right, which continues from the Seventies, expresses itself in the return of violent racist groups like the Klan and other neo-nazi formations, the rise of Christian fundamentalists and perhaps most importantly, Reagan's presidential victory and the various successes of right-wing candidates in state and local elections. With this turn of events came several related occurrences: 1) the tendency to declare social entitlement programs morally wrong and financially too costly; 2) strong and continuing demands for tax cuts, reduced social services and especially, reduced and more stringently restricted social welfare; 3) the progressive diminishing of the government's role in achieving social justice and equality for Third World peoples and the poor; and 4) the steady reversal of gains of the 60's and early 70's.

In addition to the rise of the white right in and out of government, there is a parallel rise of a Black right (Daniels, 1980). These Black conservatives who are also in and out of government serve the current Administration and right-wing thrust by supporting policies and developing arguments against the minimum wage, government intervention to correct injustices for ethnics and the poor, affirmative action, equal opportunity programs and most other programs and proposals won in the general thrust for civil rights in the 60's and early 70's. This rise of Black conservatism and the challenge it poses for the liberal civil rights approach clearly has its historical parallel in the Washington-DuBois conflict concerning approaches to Black social advancement. Like Washington, the Black conservatives reject Black protest and emphasize vocational education and self-help. On the other hand, the liberals, like DuBois, stress protest, multidimensional education and the obligation of U.S. society to live up to its claims and of government to facilitate and insure this.

In this context, the liberal and radical Black leadership have been challenged to rebuild their own organizations and the mass movement which was so effective in the Sixties. As in the 60's, the mass movement requires national organizations with adequate vision, structure and resources to meet the challenge of leadership and cooperation necessary to form a national Black united front which will stand at the center of the mass movement. Both radical and liberal organizations have attempted to build such a united front formation. The liberal forces have created the Black Leadership Forum which is made up of approximately sixteen national organizations. However, it is not well-known and is not visibly engaged in collective planning, organizing the national Black community or confronting the system. Secondly, the liberal forces often use the yearly Congressional Black Caucus Legislative Weekend structure as a means to gather, get briefings on the latest governmental policies, decisions and proposals, and to discuss possible defensive and developmental strategies. But the CBC is not really suited for activist leadership and the Weekends are more for briefings and informal exchanges than for the development of concrete action plans.

The radicals also have produced two national structures which they see as possibly providing an ideological and structural center for the mass movement necessary to define, defend and develop Black interests. Those are the National Black United Front and the

National Black Independent Political Party, both of which were formed in 1980, the former in June and the latter in November. NBIPP, as mentioned above, seeks to be a genuine party which gives Blacks a clear alternative to the two traditional parties. Following in the tradition of other Black political parties, it seeks to point out the inability of the traditional parties to meet Black needs and build a powerful alternative structure to accomplish this (Daniels, 1980; Flewellen, 1981). The Party, however, remains in the formative stages and is having the traditional problems of third parties, i.e., resources, strategy, membership, community legitimacy and electoral success. (Walton, 1972).

NBUF is the larger of the two organizations, more active and more solidly based in the national community with chapters throughout the country (Daughtery, 1981). Although it is essentially a nationalist formation, NBUF's constitution sets for itself the task of "delicately" formulating "the conservative, moderate, reform, radical and nationalist concerns, problems and goals of the varied constituencies in the Black community into a dynamic black agenda, which speaks to our collective interests as a people." This is obviously its chief task and will decide whether it succeeds and grows or flounders.

The problem of alliance and coalition is also a challenge for Blacks in the 80's. For they are a necessary complement to the building of a self-conscious and effective mass movement. Although strains developed in the traditional Black-labor-liberal coalition in the late 60's and 70's, the Black liberal forces continue to see it as vital to defense of gains and the struggle for broad social change and thus, are striving to rebuild it. And the radicals who see alliances with Third World people and labor as necessary political projects are likewise attempting to rebuild and build those and make them active and effective.

In conclusion then, the 80's promise to be a decisive decade whose conflicts and struggles will be over the shape and future of the country. Thus, the decade poses not only a challenge to Blacks, but also to other Third World peoples, progressives and liberals to be actively concerned about what kind of country this should be. Clearly, however, it is in the interest and historical tradition of African Americans to serve again as catalyst and vanguard of the struggle which resists rightist reversals of fundamental humanistic gains and begins to build a society which successfully defends and expands the national ideals of freedom, equality of access and opportunity, and social justice. As Harding (1980:231) contends, it is African Americans who must, at "so elemental a time of turning" and coming from such a rich history of social change and leadership, pose the question to themselves and others of "how do we move forward, beyond our best leaders of the past, beyond our best declarations, beyond our best actions, beyond our best dreams, to participate fully in the creation of a fundamentally new reality, in ourselves, in our people, in this nation, and in this world?"

STUDY QUESTIONS

1. What is history and what is its relevance?
2. Cite some of Egypt's major contributions to the advancement of humankind.
3. List and discuss the major empires of the Western Sudanic civilization.
4. What were some of the major contributions of the Moorish empire to Europe through Spain?
5. What are the basic factors leading to the fall of African societies?
6. What arguments does Van Sertima make to prove African presence in Olmec civilization?
7. What are some basic misconceptions about the slave trade? Discuss its impact?

8. What was the basis for slavery and some of its basic aspects?
9. List and discuss the major forms of resistance to slavery.
10. Discuss Black participation in the Civil War.
11. What were some of the basic reasons for the failure of Reconstruction?
12. What were the reasons for the Great Migration?
13. What were some of the major Black inventors and inventions during the period of industrialization?
14. What are some of the major philosophical contentions of Washington, DuBois and Garvey?
15. Discuss the New Deal period.
16. What were the two main tendencies of the 60's and what were their organizations and achievements?
17. What are some major challenges and achievements of the 70's and 80's?

REFERENCES

Introduction/African Background

Ajayi, J.F.A. and Ian Espie (eds.). (1972) *A Thousand Years of West African History,* New York: Humanities Press.

Beattie, John. (1960) *Bunyoro, An African Kingdom,* New York: Holt, Beinhart, Winston.

ben-Jochannon, Yosef A.A. (1971) *Africa: Mother of "Western Civilization,"* New York: Alkebu-lan Books Associates.

———— . (1970) *African Origins of the Major "Western Religions,"* New York: Alkebu-lan Books Associates.

———— . (1972) *Black Man of the Nile and His Family,* New York: Alkebu-lan Books Associates.

Bober, M.M. (1948) *Karl Marx' Interpretation of History,* New York: W.W. Norton & Co.

Bracey, John H. et al. (1970) *Black Nationalism in America,* New York: Bobbs-Merrill Co.

Budge, E.A. Wallis (transl.). (1960) *The Book of the Dead,* New York: University Books.

Clark, J. Desmond. (1970) *The Prehistory of Africa,* New York: Praeger Publishers.

Collins, Robert O. (1968) *Problems in African History,* Englewood Cliffs: Prentice-Hall, Inc.

Conrad, Earl. (1943) *Harriet Tubman,* Washington, D.C.: Associated Publishers, Inc.

Davidson, Basil. (1966) *A History of West Africa to the Nineteenth Century,* Garden City, N.Y.: Doubleday & Co.

_____. (1967) *East and Central Africa to the Late Nineteenth Century,* Nairobi: Longmans, Green & Co.

_____. (1959) *The Lost Cities of Africa,* Boston: Little, Brown & Co.

DeGraft-Johnson, John C. (1966) *African Glory,* New York: Walker & Co.

Diop, Cheikh Anta. (1974) *The African Origin of Civilization: Myth or Reality,* Westport: Lawrence Hill & Co.

DuBois, W.E.B. (1975) *Black Folk: Then and Now,* New York: Kraus-Thomson.

_____. (1965) *The World and Africa,* New York: International Publishers.

El Mahdi, Mandour. (1965) *A Short History of the Sudan,* London: Oxford University Press.

Fage, J.D. (1969) *A History of West Africa,* London: Cambridge University Press.

Gailey, Harry A. (1970) *History of Africa From Earliest Times to 1800,* New York: Holt, Rinehart and Winston.

Garvey, Amy Jacques (ed.) (1977) *Philosophy & Opinions of Marcus Garvey, I & II*, New York: Atheneum.

Harris, Joseph E.   (1972) *Africans and Their History*, New York: New American Library.

Jackson, John G.   (1980) *Introduction to African Civilizations*, Secaucus, N.J.: Citadel Press.

James, George.   (1976) *Stolen Legacy*, San Francisco: Julian Richardson Associates.

July, Robert W.   (1970) *A History of the African People*, New York: Charles Scribner's Sons.

Karenga, Maulana.   (1977) "Corrective History," *First World*, 1, 3, (May/June) 50-54.

_____ .   (1978)   *Essays on Struggle: Position and Analysis*, San Diego: Kawaida Publications.

_____ .   (1980) *Kawaida Theory: An Introductory Outline*, Inglewood, Ca.: Kawaida Publications.

Kling, Susan.   (1979) *Fannie Lou Hamer*, Chicago: Women for Racial and Economic Equality.

Lane-Poole, Stanley.   (1886)   *The Story of the Moors in Spain*, New York: G.P. Putnam's Sons.

Massie, Dorothy C.   (1974) *The Legacy of Mary McLeod Bethune*, Washington, D.C.: National Education Association.

McCabe, Joseph.   (1935) *The Splendour of Moorish Spain*, London: Watts and Co.

McCall, Daniel F.   (1969) *Africa in Time-Perspective*, New York: Oxford University Press.

Murdock, G.P.   (1959) *Africa: Its People and Their Culture History*, New York: McGraw Hill.

Murphy, E. Jefferson. (1972) *History of African Civilization*, New York: Dell Publishing Company.

National Educational Association. (1974) *Mary McLeod Bethune*, New York: National Educational Association.

Oliver, Roland and G. Matthews. (1963) *History of East Africa, I*, Oxford: Clarendon Press.

Omer-Cooper, John D. (1966) *The Zulu Aftermath*, London: Longmans.

Pankhurst, Richard Keir. (1967) *The Ethiopian Royal Chronicles*, Addis Ababa: Oxford University Press.

Parry, J.H. (1966) *The Establishment of the European Hegemony*, New York: Harper & Row.

Petry, Ann (1955) *Harriet Tubman*, New York: Robert Books.

Rocker, Rudolph. (1937) *Nationalism and Culture*, New York: Couici-Friede.

Rodney, Walter. (1974) *How Europe Underdeveloped Africa*, Washington, D.C.: Howard University Press.

Rogers, J.A. (1972) *World's Great Men of Color, I*, New York: Macmillan.

Shinnie, Peter L. (1967) *Meroe: A Civilization of the Sudan*, New York: Frederick A. Praeger, Inc.

Thorpe, Earl. (1971) *Black Historians*, New York: William Morrow.

Trimingham, John S. (1962) *A History of Islam in West Africa*, London: Oxford University Press.

Van Sertima, Ivan. (1976) *They Came Before Columbus*, New York: Random House.

Vasina, Jan. (1968) *Kingdoms of the Savanna*, Madison: University of Wisconsin Press.

Vilakazi, Absolam.   (1962) *Zulu Transformations*, Natal, S.A.: University of Witwatersrand Press.

Williams, Chancellor.   (1974) *The Destruction of Black Civilization*, Chicago: Third World Press.

Africans in America

Adams, Russell L.   (1969) *Great Negroes Past and Present*, Chicago: Afro-Am Publishing Co.

Aptheker, Herbert   (1959) *A Documentary History of the Negro People in the United States*, New York: Citadel Press.

_____ . (1943) *American Negro Slave Revolts*, New York: International Publishers.

_____ . (1968) *To Be Free*, New York: International Publishers.

Bauer, Raymond and Alice.   (1942) "Day-to-Day Resistance to Slavery," *Journal of Negro History*, 27 (October) 388-419.

Bennett, Lerone.   (1975) *The Shaping of Black America*, Chicago: Johnson Publishing Company.

Bernal, Ignacio. (1979) *Great Sculpture of Ancient Mexico*, New York: William Morrow & Company.

Blassingame, John.   (1979) *The Slave Community*, New York: Oxford University Press.

Brisbane, Robert H.   (1974) *Black Activism*, Valley Forge, Pa.: Judson Press.

Broderick, Francis.   (1969) *W.E.B. DuBois: Negro Leader in Time of Crisis*, Stanford: Stanford University Press.

Carmichael, Stokely and Charles Hamilton.   (1967) *Black Power*, New York: Vintage Books.

Carroll, Joseph. (1938) *Slave Insurrections in the U.S.*, Boston: Little, Brown & Co.

Carson, Clayborne.   (1981) *In Struggle,* Cambridge, Mass.: Harvard University Press.

Carwell, Hattie.   (1977) *Blacks in Science,* Hicksville, N.Y.: Exposition Press.

Clark, Kenneth (ed.) (1963) *The Negro Protest,* Boston: Harper Press.

Cleage, Albert. (1972) *Black Christian Nationalism,* New York: William Morrow & Co.

_____ . (1968) *The Black Messiah,* New York: Sheed & Ward.

Coe, Michael. (1962) *Mexico,* New York: Praeger Publishers.

Conyers, James E. and Walter L. Wallace.   (1976) *Black Elected Officials,* New York: Russell Sage Foundation.

Cruse, Harold.   (1967) *Crisis of the Negro Intellectual,* New York: William Morrow & Co.

Daniels, Ron. (1980) "The National Black Political Assembly: Building Independent Black Politics in the 1980's," *Black Scholar,* 11,4 (March/April).

Daughtery, Herbert. (1981) "An Interview," *The Black Nation, (Fall) 8-11.*

Davidson, Basil.   (1968) Africa in History, London: Macmillian Co.

De Roo, Peter: (1900) *History of America Before Columbus,* Philadelphia: J.B. Lippincott.

Diggs, Irene.   (1975) *Black Innovators,* Chicago: Third World Press.

Drake, St. Clair and Horace Cayton. (1962) *Black Metropolis,* New York: Harper & Row.

Dubois, W.E.B.   (1969) *Souls of Black Folk,* New York: New American Library.

Edwards, Harry. (1970) *Black Students,* New York: Free Press.

Elkins, Stanley. (1966) *Slavery*, Chicago: University of Chicago Press.

Emmerich, Andre. (1963) *Art Before Columbus*, New York: Simon and Schuster.

Farmer, James. (1965) *Freedom Win*, New York: Random House.

Flewellen, Kathryn. (1981) "The National Black Independent Political Party: Will History Repeat?" *Freedomways*, 21, 2, pp. 93-105.

Forman, James. (1972) *The Making of Black Revolutionaries*, New York: Macmillan Co.

Fogel, Robert and Barry Engerman. (1974) *Time on the Cross*, Boston: Little, Brown & Co.

Foster, Laurence. (1935) *Negro-Indian Relationships in the Southwest*, Philadelphia: AMS Press.

Franklin, John H. (1974) *From Slavery to Freedom*, New York: Alfred A. Knopf.

Garvey, Amy Jacques (ed.). (1977) *Philosophy & Opinions of Marcus Garvey, I & II*, New York: Atheneum.

Genovese, Eugene. (1981) *From Rebellion to Revolution*, New York: Vintage Books.

———. (1974) Roll, Jordan, Roll. New York: Pantheon Books

Gilliam, Reginald E. (1975) *Black Political Development*, Port Washington, N.Y.: Kennikat Press.

Greene, Lorenzo. (1944) "Mutiny on the Slave Ships," *Phylon*, 5 (4th qtr.)

Greider, William. (1981) "The Education of David Stockman," *The Atlantic Monthly*, (December) 27-54.

Haber, Louis. (1970). *Black Pioneers of Science and Invention*, New York: Harcourt, Brace and World, Inc.

Harding, Vincent.   (1980)   *The Other American Revolution,* Los Angeles/Atlanta: Center for Afro-American Studies/Institute of the Black World.

_____ .   (1981) *There Is A River,* New York: Harcourt, Brace Jovanovich.

Hare, Nathan.   (1972) "The Battle for Black Studies," *The Black Scholar,* 3, 9 (May) 32-47.

Harris, Joseph E.   (1972) *Africans and Their History,* New York: New American Library.

Hayden, Robert C.   (1972) *Eight Black American Inventors,* Reading, Mass.: Addison-Wesley Co.

Jackson, John G.   (1980) *Pagan Origins of the Christ Myth,* San Diego: The Truth Seeker Company.

Jairazbhoy, R.A.   (1974) *Ancient Egyptians and Chinese in America,* Totowa, N.J.: Rowman and Littlefield.

Karenga, Maulana.   (1977) "Corrective History," *First World,* 1, 3 (May/June) 50-54.

_____ .   (1978) *Essays on Struggle: Position and Analysis,* San Diego: Kawaida Publications.

_____ .   (1980) *Kawaida Theory: An Introductory Outline,* Inglewood, Ca.: Kawaida Publications.

King, Martin Luther, Jr.   (1958) *Stride Toward Freedom,* New York: Harper & Row Publishers.

_____ .   (1962) *Why We Can't Wait,* New York: Harper & Row Publishers.

Klein, Aaron E.   (1971) *The Hidden Contributors: Black Scientists and Inventors in America,* New York: Doubleday and Co.

Lawrence, Harold. (1962) "African Explorers in the New World," *The Crisis,* (June-July) 321-332.

Littlefield, Daniel Jr. (1977) *Africans and Seminoles*, Westport: Greenwood Press.

Logan, Rayford. (1954) *The Negro in American Life and Thought: The Nadir, 1877-1901*, New York: Van Nostrand Reinhold Co.

Lomax, Louis E. (1962) *The Negro Revolt*, New York: Signet Books.

Malcolm X. (1965) *Autobiography of Malcolm X*, New York: Grove Press.

———— .   (1970) *By Any Means Necessary*, New York: Grove Press.

————. (1966) *Malcolm X Speaks*, New York: Grove Press.

Marine, Gene.   (1969) *The Black Panthers*, New York: New American Library.

Martin, Tony. (1976) *Race First*, Westport: Greenwood Press.

Meier, August.   (1975) "Toward A Reinterpretation of Booker T. Washington," *Journal of Southern History*, 23, pp. 220-227.

Moon, Henry. (1972) *The Emerging Thought of W.E.B. DuBois*, New York: Simon & Schuster.

Muhammad, Elijah.   (1973) *The Fall of Africa*, Chicago: Muhammad's Temple of Islam, No. 2.

————. (1965) *Message to the Black Man in America*, Chicago: Muhammad's Temple of Islam, No. 2.

Mullin, Gerald W. (1975) *Flight and Rebellion*, New York: Oxford University Press.

Newton, Huey.   (1972) *To Die For the People*, New York: Random House.

Obadele, Imari.   (1975) *Foundations of the Black Nation*, Detroit: Songhay Press.

Peck, James.   (1962) *Freedom Ride,* New York: Simon & Schuster.

Phillips, Ulrich B.   (1963) *"Life and Labor in the Old South,"* Boston: Little, Brown & Co.

Porter, Kenneth.   (1932) "Relations Between Negroes and Indians With the Present Limits of the United States," *Journal of Negro History,* 17 (July) 287-367.

Price, Richard.   (1973) *Maroon Societies,* Garden City, N.Y.: Anchor Books.

Proudfoot, Merrill.   (1962) *Diary of a Sit-In,* Chapel Hill, N.C.: University of North Carolina Press.

Quarles, Benjamin. (1969) *Black Abolitionists* New York, Oxford University Press.

_____. (1953) *The Negro in the Civil War,* Boston: Little, Brown & Co.
_____ .   (1976) *The Negro in the Making of America,* New York: Collier Books.

Robinson, Armstead et al (eds.).   (1969) *Black Studies in the University,* New York: Bantam Books.

Rodney, Walter.   (1974) *How Europe Underdeveloped Africa,* Washington, D.C. Howard University Press.

Rogers, J.A.   (1961) *Africa's Gift to America,* New York: Helga M. Rogers.

Salaam, Kalamu ya.   (1974) "Tell No Lies Claim No Easy Victories," *Black World,* 23, 12 (October) 18-34.

Schwartz, Rosalie.   (1975) *Across the Rio to Freedom,* El Paso: Texas Western Press

Seale, Bobby.   (1970) *Seize the Time,* New York: Random House.

Sindler, Allan P.   (1978) *Bakke, DeFunis and Minority Admissions,* New York: Longman.

Sorin, Gerald.   (1973) *Abolitionism.* New York: Praeger Publishers.

Stamp, Kenneth.   (1965) *The Peculiar Institution,* New York: Alfred Knopf, Inc.

Stirling, Matthew, W.   (1939) "Discovering the New World's Oldest Dated Work of Man," *National Geographic Magazine,* 76 (August) 183-218.

Stuckey, Sterling.   (1977) "Through the Prism of Folklore: the Black Ethos in Slavery," in *American Negro Slavery,* (eds.) Allen Weinstein and Frank Gatell, New York: Oxford University Press, 134-152.

Thornbrough, E.L. (ed.).   (1969) *Booker T. Washington,* Englewood Cliffs: Prentice-Hall, Inc.

Van Sertima, Ivan.   (1976) *They Came Before Columbus,* New York: Random House.

von Wuthenau, Alexander.   (1969) *The Art of Terracotta Pottery in Pre-Columbian South and Central America,* New York: Random House.

Walton, Hanes Jr.   (1972) *Black Political Parties,* New York: Free Press.

Washington, Booker T.   (1968) *Up From Slavery,* New York: Magnum Books.

Weinberg, Meyer.   (1970) *W.E.B. DuBois: A Reader,* New York: Harper & Row Publishers.

Weiner, Leo. (1922) *Africa and the Discovery of America,* Philadelphia: Innes and Sons.

Williams, Eric.   (1966) *Capitalism & Slavery,* New York: Capricorn Books.

Williams, Robert.   (1973) *Negroes With Guns,* Chicago: Third World Press.

Wolffe, Miles.   (1972) *Lunch at the Five and Ten,* New York: Stein & Day Publishers.

Woodson, Carter G. and Charles H. Wesley. (1972) *The Negro in Our History*, Washington, D.C.: Associated Publishers.

Zinn, Howard. (1964) *SNCC. The New Abolitionists*, Boston: Beacon Press.

III
BLACK RELIGION

INTRODUCTION

Religion has always been a vital part of Black life in both Africa and the U.S. In Africa, religion was so pervasive that distinctions between it and other areas of life were almost imperceptible (Mbiti, 1970). In the U.S., the extent of Black religiousness is clear and has been well-documented (Lincoln, 1974). Although there are numerous definitions for religion, for the purpose of this chapter, religion can be defined as thought, belief and practice concerned with the ultimate questions of life (Karenga, 1980:23). Among such questions are those concerning human death, relevance, origin, destiny, suffering and obligations to other humans and in most cases, to a Supreme or Ultimate Being. Within the context of the concern with the ultimate is also the clear division between the sacred, i.e., the set apart and exalted, and the profane, i.e., the common and non-exalted (Yinger, 1970).

The religion of Black people in the U.S. is predominantly Judeo-Christian, but Islam, both Black and orthodox, and traditional African religions, are growing among Afro-Americans. Given the fact that Black religion is so predominantly Judeo-Christian, the tendency is to see it as "white religion in Black face." However, as Lincoln (1974a) and Wilmore (1973) contend, such an interpretation is grossly incorrect. For regardless of what external details of white Christianity are similar to Black Christianity, the essence of Black Christianity is different. The essence of a people's

160

religion is rooted in its own social and historical experiences and the truth and meaning they extract from these and translate into an authentic spiritual expression which speaks specifically to them. Thus, Black religion represents in its essence then, not imitation but "the desire of Blacks to be self-conscious about the meaning of their Blackness and to search for spiritual fulfillment in terms of their understanding of themselves and their experience of history" (Lincoln, 1974a:3).

AFRICAN MODELS

GENERAL THEMES

Black religion like Black people began in Africa and thus, it is important to discuss its historical forms before turning to its current expressions. The study of traditional African religions is made difficult by Europeans interpretations which exhibit a need to make Christianity seem superior and African religions primitive (Evans-Pritchard, 1965), and by African Christian interpretations which strive to make African religions more "normal" by making them look more Christian or Western (Idowu, 1975; Mbiti, 1970). To appreciate African religions, one must admit similarities and differences without seeing the similarities as "less developed" and the differences as evidence of psychological or cultural defectiveness.

Thus, if African stories of creation and gods are myths, so are Christian, Jewish and Islamic ones. Moreover, Jehovah, Yaweh and Allah are no more arguable than Nkulunkulu, Oludumare and Amma. And the abasom of the Ashanti and the orisha of the Yoruba are no less effective as divine intermediaries than Catholic saints like Jude and Christopher. All non-scientific approaches to the origin of the world and the forces operative in it are vulnerable to challenge. And the choice of one over the other is more a matter of tradition and preference than proof of any particular one's validity. Therefore, my use of Western religious examples will not be to force comparisons or contrasts, but to demonstrate parallels where appropriate which would tend to lessen a student's tendency to reductively translate African religions in a mistaken assumption of superiority for his/her own.

Although African religions are complex and diverse, there are some general themes which tend to appear in all of them. First, there is the belief in one Supreme God: Oludumare among the Yoruba, Nkulunkulu among the Zulu and Amma among the Dogon. This god is the Father in most societies, but also appears as Mother in matriarchical societies like the Ovambo in Namibia and the Nuba in Kenya. Moreover, in Dogon religion, Amma has both male and female characteristics, reflecting the Dogon concept of binary opposition as the motive force and structure of the universe (Ray, 1976:28-29).

Secondly, in traditional African religion, God is both immanent and transcedent, near and far. In this framework, then, Africans engage in daily interaction with divinities, who are seen as God's intermediaries and assistants (Mbiti, 1970). These divinities are both similar to and different from Jesus, angels and Catholic saints as intermediaries and assistants to the Supreme Being. It is this deference and exchange with the divinities which made the less critical assume Africans were polytheistic rather than monotheistic. However, evidence clearly argues against this assumption.

Thirdly, African religions stress ancestor veneration. The ancestors are venerated because of their contribution in life, their being guardians of family traditions and ethics and because they are viewed as "the best group of intermediaries between men and God" (Mbiti, 1970:108).

Fourthly, African traditional religion stresses the necessary balance between one's collective identity and responsibility as a member of society and one's personal identity and responsibility. Like religion itself, a person is defined as an integral part of a definite community, to which she/he belongs and in which she/he finds identity and relevance. Summing up this conception, Mbiti (1970:141) states that "I am because we are, and since we are, therefore I am." The Dinka have captured this stress on the moral ideal of harmonious integration of self with the community in their word *cieng* which means both *morality* and *living together*. In this conception, the highest moral ideal is to live in harmony, know oneself and one's duties through others and reach one's fullness in cooperation with and through support from one's significant others (Deng, 1973).

Another key theme in African religions is the profound respect for nature. Because humans live in a religious universe, everything that is has religious relevance. The whole world as God's creation is alive with His/Her symbols and gifts to humans, and bear witness to His/Her power, beauty and beneficence. Thus, there are sacred trees, rivers, mountains and animals (as in Western religions). Nature is not only respected because of its association with God, but also because of its relevance to humankind. The stress, then, is to show it due respect, not abuse it and live in harmony with it and the universe.

Finally, the conception of death and immortality is an important theme in African religions. Death in African religions is seen in several ways. First, it is seen as another stage in human development. Humans are born, live, die and become the ancestors. Death is thus not the end, but a beginning of another form of existence, i.e., as ancestor and spirit. Therefore, it is seen as a disruption of life rather than an end to it. After a period of mourning, then, there is celebration for the human conquest of death. For after the funeral, the dead are "revived" in the spirit world and as ancestors, are close and relevant. Secondly, death is seen as reflective of cosmic patterns, i.e., the rising and setting of the sun, and often graves are dug east and west to imitate this pattern.

Thirdly, death is seen as a transition of life to personal and collective immortality. Personally, one lives after death through four media: 1) children; 2) other relatives; 3) rituals of remembrance; and 4) great works or significant deeds. The living remember and speak one's names and deeds, and works speak of one's significance throughout time. Thus, without relatives to keep one's memory alive or significant achievements and deeds, one is what Africans call utterly dead. Collective immortality is achieved through the life of one's people and through what one means to them. For as long as they live, the person lives and shares in their life and destiny.

THE DOGON MODEL

One of the most complex and impressive African religious systems is that of the Dogon. The Dogon, who live in Mali, have astounded the world by their astronomical knowledge and impressed it with the logic and intricacy of their thought. So impressive is their knowledge, especially of the Sirius star-system, that some Europeans have argued that the Dogon's knowledge was given to them by space beings (Temple, 1976) or by mysterious Europeans (Sagan, 1979). However, Europeans did not know themselves until the 1800's what the Dogon knew about the Sirius star-system 700 years ago (Adams, 1979).

The socio-religious thought of the Dogon evolves from an elaborate cosmogyny and an extremely complex cosmology (Griaule, 1978; Griaule and Dieterlen, 1955). It is these constructions around which the Dogon understand and organize their world and seek to carry out their social and spiritual tasks. For the sake of brevity and clarity, I have tried to cut down the story of creation to its most basic elements while at the same time, trying to remain faithful to its logic and content.

In the beginning everything that would be already potentially was. The substance and structure of the universe was in Amma, the Supreme God, who was in the image of an egg and divided into four quarters containing the four basic elements of air, earth, fire and water, and the four cardinal directions - north, south, east and west. Thus, Amma was the egg of the universe and the universe and Amma were one. As egg, Amma symbolized and was fertility and unlimited creative possibility. Through creative thought, Amma traced within himself the design and developmental course of the universe using 266 cosmic Signs which contained the essence, structure and life-principle of all things. Placing the four basic elements and sacred Signs and Seeds on a flat disk, Amma set the disk revolving between the two cosmic axes. But the spinning disk threw off the water drying up the Seeds. The first creation was thus, aborted and Amma began again, deciding that this time he would make humans the preservers of order and life in the world.

Placing a Seed at the center of himself, the cosmic egg, he spoke seven creative Words. From this the Seed (matter) vibrated seven times unfolding along a spiral path, conserving itself on one hand and transforming itself on the other through alternations between opposites. Thus, the principal of twinness or binary opposition directed its movement and its form and established a pattern for the structure and functioning of the universe, i.e., up/down, man/woman, action/inaction, hot/cold, etc. From the infinitely small (seed, atom) the infinitely large (universe) evolved. The Seed, vibrating seven times and turning in a spiral fashion, extended itself in seven directions in the womb of the world, pre-figuring the shape of a human being, i.e., two directions for the head, two for the arms, two for the legs and one for the genital. Thus, the world was created in the image of humans and would later be organized around them.

Transforming the egg into a double placenta, Amma placed two sets of twins, male and female in each, again underscoring the principle of opposites which informs the structure and functioning of the universe. In the twins, He placed the sacred Signs, Words and Seeds of creation. Before gestation was completed, however, one of the male twins, Yurugu (Ogo) feeling lonely and incomplete burst through the womb to seize his female twin. Unable to acquire his twin, he rebelled against the established order of things. Imposing disorder on a orderly process, Yurugu descended into the void in an attempt to create a world himself. But his knowledge was incomplete and he could not speak the creative Words. Then, Amma, using the piece of placenta which Yurugu took as he broke from the celestial egg-womb, created the earth. This creation of earth restored the human shape of the world. The celestial egg became the head of man; the lower incomplete placenta, now earth and forming an incomplete circle, became the hips and legs; and the space and lines which divide and connect heaven and earth became the trunk and arms. Binary opposition is thus, again established in that heaven is the head (mind, spirit) and earth, the lower region of the body (the physical). Joined together, they form the structure and essence of humans.

To restore order in the world, Amma scattered Yurugu's male twin, Nommo, i.e., creative Word, over the expanse of the universe. Also, He created four other Nommo spirits from Nommo and their off-spring became the eight Ancestors of the Dogon. Amma then sent Nommo and the eight ancestors down to earth, with all species of animals and plants, and all the elements of human culture thus, laying the basis for human development and a prosperous earth. Descending, Nommo shouted out the creative Words, therefore transmitting the power of creative speech and thought to Earth, making it available to humankind. Through this power, they would be able to push back the boundaries of ignorance and disorder and impose creative order on the world. To punish Yurugu for his disorder and revolt, Amma transformed him into a Pale Fox. Deprived of his female half, Pale Fox is an incomplete and lonely being wandering through the world in a vain quest for wholeness. But as he wanders, he leaves tracks through the mysteries of life, revealing the dangers humans must avoid. Finally, sending rain to Earth, Amma made the Earth flourish and humans began to cultivate the land and cover it with ever-increasing numbers. Possessing creative intelligence through Nommo, humans walk the way of Yurugu as well, alternating between disorder and order, destruction and creation, rationality and irrationality, conformity and revolt.

There are several aspects of this cosmogonical construction which reveal the profundity of Dogon thought and its susceptibility to interesting and expansive interpretations. First, it stresses the binary oppositional character and functioning of the universe, i.e., creation, destruction, order, disorder, male/female, perfection, imperfection, self-conscious action/unconscious action, etc. This is essentially an African dialectics, posing opposites necessary to the explanation and functioning of the world. In fact, each opposite explains and necessitates the other. Thus, Yurugu rebels because he feels deprived of his female half which he needs for his wholeness. He fails because he represents action without critical consciousness and Nommo, who reflects the creative thought and action of Amma, succeeds in establishing order and promoting development. Secondly, the concept of God as the cosmic womb, already containing in the beginning everything that would come into being in Him, suggests a concept of God as the universe and of its already having at the beginning all the building material (matter) for everything in it. This reflects the scientific principle that matter was always and already here and only its forms changed and change.

Thirdly, the concept of God as egg is reflection of His fertility, productiveness and infinite creative possibilities, as well as the idea of them. As infinite creative possibility in the universe and of the universe, God is infinite in a logical and meaningful way. Fourthly, the Dogon pose God as making a mistake in the first creation and thus, maintain logical consistency even in discussing God. For God is both perfect and imperfect, male and female, thought and action and therefore reflects and reinforces the principle of binary opposition.

Also, there is a clear contention that the world is not perfect either and is in the process of *perpetual becoming*. This process again is marked by binary opposition in structure and functioning and strives toward the creative and ongoing harmonizing of the two opposites. Especially, profound and far-reaching is the concept that becoming of necessity requires rebellion or oppositional thought and action against the established order. Yurugu comes into being by breaking through the cosmic egg and thus, sets up conditions for a new world. Breaking from Amma, God, he becomes truly man rather than a cosmic baby. In this action, he reminds one of the young adult leaving his/her parents' house in order to build a world for him/herself. In a word, independence and development requires a break from the established state of things. And even though Yurugu fails to make the world, he contributed to its origin and still leaves tracks through the mysteries of life which humankind can read and from which they can learn vital lessons.

Finally, Dogon thought is clearly impressive in its stress on humans as the indispensable element in the world's becoming and functioning. As noted above, the universe was created in the image of the human personality; he/she is the world in microcosm, containing its basic elements, the four cardinal directions, and the sacred cosmic Seeds, Signs and Words. Moreover, Amma, God, could not make the world without humans, for not only did the world need man/woman to flourish, but so did God. For if God is idea and creative possibility, only man/woman can know and appreciate it. Only humans are capable of creative thought; trees will not pray or praise, and dogs do not discuss spiritual or social duties. But if God needs man/woman, the binary oppositional logic of Dogon thought requires that man/woman also needs God. For if idea and creative possibility (God) cannot exist without man/woman; man/woman cannot exist without idea and creative possibility (God).

THE EGYPTIAN LEGACY

Egypt's contribution to Western religions is a persistent and widely argued contention. Historians Yosef ben-Jochannan (1970, 1978), and John Jackson (1972) and philosopher, George James (1976) are the most well-known advocates of this position. But there are many early European writers who agree and whom ben-Jochannan, Jackson and James use in their works. Among these are Wallis Budge, Charles Vail, James Breasted, Geoffry Higgins, Gerald Massey, James Frazier, Henri Frankfort and W.M. Petrie, all which are authorities on Ancient Egypt.

John Jackson (1972) cites several legacies of Egypt to Christianity. First, he argues that the concept of Virgin and Child in Christianity is clearly based on the Virgin Isis and Child Horus of Egypt. Jackson (1972:123) states that "Gods, heroes, born of virgins, were quite common in olden times and the sources of most, if not all of these divinities seem to have been Egypt." He then quotes Jocelyn Rhys', *Shaken Creeds*, which notes that "In the catacombs of Rome, black statues of this Egyptian divine Mother and Infant still survive from the early Christian worship of the Virgin and Child to which they were converted."

Secondly, Jackson contends that Horus, the Egyptian Savior and light of the world is the model for Jesus who has similar qualities. He points out that, as Charles Vail contends in his *The World's Saviors*, there were fifteen saviors of miraculous birth which precede Jesus among which were Krishna and Gautama (Buddha) of India, Tammuz of Babylonia, Zoroaster of Persia, Quetzalcoatl of Mexico and Horus of Egypt. But of all the virgin-birth saviors, Horus appears to be the model for Jesus. In fact "on the inner walls of the Holy of Holies in the Temple of Luxor inscribed about two thousand years B.C.E. he (1972:124) states, "the birth of Horus is depicted in four scenes which suggests how much Jesus' story is modelled after Horus." These four scenes are: 1) the Annunciation, in which the God Thoth announces to the Virgin Isis, she will bear a son; 2) the Immaculate Conception in which the God Kneph (the Holy Spirit) and the Goddess Hathor mystically impregnate Isis by holding the ankh to her head and nostrils; 3) the Birth of the Son of God, Horus; and 4) the Adoration with men and gods paying homage to the child, including three kings or magi who are giving him gifts.

Also, Jackson notes how an ancient Egyptian passion play enacts the arrest, trial, death, burial and resurrection of Osiris, often used interchangeably with Horus, as Savior, providing more evidence of Christianity's borrowing of models from Egypt. Finally, Jackson points out that even the celebration of Christmas on December 25th has its roots in Egypt. For "In Egypt, three thousand years ago, the birth day of the sun God (Ra) was celebrated on the 25th of December, since it was the first day to noticeably lengthen after December 21st (the day of the winter solstice)" (Jackson, 1972:134).

Ben-Jochannan (1970, 1978) has argued at length, as the title of his book demonstrates, the *African Origins of the Major Western Religions*. Although he shows other African sources of Western religions, his main focus in this and other works stress heavily the particular Egyptian-African contribution. Ben-Jochannan (1978:xxxix) agrees with Jackson that Horus is the model for Jesus, pointing out the following similarities: 1) both Horus and Jesus had two mothers, one who conceived them (Isis, Mary) and one who raised them (Nephthys, Mary, Wife of Cleophas); 2) both had an earthly father (Seb, Joseph); 3) both were the only child in one family and one of five in the second family); 4) from age 12 to 30 there is no record of Horus' or Jesus' life; 5) Horus at 30 was baptized by Anep, Jesus at 30 by John; and 6) Horus when baptized was transformed into the beloved and only begotten son of the Father or Holy Spirit represented by a bird; Jesus underwent the same with the Holy Spirit represented by a dove.

Secondly, ben-Jochannan (1970:164-65) calls attention to the "Plagarism on Solomon's part" for borrowing so heavily from the Teachings of Amenemope (Amenophis) who lived 300 years (1405-1370 B.C.E.) before the reign of Solomon (976-936 B.C.E.). The clearest examples are found in Proverbs 22:17-29. Citing Amenemope first and Proverbs afterward the comparisons are as follows: 1) "Give thine ear and hear the words that are said; apply thine heart to apprehend them"/"Bow down thine ear, and hear the word of the wise, and apply thine heart unto my knowledge;" 2) "Beware of robbing the poor, and of oppressing the afflicted;"/ Rob not the poor because he is poor, neither oppress the lowly at the gate;" 3) "a scribe who is skillful in his business, findest himself worthy to be a courtier (an attendent at a royal court);" "seest thou a man diligent in his business, he shall stand before kings."

Although ben-Jochannan cites more, these are illustrative. Moreover, Griffith (1926) confirms ben-Jochannan's contentions and cites approximately twenty more borrowings including the "planted by the rivers of water" analogy, found in Psalms 1:3 and Jeremiah 17:18. He concludes that this borrowing was not abnormal, for "when the Hebrews were becoming civilized under Solomon and his successors, they looked especially to Egypt and Babylonia for instruction in the arts of life..."

Finally, ben-Jochannan argues that the Ten Commandments (700 B.C.E.) of Judeo-Christian religions are derived from the 147 Negative Confessions (4100 B.C.E.) found in the Egyptian Book of the Dead (Budge, 1969:572ff). These were Declarations of Innocence that one should make "so that he may be separated from every sin which he has committed and may behold the face of the Gods." Ben-Jochannan (1970:68-69) lists seven Declarations of Innocence (Negative Confessions) which correspond to the Hebrew Commandments, i.e., "1) I have not committed theft; 2) I have not uttered falsehood; 3) I have not slain man or woman; 4) I have not defiled the wife of a man; 5) I have not cursed God; 6) I have not violated sacred times and seasons; 6) I have not increased my wealth except with such things as are my own possessions." These correspond to the Judeo-Christian Commandments against theft, lies, murder, adultery, blasphemy, violation of the Sabbath, and coveting what is not one's own.

George James (1976) argues in his major work, *Stolen Legacy*, that it is out of Egyptian socio-religious philosophy that so-called Greek philosophy came. In fact, he (1976:1) contends at the outset that "The term Greek philosophy, to begin with is a misnomer," since it is essentially a derivative from the Egyptian socio-religious educational and philosophical system called "the Egyptian Mysteries System." Realizing the awesome burden of proof such a contention incurs, James develops historical, textual and conceptual evidence to support it.

In terms of historical evidence, James cites the following. First, the teaching of the Egyptian Mysteries System was the source of higher education in the ancient world with students from Europe, Asia and other parts of Africa studying there. Not only did the Greeks study there but also Jesus and Moses. As a result, they returned to their various countries to set up EMS schools or variations of them. Secondly, Pythagoras, from whom all Greek philosophers borrowed, studied in Egypt as did Thales, Democratus, Plato, Diogenes, Timaeus and Herodotus and all confirm this in their writings. Thirdly, other Greek philosophers - Anaximander, Anximenes, Parmenides, Zeno and Melisus studied in Ionia in Asia Minor, a stronghold of EMS schools.

Fourthly, immigration of Greeks to Egypt for education began as early as 525 B.C.E. after the Persian invasion of Egypt. Fifthly, the conquest of Egypt by Alexander (333 B.C.E.) prepared the way for greater absorption of Egyptian knowledge from its schools and libraries. In fact, the school of Aristotle moved from Athens to Egypt, converted the Egyptian Royal Library to a research center and university and compiled a vast body of scientific and other knowledge from documents and oral instruction from Egyptian priests, and called it the history of Greek philosophy. Sixthly, there is an historical and logical problem of establishing that Aristotle wrote 400 to 1,000 books and learned from Plato who learned from Socrates a math, science, politics and economics Socrates did not know. Historical evidence says Alexander gave Aristotle money to buy books on science, but in order to obtain them they had to be in existence, and if they were in existence, he cannot be credited with having written them. In fact, he got them from the libraries of Egypt. Finally, the persecution of Greek philosophers for teaching *foreign* doctrines and the edicts of Roman emperors Theodius (4th cent.) and Justinian (6th cent.) which abolished EMS in Greece as well as Egypt, point strongly to the historical link between the two.

The textual and conceptual evidence shows also the historical link and borrowing. First, the Memphite Theology (C. 4,000 B.C.E.) with its three part text on Gods of Chaos, Gods of Creation and Primate of the Gods, contain within it concepts the Greeks appear to have borrowed. In sum, these borrowings are: 1) the concept of summum bonum - highest good and discipline and cardinal virtues which make humans gods (Aristotle, Socrates, Plato); 2) the EMS curriculum, i.e., the Seven Liberal Arts, the Sciences of the 42 books of Hermes; the Sciences of the Monument (Architecture, Masonry, etc.), the secret Sciences (numerical geometric and religious symbolism), and the Social Order and its Protection (social sciences); 3) proof of God, used by Aristotle, i.e., purpose in the universe and God as the Unmoved Mover; 4) concept of the Soul, immortality and salvation; 5) concept of the key elements - air, earth, fire, water; 6) the principle of opposites in the structure and functioning of the universe (dialectics); 7) the concept of creation as a product of Nous (mind, intelligence) and logos (creative utterance); 8) the concept of the atom as the basic building block of the universe (from the God, Atum, whose name and attributes are the same as those ascribed to the atom.) "This is the legacy of the African continent to the nations of the world," James (1976:151) concludes. And since it is she who "has laid the foundations of modern progress...she and her people deserve the honor and praise which for centuries have been falsely given to the Greeks."

Finally, J.A. Rogers (1972) credits Pharoah Akhenaton (c. 1350 B.C.E.) with making significant contributions to religious development. He (1976:57-66) states that 1,300 years before Jesus, Akhenaton taught and lived "a gospel of perfect love, brotherhood and truth. Two thousand years before Muhammad, he taught the doctrine of One God." And "three thousand years before Darwin, he sensed the unity that runs through all living things." Breaking from the Egyptian stress on many Gods with one supreme God, Akhenaton stressed the worship of One God. "A thousand years before Moses wrote the Second Commandment banishing graven images of God, Akhenaton did so." Moreover, Akhenaton's God "unlike that of Moses was not a jealous God, but a God of Perfect Love, a God compassionate even toward the chicken that 'crieth in the egg shell'." Others have suggested that his psalms were the model for David's whose were written 500 years later and Rogers points out the similarity. Finally, Rogers notes that Akhenaton advanced the concept that "the Kingdom of God is within you," centuries before Jesus did. Again, as in so many areas, Egypt's legacy proves itself profound and far-reaching. And it is for this reason Europe for so many years taught that Egypt was European rather than African in both color and culture.

THE CHRISTIAN MODEL

REASONS FOR CONVERSION

It is common knowledge that African Americans were converted to Christianity in slavery. But what is less known and less discussed are the reasons for the conversion both from the point of view of the slaveholders and the enslaved Africans. The slaveholders reasons for Christianizing the enslaved Africans began with their perception of Christianity as a way to reinforce and maintain dominance.

Thus, in 1743, a white minister prepared a book of dialogue for slaveholders to teach enslaved Africans which stressed contentment and thanks for being enslaved and ended saying "I can't help knowing my duty. I am to serve God in that state in which he has placed me. I am to do what my master orders me" (Frazier, 1974:19). As the indoctrination progressed, then, slaveholders soon discovered that many of the most amenable and submissive enslaved Africans were those who were Christians.

Secondly, the slaveholders were equally and at times more so, interested in uprooting Africans from their own religious heritage, in order to deprive them of cultural distinction and motivation for revolt. As Frazier (1974:17) points out, "whites were always on guard against African religious practices which could provide an opportunity for slave revolts, and they outlawed such practices." Finally, slaveholders converted Africans because they and other whites believed it was their duty to bring light to "benighted and lost" heathens. It was, in a word, based on a culturally chauvinist assumption that their religion was the only real and correct one and that all others were pagan and an abomination to their intolerant and jealous God.

Although many Africans accepted Christianity, many others resisted it for a long time, maintaining their commitment to traditional African religion or Islam. Moreover, most of those who accepted Christianity transformed it in their own image and interests (Blassingame, 1979; Wilmore, 1973). Given the importance of religion to Blacks and the reverence they had for their God, one must raise the question, what compelled them to exchange their God for that of the slaveholder?. The first reason for Afro-American conversion to Christianity was obviously the conquest and coercion by the slaveholder. Alex Haley's (1976) description of the brutally coerced transformation of Kunta Kinte into Christianized Toby in his popular family saga, *Roots*, is representative of the process. Moreover, at one point as Frazier (1974:15) notes, the slaveholder and the "missionaries recognized its difficulty of converting adult Africans and concentrated their efforts on children."

Secondly, Africans began to accept Christianity more as they gradually began to accept the slaveholders religious and cultural contentions which posed Christianity and the Christian God more powerful. This gradual acceptance was encouraged by the fact of their enslavement, the religious doubt and self-doubt it raised, the gradual loss of historical memory and the end of revivifying contacts from Africa through the end of the slave trade. Thirdly, Christianity came to be seen as a coping strategy on the social and psychological level. Socially acceptance meant avoidance of humiliation, punishment and beatings reserved for recalcitrant "heathens." Psychologically, it meant a transferred hope for deliverance, which the old religions seemed unable to fulfill.

Fourthly, Christianity and the religious meetings it allowed became, even under severe restriction, a means of establishing and maintaining a sense of community. This was a time for the enslaved Africans to meet, to reinforce bonds between them, discuss hopes, problems and also, as in the Turner, Vesey and Prosser revolts, a time to plan liberation strategies. Finally, after years of forced conversion and tentative and partial acceptance, Christianity became a heritage, and subsequent generations born in a Christian context simply accepted it. However, it is important to stress that inspite of this conversion to Christianity, Africans did not accept it totally in its racist slavery-supporting form. In fact, "a distinctive African American form of Christianity - actually a new religion of an oppressed people - slowly took root in the Black community" (Wilmore, 1973:36). This new "Black folk religion carried within its perspectives a definitive moral judgment against slavery and a clear legitimation of the slaves' and later the freedman's struggle against the forces of injustice and inequality."

THE HISTORICAL ROLE OF THE CHURCH

The role of the Black church in African American life has been substantial and enduring since its inception (Woodson, 1945). Although Frazier (1974) divides the church into the "invisible church" in slavery and the institutional church which began with the founding of the African Methodist Episcopal Church in 1787 and the first African Baptist Church in 1788, for the purpose of this section and to stress historical continuity, the division will not be made. Moreover, although the Black church has rightly been and continues to be accused of support for the established order at various times (Washington, 1964), it does have a history of social activism and social service of which it can be proud (Lincoln, 1974; Wilmore, 1975). And it is this history which will be stressed.

The Black church obviously began as a spiritual sanctuary and community against a violent and destructive character of the slave world. And even after slavery, it remained a wall of defense and comfort against racism and its accompanying attacks on Black dignity, relevance and social worth. Secondly, the Black church served as an agency of social reorientation and reconstruction, providing reinforcement for the old values of marriage, family morality and spirituality in the face of the corrosive effects of slavery (Blassingame, 1979).

Thirdly, the church became a center for economic cooperation, pooling resources to buy churches, building mutual aid societies which provided social services for free Blacks and purchasing and helping resettle enslaved Africans, and setting up businesses for economic development. Fourthly, the church engaged in both public and internal educational projects, setting up schools and training ministers and teachers and raising funds to carry these projects. Finally, the Black church from its earliest days as an invisible spiritual community, supported social change and struggle, providing leaders and leadership at various points in the struggle for Black liberation and a truly higher level of human life.

THE KING MODEL

The death of Bishop Henry M. Turner left the Black community with "no clergyman of his stature who could, by temperament or ideology, assume the leadership role he played in a persistant but unsuccessful attempt to radicalize the Black church" (Wilmore, 1973:187). Turner had been an advocate of the social role and responsibility of the church and religion, had engaged in a merciless criticism of U.S. society, and advocated the Blackness of God, draft resistance, armed self-defense and emigrationism. Not until King did another Black Christian leader rise to his level of relevance and social effectiveness. "It was Martin Luther King," Lincoln (1974:114) observes, "who made the contemporary church aware of its power to effect change." Moreover, he also revived its tradition of self-conscious social activism and thus, broke it from the moderate accommodating tendency which was also a part of its history and which it had exhibited since the death of Turner.

King developed a theory and practice which combined the best of Black religion with socially-focused concepts borrowed from Ghandi, Thoreau, Hegel, Rauschenbush, Tillich and others (King, 1958, 1963, 1964, 1967). Within his socio-political philosophy, five key concepts stand at its core. First, King posed Blacks as a people whose suffering and social situation has prepared them for and in fact, gives them a divine historical mission of not only liberating themselves, but also of restructuring and spiritualizing U.S. society.

Secondly, King argued that Blacks had both the moral right and responsibility to disobey unjust laws in their resistance to social evil. This stress, as Walton (1976:44) notes, combines Henry David Thoreau's concept of "the rightfulness of civil disobedience", Jesus' stress on humanity, forgiveness and love, and Ghandi's stress on loving non-violence as a method of social transformation. "Your highest loyalty is to God," King (1963:128) stated, "and not to the mores, or folkways, the state or the nation or any man-made institution." Thus, when any of those "conflict with God's will, it is your Christian duty to oppose it."

Closely related to the above concept is King's contention that it is immoral and cowardly to collaborate in one's own oppression. "To accept passively an unjust system is to cooperate with that system," he (1958:188) maintained. And in doing this, "the oppressed becomes as evil as the oppressor." Moreover, such non-action says "to the oppressor that his actions are morally right." Thus, he (1958:189) concludes, acquiescence to oppression is not only morally wrong and corruptive, "it is (also) the way of a coward."

Fourthly, King posed the necessity of religion having a social as well as spiritual function. Having read Walter Rauschenbush's *Christianity and the Social Crisis*, he (1958:72) developed "a theological basis for the social concern" which he felt religion should have "as a result of his early experiences." Therefore, he stressed that true religion was obligated to deal "with the whole man, not only his soul, but his body, not only his spiritual well-being but his social well-being." A final core concept in King's socio-political philosophy was his contention that human nature is perfectable through struggle. He (1958:82) asserted that Hegel's "analysis of the dialectical process...helped me to see that growth comes through struggle." Central to this concept is the emphasis on "creative tension," non-violent struggle which not only changes the oppressor, but also the oppressed in the process.

King's socio-political philosophy was important to Black religion and the Civil Rights Movement in several ways. First, it gave religious sanction to social resistance-although of the non-violent type and thus, spiritually inspired an oppressed people who would not have been moved as deeply by other doctrines in their quest for freedom. Secondly, it made social passivity immoral, an act in contradiction with the will of God and His desire for truth, freedom and justice in the world, and therefore, reinforced the need to resist social evil. Thirdly, it placed on preachers a continuing responsibility and pressure to take an active stand in the Movement and make religion more socially relevant. And finally, King's socio-political philosophy served as a transition in Black religion which encouraged self-criticism and pointed toward a Black liberation theology.

BLACK LIBERATION THEOLOGY

In July 1966 and in the midst of the period of Black urban revolts, a group of Black clergy met in Harlem to develop a position on the struggle for Black power in the U.S. There, they assumed a position which made a definitive contribution to the emergence of Black Liberation Theology. Breaking from King's negative position on Black power as 'nihilistic', they affirmed the right and need of Black power, critized the Black church for too often steering "its members away from the reign of God in this *world* to a distorted and complacent view of an *otherworldly* conception of God's power" and committed themselves to "use more of the resources of our churches in working for human justice in places of social change and upheaval" where God is truly already at work. This statement and other highly significant Black Liberation Theology documents appear in Wilmore and Cone's (1979) excellent documentary history of Black Theology from 1966 to 1979. Finally, the body of clergy who began in 1966 as the National Committee of Negro Churchmen changed their name to the National Committee of Black Churchmen and became the practical expression and representative of the new Black Liberation Theology.

Black Liberation Theology, however, did not come into being by itself. It evolved from several fundamental sources. First, it was developed in response to the dynamics of the decade of the 60's with its stress on Blackness and social activism and struggle. The 60's demanded a redefinition of the world in Black images and interests and Black religion was no exception. Also, the 60's demanded active engagement in the Black struggle for liberation and a higher level of human life and challenged the church to participate or disband. Secondly, Black Liberation theology was inspired by both emulation and criticism of King. King's stress on the social relevance and role of religion and on active engagement in the struggle against social evil were accepted and applied, but his stress on non-violence was challenged or played down, his denunciation of Black power rejected, and his emphasis on redemptive suffering translated as redemption through liberating struggle.

Thirdly, Black Liberation Theology evolved from an ongoing internal criticism and push for a more relevant religion in light of the activist tradition of the Black church as well as the temper of the times. This process was given support and intensified by the dynamics of the 60's and forced Black churchmen and women and theologians to redefine the meaning and role of God in history and His relationship to Black oppression and struggle for liberation. Finally, Black Liberation Theology helped inspire and was in turn inspired by Third World theology (Wilmore, 1979). Especially key here is Latin American Liberation Theology represented by Gustavo Gutierrez (1974, 1973) and Sergio Torres (1981, 1976) who translate religion in the most socially relevant and demanding ways.

One could argue there is a distinction between Black Theology and Black Liberation Theology, the former being all forms of Black systematic religious thought and the latter being one particular form of it. However, this distinction will not be made; for the quest for a Black Theology is firmly and clearly rooted in the search for religious answers to the questions of Black Liberation. Some of the major writers who have sought to pose and answer such questions are Gayraud Wilmore (1973), Major Jones (1974, 1971), William Jones (1973), J. Deotis Roberts (1974, 1971), Joseph Washington (1967), and Joseph Johnson (1978, 1971).

In addition to the above writers, two others stand out as definitive of the two trends in Black Liberation Theology, i.e., Black nationalist Christianity and Black Christian nationalism. These are James Cone (1969, 1970, 1975) and Albert Cleage, Jr. (1969, 1972). Moreover, both Cone and Cleage were key to the development of Black Liberation Theology. Cone, a professor of systematic theology at Union Theological Seminary, "more than anyone else...set the tone and described the context of Black Theology with the publication of his first book *Black theology and Black Power* in 1969" and helped shape the movement as a practical project (Wilmore and Cone, 1979:77). Cleage, the dean of Black Nationalist Christians and founder and head of the Shrine of the Black Madonna as early as 1963 "was also an active member of the NCBC almost from its inception and took part in the first theological discussions of the new movement of militant Black clergy in 1967" (Wilmore and Cone, 1979:67). Given their relevance to and work in this theoretical and practical thrust, their contentions can serve as a framework for discussion of Black Liberation Theology in general.

Establishing the bases for a Black Liberation Theology, Cone maintains that it must above all speak to the condition and struggle of Black people. "Black Theology has as its starting point the Black condition," he (1969:118) asserts. "It is a theology which *confronts* white society as racist Antichrist, communicating to the oppressor that nothing will be spared in the fight for freedom." (1969:135).

Secondly, Cone (1970:120) insists on the Blackness of God and Jesus. "The Blackness of God and everything implied by it in a racist society is the heart of Black Theology's doctrine of God." For "there is no place for a colorless God in a society (where) people suffer precisely because of their color." Thirdly, Cone (1970:116) argues that the God of Black Liberation Theology is and must be "the God of and for the oppressed of the land who makes himself known through their liberation." For Cone (1969:47) then, Black power and Black liberation are "doing God's work in history by righting the wrongs done against his people..." Thus, Blacks become God's covenant community. His latest book, *God of the Oppressed* (1975), reaffirms this stress on God's role in Black life and history as dictated by biblical assertions.

A fourth contention of Cone is the need for vindication of the Black church and the call upon it to recapture its radical tradition in the struggle for freedom, justice and equality. Citing Henry Garnet and Nat Turner as models, he (1969:94) argues that "the Black church was born in protest" and "in this sense, it is the precursor of Black Power." The need, then, is to revive this "heritage of radical involvement in the world." For "this past is a symbol of what is actively needed in the present" (1969:112-113). Finally, rejecting non-violence as "a technique of the rich to keep the poor poor," Cone declares that "if the system is evil, then revolutionary violence is both justified and necessary to end it." In fact, "sacrificing love" must be revolutionary love which "may mean joining a violent rebellion" (1969:113).

Cleage (1968:38) maintains at the outset that the Judeo-Christian heritage is a stolen heritage that must be recaptured. For "the white man captured the religion of a Black Nation (Israel), the revelations of a Black God, the teaching of a Black Messiah (Jesus) and he used them to keep Black men enslaved." This contention already leads Cleage to his second contention that God is and must be Black - as of course, is Jesus. Thirdly, Cleage (1972:3-4) argues for a rejection of the "Pauline perversion" of God's words in the New Testament with its emphasis on loving submission and concentration on the Old Testament's emphasis on struggle and liberation. The need is to make a distinction between salvation (spiritual) and liberation (social), and to struggle to eliminate "oppression, powerlessness and the white man's *declaration of Black inferiority* through Black unity" within the framework of Black Christian nationalism.

Fourthly, like Cone, Cleage identifies the church as a key instrument in the liberation of Blacks. Thus, he (1972:xxxiv) calls for Blacks to "rediscover the historic roots of Christianity, strip from them the mystical distortions and... bring the Black Christian church into the liberation struggle and make it relevant to the lives of Blacks."

Finally, Cleage (1972:403) argues that there is a dual aspect to the liberation struggle, an internal as well as external dimension. Given Blacks' history of oppression, they "have two beasts to fight: the beast within and the beast without." Externally, their enemy is whites, in fact, white Christians (Cleage, 1968:55).For "...within the system in which we live, we are not only separate, we are in conflict. We seek our freedom in a power struggle against them and in the context of this struggle, they are the enemy." Internally, the struggle is against what white society has made them, i.e., individualistic, addicted to mysticism about God and using religion as psychic relief rather than inspiration to actively seek liberation.

In sum then, Black Liberation Theology is centered around several core contentions which appear in varying and similar forms in most writings on it. Among these are: 1) the need for a God in Black people's own image and interest, i.e., Black and of and for the oppressed; 2) the imperative that religion must reflect the interests of Black and concretely and actively benefit them; 3) the contention that Blacks are a ''chosen people'' or ''covenant community'', i.e., have a special relationship with God; 4) the recognition of the Black church's radical history and a call for its resuming this role in the liberation struggle of Black people; and 5) the indispensability of social struggle to liberate Blacks - socially and spiritually - and realize God's will to bring truth, freedom and justice to society and the world.

THE ISLAMIC ALTERNATIVE

Islam is clearly the largest and most effective religious alternative to Christianity among Blacks. In fact, as Lincoln (1974:154) contends, ''It has an evitable appeal to Blacks who have difficulty with American Christianity because of its racism, and with the Black Christian church because of its posture of accommodation.'' Beginning in 1913 with Noble Drew Ali's establishment of the Moorish Science Temple and growing to its highest point in the early 60's in the context of the Nation of Islam, headed by the Hon. Elijah Muhammad, Islam has become a major religion among Afro-Americans. Moreover, it has served as a creative challenge to Black Christianity in its internal criticism and struggle to create a more socially relevant religion, as expressed in Black Liberation Theology.

THE MOORISH SCIENCE TEMPLE

In 1913, Noble Drew Ali established the Moorish Science Temple in Newark, New Jersey and began to teach a synthesized version of orthodox Islam, Garveyism, Christianity and various extractions from oriental philosophy (Bontemps and Conroy, 1945:175). From Newark, Ali's teachings spread to the northern cities of Detroit, Harlem, Chicago, Pittsburg, Philadelphia and various cities in the South, eventually embracing an estimated membership of 20-30,000 (Lincoln, 1961).

The main contentions of Noble Drew Ali's religious nationalism were that: 1) the key to the salvation and liberation of African people in the U.S. lay in the discovery and acceptance of their national origin as Moors; 2) Islam was "the only instrument for (Black) unity and advancement"; 3) whites were the opposite of and negative to Blacks and were soon to be destroyed; 4) the need to obey the law and refrain from radicalism; and finally, 5) the essentiality of love, harmony and peace in the world and especially among Blacks.

As Essien-Udom (1964:76) maintained, Ali's basic contentions and principles laid a basis for the Nation of Islam which came into being after it. His stress on name, land and nationality, his division of the world into dark and white peoples, his political conservatism and his conception of divine retribution of Allah on whites all find subsequent expression in the ideology and practice of the Nation of Islam. However, although the Black Islamic tradition owes its origins to Noble Drew Ali, it realized its most definitive development and recognition under the Hon. Elijah Muhammad and the Nation of Islam.

THE NATION OF ISLAM

The Nation of Islam began in 1930 with the splitting into two factions of the Moorish Science Temple, one following a newcomer to Detroit, W.D. Fard, and the other faction remaining faithful to Ali. Those following Fard eventually deified him when he disappeared in 1933 and became the founding members of the Nation of Islam under the leadership of Messenger Elijah Muhammad (Lincoln, 1961:181-182).

The first and most fundamental aspect of the socio-religious thought of Muhammad is the posing of Islam as the true religion of Black people and Christianity as the religion of their opposite and enemy, white people. Islam is a Black religion because it means submission to the will of Allah and Black people are submissive to God by nature. Secondly, it is the "religion of freedom, justice and equality" and thus, serves Black people's interests better than Christianity which "is a white man's religion and...contains no salvation for the Black man" (Muhammad, 1973:8,4).

The second aspect of Muhammad's socio-religious philosophy is his contention that Allah (God) is in reality a Black man and the Black man is God. As Lincoln (1961:73) observed, "all Black men represent Allah or at least participate in Him for all Black men are divine." Thirdly, Muhammad argues that Black people are a chosen people who are righteous by creation" and "righteous by nature".

Reversing the religious and world order ideologically in a way no one else had done, Muhammad defined the white man as the devil. By this he meant two things: 1) that logically if God is Black, the devil of dialectical necessity must be white; and 2) that if the devil means the embodiment of evil, the historical record of the white man both exposes and confirms his true identity. Thus, he (1965:134) states, that the white man's claim to be God or his chosen is in fact a lie. It is this part of Muhammad's doctrine of deliverance the God-devil thesis which has proved the most controversial and at the same time and most effective organizing principle.

Fifthly, Muhammad argued that separation on the social and political level from whites was a divine imperative. This he (1965:273-275) argues is necessary in order for Blacks to avoid the corruptive influence of white civilization which is "floating in corruption", to avoid the divine destruction Allah has for America, and to establish a nation in their own image and interests. Also, Muhammad stressed the need for economic self-help and racial solidarity. To accomplish this, Muhammad calls for "a united front of Black men of America" who will join hands in a program of economic, political and spiritual upliftment of Black people. Lastly, Muhammad stressed the need for racial and Islamic solidarity throughout the world. He argued that all Third World people were original people and that they were destined to unite inspite of the evil influence of the West which divided them.

SCHISM, TRANSFORMATION AND REBUILDING

THE SCHISM. In 1963 the NOI began to show signs of unravelling as evidenced by the underlying reasons for the suspension and eventual ouster/resignation of Malcolm X from it. His ouster/resignation had a tremendous impact on the NOI and the Black Movement and indicated a series of problems that would eventually lead to factionalization and transformation of the NOI. Although the NOI gave the reason for Malcolm's suspension as his disobeying an order not to comment on the Kennedy assassination, the underlying political basis for it was the conflict between two major tendencies in the NOI, the radicals represented by Malcolm and the conservatives represented by the ruling stratum in charge of daily administration, with both vying for and dependent on Muhammad's decisions and support for victory in the daily battles and the ultimate struggle itself. As I (1982:5) have argued in a paper on the conflict, four major factors appear to have shaped and fed the conflict. First, the transformation of the NOI from a small marginal group to a multi-million dollar budget and huge bureaucracy changed both its political character and its conception of what was politically acceptable. As Lincoln (1961) predicted and Lomax

(1964) reported, the ruling stratum became increasingly conservative in its desire to protect its gains and Malcolm could not adjust to the new conservatism.

Secondly, then, the conflict was shaped by the ruling stratum's fierce opposition to Malcolm. Although they recognized his worth and significance to the NOI, they resented and opposed him because of: 1) his moral posture against the corruptive materialism which permeated the ruling stratum; 2) his unwillingness to moderate his radicalism in the face of changed circumstances; and 3) the likelihood of his succeeding Muhammad and establishing a radical position. Thirdly, the conflict was shaped by the ruling stratum's ability to eventually alienate Muhammad and Malcolm inspite of their prior closeness. This was achieved essentially by their being in the pivotal position of daily administration and thus of briefing the Messenger everyday and arguing Malcolm's refusal to moderate his disruptive radicalism and to accept Muhammad's divine authority.

Having been convinced of these charges, Muhammad suspended Malcolm at first and later denounced him. Malcolm in turn denounced the NOI and Muhammad and the ensuing conditions set the stage for his assassination. Finally, evidence suggests that the FBI had a significant role in provoking and sustaining the leadership struggle within the NOI. For as early as 1959, it had placed people in the leadership stratum. Moreover, Cointelpro documents obtained through the Freedom of Information Act reveal the FBI's decision to divide the NOI and either transform it or destroy it.

TRANSFORMATION. After Muhammad's death in 1975, the NOI underwent a drastic transformation and fragmentation involving severe criticism of Muhammad, rejection of early Muslim belief on whites, and the introduction of a strong Americanism and orthodox Islam. (Muhammad, 1980). This process "has its roots in the unsolved political economic problems which shaped and fed the conflict between Malcolm and the ruling stratum'' (Karenga, 1982:339). In other words, ''the non-engagement, isolation and general conservatism which Malcolm fought in the 60's expresses itself in similar forms in the 70's and today with the added dimensions of Americanism and orthodox Islam advocated by Muhammad's son Wallace.'' In addition to the above factor, four others contributed to the transformation (Karenga, 1981:339ff). A second factor contributive to the transformation then was the ideology and structure of the Nation itself. The theocratic leadership structure based on divine wisdom and authority allowed for corrupt officials to act without check, denied mass participation in decision-making and debates, and prevented criticism necessary to check the transformation carried to its ultimate by Wallace and the ruling stratum. Also, the ideological tendency toward non-engagement in social struggle, obeying laws and the stress on material acquisition cultivated an appreciation for political conservatism and vulgar materialism of the ruling stratum (Lincoln, 1961; Essien-Udom, 1964).

A third contributing factor was the leadership style and problems of succession of Imam Wallace Muhammad who succeeded his father. Wallace's leadership style leaned toward decentralization and orthodox Islam even before his father's death. Once at the helm, he reshaped the Nation. Also, his problems of succession were ones of establishing his authority; creating a new image of the NOI; and winning new converts and allies. Thus, he disavowed his father's divine authority and his God, disbanded the paramilitary arm, the Fruit of Islam, eliminating a possible challenge and changing the military or coercive image of the NOI. Moreover, he changed the doctrine of the NOI from religious Black nationalism to Americanism and orthodox Islam, winning new converts and allies who once opposed the race-and-earth focused religious doctrine of his father. Finally, as argued above, there is evidence of the

U.S. government's intervention and role in the process of transformation and fragmentation. From positions at the top, it appears they not only provoked conflict and helped eliminate the radicals, but encouraged the transformation which insured an accommodationist religious structure.

THE REBUILDING. Although Minister Louis Farrakhan the national spokesman after Malcolm, had at first gone along with the transformation, he eventually objected. In 1978, he announced publicly that he could no longer accept in silence the transformation of the Nation and its members. He listed among other things the following which he found intolerable: the ingratitude and disrespect for Messenger Muhammad which the transformed NOI was exhibiting; its open admission of whites; the deterioration of discipline and the emphasis on orthodox Islam as opposed to a people-specific Islam for Blacks which Muhammad had developed (Overbea, 1978:9).

To offset the disintegration he perceived in the NOI which was then called the World Community of Islam in the West, Farrakhan moved to rebuild the NOI in its original Black image. He formed discussion groups around the country, lectured, published and republished the Messenger's works, reproduced tape recordings of the Messenger and himself, started a newspaper, The Final Call, and began to rebuild mosque structures and leadership cadres across the country. At the heart of his efforts to rebuild the NOI is the struggle to rescue and reconstruct the image of Messenger Muhammad. To accomplish this, Farrakhan argues: the truth and currency of Muhammad's message; his moral and material achievement and the praiseworthiness of his character as a leader (Karenga, 1981:379). The success of Farrakhan in rebuilding the NOI will depend on several factors: 1) his own leadership capacity; 2) the extent of opposition from other Islamic groups claiming the Messenger's mantle; 3) his success in building a capable and committed cadre; and finally, 4) his ability to relate positively and effectively to the larger Black community.

STUDY QUESTIONS

1. Define religion and list some of its negatives and positives.
2. What are some general characteristics and general themes in African religions?
3. Discuss the ideas suggested by Dogon cosmogony.
4. What is the Egyptian legacy?
5. Why did Blacks convert to Christianity?
6. What has been the historical role of the church?
7. Cite some basic contentions of King's socio-political philosophy and his ideological impact on Black religion and the Movement.
8. Who are two major Black Liberation Theologians and what are some of their basic contentions?
9. Discuss the contentions and religious legacy of the Moorish Science Temple to the Nation of Islam.
10. Discuss the contentions of Messenger Muhammad.
11. What factors contributed to the conflict between Malcolm X and the NOI?
12. What were the factors which contributed to the transformation of the NOI?

REFERENCES

Adams, Hunter III. (1979) "African Observers of the Universe: The Sirius Question," *Journal of African Civilization*, 1, 2 (November) 1-20.

ben-Jochannan, Yosef. (1970) *African Origins of the Major "Western Religions,"* New York: Alkebu-lan Books Associates.

_____ . (1978) *Our "Black Seminarians" and "Black Clergy" Without A "Black Theology"*, New York: Alkebu-lan books Associates.

Blassingame, John W. (1979) *The Slave Community*, New York: Oxford University Press.

Bontemps, Arna and Jack Conroy. (1945) *They Seek A City*, Garden City, N.Y.: Doubleday, Doran and Company, Inc.

Budge, E.A. (trans.). (1960) *The Book of the Dead*, New Hyde Park, N.Y.: University Books.

Cleage, Albert Jr. (1972) *Black Christian Nationalism*, New York: William Morow and Co.

_____. (1968) *The Black Messiah*, New York: Sheed and Ward.

Cone, James. (1969) *Black Theology and Black Power*, New York: Seabury Press.

_____. (1970) *A Black Theology of Liberation*, Philadelphia: Lippincott Co.

_____. (1975) *God of the Oppressed*, New York: Seabury Press.

Deng, Francis. (1973) *The Dinka and Their Songs*, Oxford: Clarendon Press.

Essien-Udom, E.U. (1964) *Black Nationalism*, New York: Dell Publishing Co.

Evans-Pritchard, E.E. (1965) *Theories of Primitive Religion*, London: Oxford University Press.

Fauset, H. (1944) *Black Gods of the Metropolis*, Philadelphia: University of Pennsylania Press.

Frazier, E. Franklin. (1974) *The Negro Church in America*, New York: Schocken Books, Inc.

Griaule, Marcel. (1978) *Conversations with Ogotemmeli*, New York: Oxford University Press.

Griaule, Marcel and Germain Dieterlen. (1965) "The Dogon," in *African Worlds*, (ed.) Daryll Gord, London: Oxford University Press, 83-110.

Griffith, F.L. (1926) "The Teachings of Amenophis," *Journal of Egyptian Archaeology*, XII, 191-231.

Gutierrez Gustavo. (1974) *The Mystical and Political Dimensions of the Christian Faith*, New York: Hurder & Hurder.

_____. (1973) *A Theology of Liberation*, Maryknoll, New York: Orbis.

Haley, Alex. (1976) *Roots*, New York: Dell Publishing Co.

Harding, Vincent. (1969) "The Religion of Black Power," in *The Religious Stratum, 1968*, (ed.) Donald Cultler, Boston: Beacon Press.

Idowu, E Bolaji (1975) *African Traditional Religion*, Maryknoll, New York: Orbis Books.

Jackson, John (1972) *Man, God, and Civilization*, New Hyde Park, New York: University Books.

James, George. (1976) *Stolen Legacy*, San Francisco: Julian Richardson Associates.

Johnson, Joseph. (1978) *Proclamation Theology*, Shreveport: Fourth District Press.

_____. (1971) *The Soul of the Black Preacher*, Philadelphia: United Church Press.

Jones, Major J. (1971) *Black Awareness*, Nashville: Abingdon Press.

_____. (1974) *Christian Ethics for Black Theology*, Nashville: Abingdon Press.

Jones, William R. (1973) *Is God a White Racist?*, Garden City, New York: Anchor Press/Doubleday.

Karenga, Maulana. (1981) *Afro-American Nationalism: An Alternative Analysis,* unpublished manuscript.

_____ . (1980) *Kawaida Theory: An Introductory Outline,* Inglewood, Ca.: Kawaida Publications.

_____ . (1982) "Malcolm and the Messenger: From Psychological Assumptions to Political Analysis," *The Western Journal of Black Studies,* 6,4, (winter) 193-201.

King, Martin Luther, Jr. (1963) *Strength To Love,* New York: Harper & Row.

_____ . (1958) *Stride Toward Freedom,* New York: Harper & Row.

_____ . (1967) *Where Do We Go From Here: Chaos or Community,* New York: Harper & Row.

_____ . (1964) *Why We Can't Wait,* New York: Harper & Row.

Lincoln, C. Eric. (1974a) *The Black Church Since Frazier,* New York: Schocken Books, Inc.

_____ . (1974b) *The Black Experience in Religion,* Garden City, New York: Anchor Books.

_____ . (1961) *The Black Muslims in America,* Boston: Beacon Press.

Malcolm X. (1966) *The Autobiography of Malcolm X,* New York: Grove Press.

Marx, Karl and Frederick Engels. (1964) *On Religion,* New York: Schocken Books, Inc.

Mbiti, John S. (1970) *African Religions and Philosophy,* Garden City, N.Y.: Anchor Books.

Muhammad, Elijah. (1973) *The Fall of America,* Chicago: Muhammad's Temple of Islam No. 2.

_____ . (1965) *Message to the Black Man in America,* Chicago: Muhammad's Temple of Islam No. 2.

_____. (1965) *Message to the Black Man in America,* Chicago: Muhammad's Temple of Islam No. 2.

Muhammad, Wallace D. (1980) *As the Light Shineth From the East,* Chicago: Wallace D. Muhammad Publishing Company.

Overbea, Luix. (1978) 'Leader Quits Black Muslims,'' *Christian Science Monitor* (June 13).

Ray, Benjamin C. (1976) *African Religions,* Englewood Cliffs, N.J.: Prentice-Hall, Inc.

Roberts, J. Deotis. (1974) *A Black Political Theology,* Philadelphia: Westminster Press.

_____. (1971) *Liberation and Reconciliation,* Philadelphia: Westminster Press.

Rogers, J.A. (1972) *World's Great Men of Color, Volume I,* New York: Macmillan.

Sagan, Carl. (1979) *Broca's Brain-Reflections on the Romance of Science,* New York: Random House.

Temple, Robert. (1976) *The Sirius Mystery,* New York: St. Martin's Press.

Torres, Sergio. (1981) *The Challenge of a Basic Christian Community,* Maryknoll, N.Y.: Orbis Books.

_____. (1976) *Theology in the Americas,* Maryknoll, N.Y.: Orbis Books.

Walton, Hanes Jr. (1976) *The Political Philosophy of Martin Luther King, Jr.,* Westport, Conn.: Greenwood Press.

Washington, Joseph. (1964) *Black Religion,* Boston: Beacon Press.

_____. (1967) *The Politics of God,* Boston: Beacon Press.

Wilmore, Gayraud S. (1973) *Black Religion and Black Radicu.'ism,* Garden City, N.Y.: Anchor Books.

_____ . (1979) "The Role of Afro-America in the Rise of Third World Theology: A Historical Reappraisal," in *African Theology En Route*, (eds.) Kofi Appiah-Kubi and Sergio Torres, pp. 196-208.

Wilmore, Gayraud S. and James H. Cone (eds.). (1979) *Black Theology*, Maryknoll, N.Y.: Orbis Books.

Woodson, Carter G. (1945) *The History of the Negro Church*, Washington, D.C.: Associated Publishers.

Yinger, Milton. (1970) *The Scientific Study of Religion*, N.Y.: Macmillan.

IV
BLACK SOCIAL ORGANIZATION

INTRODUCTION

Black social organization is essentially the structure and functioning of the Black community as a whole as well as the various units and processes which compose and define it, i.e., family, groups, institutions, relations, views and values, economics, politics, conflict and change, etc. Thus, Black social organization is the subject matter of Black sociology which directs itself to the study of Black social reality from a Black perspective. The need for a Black perspective evolves inevitably from the fact that U.S. society is a society divided and organized along racial lines, that the ideology and/or social theory which rules in academic and social circles is the ideology of the ruling race/class, and that this ideology or social theory is more of an apologia for the established order than a critical analysis of it. Therefore, it becomes important that Blacks who are concerned with political, economic and cultural emancipation have an emancipatory social science which is Afrocentric. As Staples (1973:168) argues, "If white sociology is the science of oppression, Black sociology must be the science of liberation."

As an emancipatory social science, Black sociology offers both critiques and correctives. Continuing the tradition of DuBois (1967), Frazier (1957), Cox (1970), and Hare (1965), Black sociology has set for itself several basic aims: 1) to rescue Black life from the racist interpretations which pose it as pathological and pathogenic, and

198

redefine it in its multidimensionality and variousness; 2) to create new concepts, categories, analytical frameworks and bodies of data that enhance understanding of both Black reality and the larger reality of U.S. society; 3) to make ongoing critical analyses of the structure and functioning of U.S. society, especially in terms of race, class and power; 4) to join severe criticism of internal forces negative to Black progress and liberation with criticism of negative external forces; and 5) to discover, develop and reveal possibilities of social change inherent in both the Black community and the larger society (Ladner, 1973; Staples, 1976; DuBois, 1975).

Since Black sociology is so inclusive a social science, only a small selection of its concerns can be treated in this chapter. Other major concerns such as politics, economics and social psychology of the Black community will be treated in the other appropriate chapters. The selected concerns which follow are fundamental to understanding Black social organization and are also reflective of issues and problems which are directly related to Black subordination and oppression in U.S. society and Black struggle to end this condition.

THE PROBLEM OF GHETTOIZATION

The Black community, like other communities is defined by its sharing of common space, experiences, view and value systems, social institutions and self-consciousness. Its common space, however, is a bounded area of living, i.e., a ghetto, which not only closes Blacks in the community, but simultaneously shuts them out from the access and various opportunities available in the larger society. Even when Blacks move beyond the original bounded areas and form what is called "gilded ghettos" in integrated areas, these outskirt communities "also become linked to the central Black area," as whites leave and other Blacks move in (Glasgow,

1981:34). Moreover, even outside the ghetto physically, Blacks are defined and treated as the majority who are still in the ghetto with allowable variations.

W.E.B. DuBois (1967) pioneered the scientific study of Black urban life with a major work, *The Philadelphia Negro*, in 1899 and in 1945, St. Clair Drake and Horace Cayton (1962) produced the first major study which was a systematic and scholarly investigation of the Black ghetto itself. During the 60's, Kenneth Clark (1965) contributed *Dark Ghetto: Dilemmas of Social Power* which gave an incisive overview of the problems of ghetto life using Harlem as a model.

What appears, then, from DuBois', Drake's and Cayton's, and Clark's analyses, along with others is a social reality defined by six basic dimensions. First, the ghetto is territorial, i.e., residential, bounded and segregated. Inspite of Wilson's (1979) findings of increased Black suburbanization, Rose (1976) shows that in five major cities, it was simply the expansion of the central city areas or increase in the Black population already in the suburbs. Moreover, Clay (1981:89) reports that suburban migration is limited essentially to the middle class and generally "produces a resegregation pattern where Blacks are concentrated in a few suburban enclaves." Secondly, the ghetto is racial/ethnic, i.e., essentially Black and a product of a racist society which poses race as a central criteria for determining life-chances, opportunities, social status and human worth. Thirdly, the ghetto is socio-economic, i.e., marked by what Clark (1965:27ff) calls economic and social decay. Clark lists as symptoms of ghetto life poor education, poor housing, unemployment, drug addiction and alcoholism, frequent illness and early death, and crime, all accented by "the primary affliction of inferior racial status "in a racist society".

Fourthly, the ghetto is institutional, i.e., it has a complex of community institutions, organizations and enterprises which are both a positive and a negative (Spear, 1967). The positive aspect of them is that they are structures necessary for self-determined maintenance and development. But the negative aspect is that they are often not strong enough to fulfill their function or fail to use their strength adequately for social advancement and change.

Fifthly, the ghetto is clearly political, i.e., both an expression and product of Black powerlessness to prevent its establishment or end its existence. This powerlessness is obviously related to the ghetto's structural incapacity to define, defend and develop it interests as alluded to above. For without strong community structures to resist imposition and advance Black interests, external interests will most likely be imposed. Thus, the ghetto is controlled from outside and it is this external control joined with other factors of ghetto life which have led some to argue that it is an internal colony (Cruse, 1968; Clark, 1964).

Finally, the ghetto is psycho-cultural, i.e., defined by views, values and self-consciousness negative to its development and transformation into a free, proud and productive community (Clark, 1965; Karenga, 1980). Although the psychological aspect will be discussed at length in the chapter in psychology, the cultural dimensions which are directly related will be discussed below . In conclusion, then, it is this fact of ghetto life, the negatives which emerge from it and the solutions posed to correct them and develop a higher level of life that form the core of sociological inquiry and prescription.

THE RACE/CLASS QUESTION

One of the most pressing questions in Black sociology is the significance of race and class in Black life. The significance of the question rests not only in its relevance to understanding Black oppression, but also in its relevance in developing strategies for liberation. For depending on the weight each or both are given, the Black community correctly or incorrectly grasps the character of its

oppression and the theoretical and practical requirements necessary to end it. Thus, since the late Seventies the debate has intensified concerning which is most important — race oppression or class
oppression and how the two interact and relate (Washington,
1979; Willie, 1979).

The focus on class as the fundamental unit of social analysis
and the key determinant in social life has been provided most
definitively by the sociology of Marxism (Bottomore and Rubel,
1964). Marx argued essentially that the shape and functioning of
society was determined by its economic foundation and that class,
as a socio-economic category, was basic to the understanding of
society and history. Furthermore, he contended that productive
systems establish given economic roles — farmer, trader, indus-
trialist, worker — and that each group of persons which stands in
the same relationship to the means of production (raw materials,
factories, machines, etc.) form a class. As a class, each did the same
work, had the same basic interests ("real" as opposed to "perceived") and often engage in conflict with other classes. This conflict between classes, he argued, is the motive force of history.
Finally, he contended that the economic foundation was the *base*
from which the *superstructure* (law, religion, politics, ideology, etc.)
rose and upon which it rested.

From this materialistic (economic) interpretation of society
and history evolved two basic Marxist interpretations of the interaction of race and class, the orthódox Marxist theory (Cox, 1970;
Reich, 1981) and the split labor-market theory (Bonacich, 1972).
Orthodox Marxist theory argues that racism is a reflection of the
manipulation of workers by the capitalist class to divide them along
racial lines and reduce their capacity to struggle against the system. This results in encouraging discrimination against Blacks,
arguing their inferiority, use of Blacks as a surplus, marginal low-
paid working force, and establishing a privileged better-paid
racist white labor force. Thus, racism is a function of class struggle,

not an independent variable itself. The split labor-market theory argues that racial antagonism begins in the labor-market split along racial lines when business promotes worker competition to displace higher paid labor. If the labor-market split is along racial lines with whites' being the higher-paid and Blacks being the lower-paid labor, class antagonism is transformed into racial antagonism in which whites fight to neutralize or eliminate occupational competition with Blacks.

Both of these class theories of race fail to perceive that race and class interact dynamically as variables in social conflict and position. Although the orthodox Marxist view blames the capitalist and the split labor-market theory places the essential burden on the white worker, there are clearly cases where both white capitalists and white workers join to oppress or discriminate against Blacks and other Third World people. Moreover, sometimes it is done for reasons of race and other times for reasons of class and still at other times for both reasons of race and class. Also, in a racist society the class position of a person is greatly determined by his/her race. This is what Fanon (1968:40) meant when he wrote that in the racist context of the colony, race is the key determinant.

Blauner (1972:31) also calls attention to the fact that often in a racist society, racial exploitation and/or control becomes "an end itself, despite its original limited purpose as a means to exploitation and privilege." Finally, Turner (1979:31) argues that racism has become so endemic and historically rooted in U.S. society and its institutions that "it exists apart from and in some cases inspite of, the social attitudes of the people who administer these institutions." Thus, the factor of "covert or institutional racism has a dynamic of its own, despite the vagaries of prejudice and bigotry, real as they are." Given all the above contentions concerning race and class and their interaction and relation, it is clear that racism cannot be reductively translated as a function of class or class struggle. Such a position obscures the complexity and variousness

204   Black Social Organizations

of their interplay and their separate relevance as factors in a racist-capitalist society (Turner, 1979).

There are other positions on race and class, but they will be covered in chapter VI on economics. However, it is important to note in conclusion, that one of the reasons many social scientists and others have in identifying racism is that their definition is deficient. Marxists and non-Marxists tend to see racism as simply attitudes or ideology rather than as multi-faceted involving ideology, structure and practice. (Allen, 1974).

Racism is essentially a system of denial and deformation of the history and humanity of Third World people (people of color) and their right to freedom based exclusively or primarily on the specious concept of race (Karenga, 1981). Stripped of all its cultural and scientific mystification, race is a bio-social category designed to assign human worth and social status, using Europeans as the paradigm of humanity and social achievement. Racism, then, which begins with the creation and mystification of race, is social thought and practice which expresses itself in three basic ways, i.e., as: 1) imposition, i.e., conquest of a people, and interruption, destruction and appropriation of a people's history and productive capacity in racial terms; 2) ideology, i.e., an elaborate system of pseudo-intellectual categories, assumptions and contentions negative to Third World peoples and serving as justification of the imposition and reinforcement of the institutional arrangement; and 3) institutional arrangement, i.e., a system of political, economic and social structures which insure white power and privilege over Third World peoples.

THE ISSUE OF CULTURE

Although the question of culture had been raised during the Harlem Renaissance in the 20's, it was during the 60's that the Black community became increasingly concerned about the possession, meaning, reappropriation and reconstruction of their culture. The shift away from integration as the main Movement goal and the resurgence of Black nationalism brought with it a renewed interest in Black culture, its role in life and struggle and a profound and pervasive commitment to revitalize, reconstruct and construct it. Expressive of this thrust were the struggle for Black Studies which demanded recognition of Black contribution to society and the world, the look to Africa for inspiration and models and the proliferation of creative artist groups, study groups, literature and institutions which focused on culture. This thrust was both reactive and proactive, defensive and developmental. It sought not only to halt and reverse the racist attempt to negate Black culture, but also to rebuild and build a system of views and values which aided Blacks in their struggle for liberation and a higher level of human life.

Many racist, liberal and Marxist social scientists argued that Blacks had no real culture, that slavery destroyed it, and that what passed as Black culture was simply a pathological reaction to whites, a duplication of them or an expression of lower-class culture rather than a specific Black culture (Liebow, 1967; Berger, 1967). Myrdal (1944:927-930) argued that the Black person is "an exaggerated American" and essentially a "pathological" reaction to whites. Ellison (1966:316-317) responding to Myrdal stated that Myrdal misjudges Blacks' creativity and adaptive vitality. He posited that Blacks could not possibly "live and develop for over three hundred years simply by reacting." On the contrary, Blacks have made self-conscious and self-constructive efforts which have contributed to American culture, not simply borrowed from it.

Glazer and Moynihan (1963:52) argued that the key to understanding Blacks is to recognize they cannot view themselves as other ethnic groups who have a culture. For the Black person "is only an American and nothing else. He has no values and culture to guard and protect." Such a contention was challenged by the Black cultural Revolution of the 60's which not only reaffirmed Black culture and its difference from white culture in terms of life-goals, worldview and values, but also the need to draw on its African and mass sources to recreate and revitalize it and use it as a weapon in the Black Struggle (Karenga, 1967, Gayle, 1971).

Harold Cruse (1967) in his massive study of culture and politics in Harlem, made a profound contribution to the focus on cultural revitalization and struggle. He maintained that cultural oppression is tightly interlocked with political and economic oppression. For cultural control facilitates political control which in turn insures economic control. Thus, he argued instead of placing higher priority on any one of the three factors of culture, politics and economics, the three must be welded together into a dynamic synthesis and social strategy. Stressing the essentiality of culture to political and economical struggle, Cruse (1967:12) maintained that "as long as the (Afro-Americans') cultural identity is in question or open to self-doubt, then there can be no positive identification with the real demands of his political and economic existence." Therefore, Cruse (1967:475) argues that "there can be no real Black revolution in the U.S. without a cultural revolution as a corollary to the scheme of 'agencies for social change'." He concludes, calling on the Black intellectuals to solve their historical crisis, i.e., alternating between integrationist fantasies and nationalist demands when rejected by whites, and guide the masses to liberation and higher levels of life.

As argued in chapter II in the section on the Sixties, Kawaida theory stood out as the most structured and influential theory of the Black Cultural Revolution. Kawaida (Karenga, 1980,1978b) contends that the key crisis in Black life is the cultural crisis, i.e., a crisis in views and values. This crisis was caused by several factors, among which are enslavement and deculturalization, the ideological hegemony (dominance in the realm of ideas and values of the ruling race/class) and the growth of popular culture at the expense of national culture.

The need then is for a cultural revolution which will prepare the Black masses for a political struggle to end the social conditions which deny and deform their history and humanity. The cultural revolution, Kawaida states, precedes and makes possible the political revolution and also sustains it. By cultural revolution is meant "the ideological and practical struggle to transform persons and people and to build structures to insure, maintain and expand that transformation" (Karenga, 1982:2) . Whereas political revolution is the struggle to seize and reorder the unequal power and wealth in society, cultural revolution is the process which makes it possible and sustains it with transformed self-conscious participants, i.e., self-conscious agents of their own liberation.

Cultural revolution implies and also means revitalizing, creating and recreating culture (Karenga, 1967). Kawaida defines culture as the totality of a people's thought and practice, which occurs in seven basic areas: mythology (sacred and secular), history, social organization, economic organization, political organization, creative production (arts and science), and ethos (collective self-definition and consciousness). It is on these seven levels, Kawaida contends, that Black people must rebuild themselves by rebuilding their culture, so that each area is in both their *image* and *interests*. For it is a political fact that the greater the difference between the culture of the oppressed and the oppressor, the greater the difficulty of dominance and the capacity for resistance.

Finally, Kawaida, in the tradition of DuBois (1969), Frazier (1973), and Cruse (1967), posits that the cultural and political struggle must be led by a self-conscious vanguard who commits class suicide and identifies with the aspirations of the masses. This vanguard will build on the strengths of Black culture, i.e., its adaptive vitality, strong emphasis on expressive values, empathetic sharing, durability, humanism and creativity, and expand them. Moreover, the vanguard must create an Afro-centric ideology or social theory which negates the ruling race/class ideology and provides the basis for a critical Afro-centric conception of reality and the possibilities and methods of changing it. Kawaida contends that this vanguard must also urge the self-conscious creation of a national culture which not only distinguishes Blacks from their oppressor, but also aids them in their rescue and reconstruction of their history and humanity and enables them to contribute to human history and achievement in their own unique way.

THE BLACK FAMILY

At the heart of social organization is the way a people organizes its relationships. In fact, another way to define social organization is as "ways of teaching, structuring, validating, changing and expanding social behavior and relationships" (Karenga, 1980:35). The focus of social organization is thus on the socialization process, i.e., the value and vision orientation designed to instruct and enhance personal and collective behavior and relationships. Nowhere is this more clear than in the discussion of the Black family. For if the Black family is the smallest example of the nation, i.e., Black people, its strengths and weakneses greatly determine the capacity of Black people to achieve the social tasks they pose for themselves.

The assessment of the Black family's strength and weakness pervade social science literature. In fact, much of the literature, if not most, can be assigned to either one school of thought and research or the other (Willie, 1970; Staples, 1978; McAdoo, 1981). These two approaches to the Black family may be termed the pathological-pathogenic and the adaptive-vitality approaches. The first is predicated on the assumption that the Black family is either pathological or pathogenic or both. That is to say, it is not only a dysfunctional and sick social unit, but produces sick and dysfunctional members of society.

Frazier (1939), unwittingly helped lay the basis for the pathology school in his research on the Black family. He believed that slavery, urbanization and racism prevented perpetuation of the African family relations and forms and imposed severe strains on the Black family's ability to function effectively. Thus, it developed negative situational adaptations to handle this legacy of oppression and exploitation. From this, he notes, came the matriarchal character of the Black family with its strong women and ineffective and marginal men; its unstable marriages; the prevailing norm of casual sex, and the loss of folk culture cohesiveness in the urbanization process.

Daniel Moynihan (1965), using largely census data, tried to confirm Frazier's conception by statistics. Although Frazier had pointed to the social causes of Black family problems, Moynihan blamed social problems on the Black family. Making a generalized indictment of Black families, he (1965:5) argued that "at the heart of the deterioration of the fabric of (Black) society is the deterioration of the (Black) family." Citing Frazier as if to escape the charge of racist sociology, Moynihan charged that the Black community was plagued by pathological and pathogenic families marked by and conducive to matriarchy, broken and ineffective males, delinquency, economic dependency, poor academic performance, unwed motherhood, etc.

The adaptive-vitality school contends that adaptation by Blacks to socio-economic pressures and limitations must not be seen as pathologies, but as strength, i.e., adaptive vitality. Billingsley (1968), Blassingame (1972), Young (1970), Hill (1972), Nobles (1978), Staples (1978) et al represent this school. Among the propositions they argue are the following: 1) that the Black family is unique and cannot be fitted into a white formula for analysis; 2) that it was not totally destroyed in slavery; 3) that it has proved its durability and adaptive vitality in the face of severe oppression, and thus, is a strong and functional social unit.

Staples (1971:133) notes that one of the major problems with the traditional approaches to the study of the Black family has been their tendency to fix it in a white-middle class formula. He argues that the result of this subjective approach "has been that the Black family continues to be defined as a pathological unit whose unique way of functioning sustains the conditions of its oppression." Billingsley (1970:132-133) also critized white social science for focusing almost exclusively on lower income families and ignoring the majority of stable Black families and blaming lower-class families for their victimization by society. Although, he concedes lower-class family negatives while praising upper-class positives, he nevertheless argues these negatives are socially-rooted. Moreover, he stresses that many misunderstood features of the Black family are sources of strength and raises questions concerning politically suspect conclusions which have social policy implications.

Although proponents of the adaptive vitality approach do not agree on the degree of African influence on Afro-American culture and family, there is agreement that slavery did not destroy all. Early studies by DuBois (1969) and Carter G. Woodson (1936), as well as Herskovits (1941) showed a legacy from Africa as well as from slavery in Afro-American culture and social institutions. More recently, Blassingame (1972) found African survivals in courtship practices, dance, familial roles, folktales, language, music, names, proverbs, and religious beliefs and practice. Blassingame asserted that it is important to realize that "Whatever the impact slavery had on (Blacks') behavior and attitudes, it did not force them to concentrate all their psychic energy on survival." On the contrary, they showed remarkable adaptive vitality in the system and inspite of the end of contact with Africa when the slave trade ended, the enslaved African "was able to retain many cultural elements and (for a while) an emotional contact with his motherland."

Nobles (1978, 1981) posits that Africanity or Africaness is clearly evidenced in Afro-American families. He (1978:22) cites "the actuality of black kinship bonds and the sense of extended family" as an example of this as well as an egalitarian quality to relationships and a profound commitment to the survival of the family (ethnic group). Moreover, he sees Africanity in Blacks' affective rather than economic approach to family life and their sense of collectivity rather than the individualism which is endemic to European culture.

Finally, Sudarkasa (1980, 1981) asserts that both African and slavery legacies exist. She (1981:37) states that "just as surely as Black American family patterns are in part an outgrowth of the descent into slavery, so too are they partly a reflection of the archetypical African institutions and values that informed and influenced the behavior of these Africans who were enslaved in America." Also she (1981:39) notes, that although there are "relatively few 'traces' of direct *institutional transfer* from Africa to America," there are "numerous examples of the *institutional transformation* from Africa to America." Thus, she tends to support Blassingame's contention that Africans were able to build viable and creative syntheses out of African and European culture. Sudarkasa essentially poses the concept and force of consanguinity or bloodtie kinship as an enduring Africanism as well as the extended family of which it is an expression. "The extended family networks that were formed during slavery by Africans *and their descendents* were based on the institutional heritage which Africans had brought with them to this continent," she (1981:45) contends. And the specific forms they assumed depend on the cultural, economic and political circumstances in which Blacks found themselves.

The proponents of the adaptive-vitality model and approach are concerned also that the Black family be viewed and studied as a distinct institution with its own historical tradition and characteristics, not as a pathological or defective variation on the Euro-American theme. Although some make a distinction between *alternative* and *adaptive* strategies and forms developed by Black families to meet the challenge of an oppressive social life, that distinction is not made here. As Sudarkasa (1981:37) has noted, the two characterizations of Black families are not mutually exclusive and represent false dichotomies. For adaptive strategies and behavior contribute to the development of alternative formations as the history of the Black family shows. I have used the term adaptive vitality which is the "ability to adjust structurally and ideologically in confrontation with society without losing its distinct character," to absorb stress and strain and bounce back with vigor. It is the ability to push past simple survival and develop continuously (Karenga, 1980:52). It is in the context of the above clarification that the strengths of Black families which proponents of the adaptive-vitality school are presented and have meaning.

Although Staples, Ladner (1972), Billingsley, Nobles and others have listed various strengths of Black families, the classic study on this is Robert Hill's (1978) book of the same title, *The Strengths of Black Families*. Hill (1978:3) defines family strengths as "those traits which facilitate the ability of the family to meet the needs of its members and the demands made upon it by systems outside the family unit." Having done this, he lists five strengths which examination of literature on Black families reveal as having been "functional for their survival, development and stability" (1978:4): 1) strong kinship bonds which is stronger among Blacks than whites and expresses itself by absorption of relatives, especially minors and the elderly in various families; 2) strong work orientation, i.e., "the Black poor still are more likely to work than the white poor"; 3) the adaptability of family roles, i.e., male and female can assume each other's household roles in the event of absence, illness, etc.; 4) high achievement orientation, i.e., the majority of low-income students and their parents have college aspirations; and finally, 5) religious orientation.

In criticism of the adaptive-vitality proponents, Nathan Hare (1976) contends the strength-of-the-family school may have unwittingly created their own negatives while challenging the negatives of the pathology-pathogenesis school. First, he (1976:9) states that strength-of-the-family orientation "prohibits any recognition of pathological consequences of our oppression" and thus, undermines the thrust of corrective action. Secondly, Hare (1976:10) argues that such an approach "fails to incorporate a power-conflict model appropriate to advocates of social change." Finally, Hare (1976:11) contends that the strength-of-the-family approach helps "make it easier for an oppressive society to ignore the heinous conditions it imposes on the Black family." He stresses that he is not advocating victimology, but he has problems with claiming all is well with the Black world at the expense of social criticism.

Hare's contentions point to a serious dilemma of Black scholarship, i.e., how does one prove strength in oppression without overstating the case, diluting criticism of the system and absolving the oppressor in the process? Likewise, the parallel dilemma is how does one criticize the system and state of things without contributing to the victimology school which thrives on litanies of lost battles and casualty lists, while omitting victories and strengths and the possibilities for change inherent in both Black people and society? The answer to these questions are not easily achieved. The tasks of an emancipatory social science are to develop a critical and balanced analysis which reveals Black strengths and weaknesses as well as a prescription for self-conscious action to free themselves and to shape reality into their own image and interests. Such, then, is the central task of an emancipatory Black social science.

BLACK MALE/FEMALE RELATIONS

This is a revised and shortened version of the article which appeared first in Black Male/Female Relationships, *vol. 2, no. 1 (1979) under the title of "The Black Male/Female Connection".*

Male/female relationships are of fundamental and enduring concern and importance for several reasons: 1) because of their species character, i.e., their indispensability to the maintenance and development of the species; 2) they are a measurement of our humanity, i.e., how far humans are from the animal world; 3) they are a measurement of the quality of social life of any given society, i.e., the treatment of women in relationships and by extension in society becomes as Toure (1959:72) notes, "...a mirror that reflects the economic and social conditions, the level of political, cultural and moral development of a given country"; 4) they are a measurement and mirror of personal development and identity, i.e., a revelation of who persons really are; and finally, 5) they are, a measurement of a people's capacity for struggle and social construction, for as a fundamental unit of the nation, their strengths and weaknesses determine the nation's capacity to define, defend and develop it's interest. (Karenga, 1978a).

One does not have to be as bitterly negative as Wallace (1979) and Shange (1977) to admit that there are substantive problems concerning Black male/female relationships (Karenga, 1979). The lack of relationships due to the scarcity of men (Jackson 1978) and the games one has to play to begin and sustain relationships (Staples, 1978) poses significant problems. Moreover, the quality and future of those relationships that exist are open to continuing question and challenge, given the social stress and strain with which they are daily confronted (Staples, 1981). Also, there is the obvious need for a new family form, i.e., an extended family, to correct the deficiencies of the nuclear family and lay the basis for a more proactive and mutually beneficial exchange (Karenga, 1978a: 87-89; Madhubuti, 1980). But who that family should include and the criteria for inclusion as well as the moral minimum value system it should operate by for maximum mutual benefit are still to be developed and agreed upon.

However, in discussing the problems of Black male/female relationships, it is important to keep in mind at least four fundamental facts. First, Black male/female relationships like Black families are no more problem ridden or pathological than Jewish and Gentile families and male/female relationships. In this regard, it might help to remember that Sigmund Freud's studies on personal and family pathology were done among Jews and Gentiles, not among Blacks or other Third World people.

Secondly, it is important to recognize that real life unavoidably involves problems and problem-solving. The point, then, is not to be without problems, but to be resourceful in devising solutions. Thirdly, it is important to recognize that not all Black male/female relationships are in turmoil and trouble. However, there are enough relationships in turmoil and trouble and enough persons without relationships to make the question of Black male/female necessary for discussion.

Finally, it is of equal importance to realize that any criticism of Black male/female relationships is at the same time and in equal measure a criticism of U.S. society which has shaped them to fit and function ''properly'' in it. For social conditions create both social consciousness and social conduct and failure to recognize this can lead one to see racial defects where social ones are more real and relevant.

It is this final contention that serves as a key point of departure for any serious analysis of Black male/female relationships. For to say we are products of our social conditions is to say the same thing about our relationships. Analyses of the major defects in Black male/female relationships clearly reveal their social rather than genetic or purely personal basis. Thus, to understand the negatives of our relationships we must understand the negative characteristics of society which have shaped them.

These negatives of U.S. society are defined by and derived from three major structural and value systems: capitalism, racism and sexism. Capitalism is a socio-economic system defined by private ownership of the means to satisfy human needs and the ruthless and continuous pursuit of profit which turns virtually everything into a commodity, i.e., an object for sale and purchase. Racism is a system of denial and deformation of a people's history and humanity based primarily or exclusively on the specious concept of race and racial hierarchies. Sexism is the social practice of using gender or sex as the key determinant in establishing, maintaining and explaining relationships and exchanges. In others words, it is a system of assumptions and acts, theories and practices which imply and impose unequal, oppressive and exploitative relationships based on gender or sex.

Capitalism, then, turns relationships and parts of relationships into commodities and utilitarian arrangements. Racism engenders self-hate, self-doubt and pathological fixation on the white paradigm. And sexism encourages artificial personal power over women as a substitute for real social power over one's destiny and daily life. The result of these three structural and value strains on Black male/female relationships expresses itself as a transformation of the relationships into what can be best described as *connections*. A connection is a short-term or tentative association which is utilitarian and alienated and is designed primarily for the mutual misuse of each other's body. A quality relationship on the other hand is a long-term, stable association defined by its positive sharing, its mutual investment in each other's happiness, well-being and development.

There are four basic connections which plague male/female relationships in the U.S. and by logical extension Black male/female relationships: 1) the cash connection; 2) the flesh connection;

3) the force connection; 4) the dependency connection (Karenga, 1978a). The cash connection grows out of the commodity character of society. It is informed by several capitalistic assumptions among which are: 1) everything and everyone has a price; 2) anything you can't buy ain't worth having anyhow; 3) what you invest money or material assets in is yours; and 4) money is the measure of and solution to everything.

In such a context, mothers tell their daughters to look for and marry someone who can "take care" of them, as if they were disabled; women sell themselves to men, exchanging sex for economic security and call it marriage; teenage men invest in young women with a movie and a Mac burger and demand their bodies in exchange; and male idiots claim the right to rule and ruin the lives of their wives and children on the basis of the money they bring in. Money and material considerations, then, form the basis for the cash connection and diminish the chances for a quality relationship which is conscious of but not ruled by material considerations.

The flesh connection grows out of the pornographic character of society and is defined as an association based on purely or predominantly on the pursuit of sex. This connection focuses on the body and all the perverse things one can do with all or selected parts of it. Pornography, as a definite social thought and practice and as the essence and source of the flesh connection, expresses itself in five basic ways: 1) as species alienation, i.e., man alienated from and oblivious of his species half; 2) objectification of the species half, turning a natural partner into an object of use and disuse; 3) fragmentation of the body, i.e., hacking the body into usable pieces and rejecting the wholeness of the human personality; 4) brutalization, most viciously expressed in the sado-masochistic vulgarities society at its most violent and alienated level has produced; and 5) a sexual commodity form, i.e., the joining of the cash and flesh connection through the packaging and peddling of the human body.

A third connection is the force connection which rises out of the violent and oppressive character of society. Historically, men have used their greater physical strength to subdue women and win arguments they would otherwise lose. Moreover, the flesh and force connection merge in the act of rape which is not so much sexual as it is psycho-cultural and physical. For above all, it is an act of domination practiced by husbands, friends and strangers (Karenga, 1978a:15).

Also, there is social or ideological coercion which forces women, through censure and labelling, into traditional roles. Finally, the force connection expresses itself in economic coercion. This operates on the principles that he who controls the means to satisfy human needs controls at the same time the humans with those needs.

The fourth and final connection which challenges and often denies quality Black male/female relationships is the dependency connection. This connection is the logical and inevitable result of the others. After a woman has been transformed into a commodity, reduced to parts of her body and physically or ideologically whipped into compliance, she can only be dependent. Like all slaves and servants, she becomes a set of reactions to her slavemaster, a defender of his definitions and treatment of her. Thus, interdependence, a key value in quality relationships, becomes impossible and the connection becomes the model rather than the deviance (Nobles, 1978).

Given the seriousness of problem, it is only logical to ask what is the solution? The solution like the problem has both a personal and social dimension and requires transformation on both levels. Although, I have argued that conditions create consciousness, consciousness and the social practice that it engenders can and often do create conditions. Certainly, capitalism, racism and sexism shape our relationships, but they are systems created and maintained by humans and they can be changed and rebuilt by humans.

Without such a proactive conception of human possibility, neither personal nor social change is possible.

But the struggle to change systems must begin with the struggle of a people to change themselves, i.e., their own views and values and the negative and non-productive ways they have organized and live their daily lives. Only then can they self-consciously rebuild their relationships and begin to change the social conditions which deform and deny these relationships.

The solution to deficient relations, then, is rooted in the creation, acceptance and practice of a new value system. Both Ladner (1971:269) and Staples (1981:231-232) argue the need for a value system which rejects and counters the standards of the dominant society. "We must seek other alternative and more viable standards," Ladner (1971:269) asserts. For the U.S. model "which purports to be the exemplary one" is not only negative to Black interest, but also "is in the process of internal destruction, and there is little within it which seems worthy of salvaging." This requires an alternative value system which calls for a redefinition of reality in Blacks' own interest and image, for a new definition of man and woman and the kind of relationships they ought to have.

Real relationships must begin with terms clearly stated, and grow and are reinforced by common values, common interests and aspirations, quality commitment, support structures, continuous renewal, and common struggle for liberation and a higher level of human life (Karenga, 1980:47-48). For in the final analysis, the call for an end to deformed and defective relationships, must be a call for an end to the social conditions which created and sustain them. One must begin with a *moral minimum* that cannot be compromised, a set of values which are resistant to revision because they are at the very roots of the relationship. Prohibition against violence; full, free and frank discussion; egalitarian exchange; collective decision-making; and shared responsibility in love and struggle must be a part of that moral minimum, if a relationship is to be real and mutually beneficial.

This, however, is just a beginning and outline of possibilities. The realities will be built by those *New Africans* in U.S. society who dare to be other than their immediate and social conditions encourage them to be. Essentially, I concur with Staples' (1981:232) contention that "Now we stand at the crossroads of a major decision about which way we will proceed to order our lives." The choice is clearly between the continuation of the current social and personal state of things or self-conscious intervention to change it and build a better society and system of relationships. And as Staples concludes, "Whatever the decision may be, we should not be deluded into believing that the consequences are individual ones. The future of the race may be at stake."

STUDY QUESTIONS

1. Define social organization.
2. What are some basic aims of Black sociology as an emancipatory social science?
3. What are the basic characteristics of the ghetto?
4. What are possible resource structures and some proposed solutions to problems of the ghetto?
5. Discuss the race/class controversy.
6. What is racism? Discuss its three basic aspects.
7. Discuss Kawaida's position on cultural revolution.
8. What are the two basic approaches to the study of the Black family? What are their basic concerns and contentions?
9. What are Hare's contentions about the strength-of-the-family advocates and the problems these pose for critical and emancipatory social science?

10. What are the reasons male/female relations are so important?

11. What four fundamental facts must be kept in mind when discussing Black male/female relations?

12. What three structural and value tendencies of U.S. society help shape male/female relations?

13. What are the four basic connections in male/female relations?

14. What are some basic solutions to the problem of male/female relations?

REFERENCES

Allen, Robert (1974) *Reluctant Reformers*, Washington, D.C.: Howard University Press.

Berger, Bennett. (1967) "Soul Searching," *Trans-Action*, (June) 54-57.

Billingsley, Andrew. (1970) "Black Families and White Social Science," *Journal of Social Issues*, 26, 3 (Summer) 127-142.

Billingsley, Andrew. (1968) *Black Families in White America*, Englewood Cliffs, N.J.: Prentice-Hall, Inc.

Blassingame, John. (1972) *The Slave Community*, New York: Oxford University Press.

Blauner, Robert. (1972) *Racial Oppression in America*, New York: Harper & Row, Publishers.

Bonacich, Edna. (1972) "A Theory of Ethnic Antagonism: The Split Labor Market," *American Sociological Review*, 37 (October), 547-559.

Bottomore, T.B. and Maximilien Rubel. (1964) *Karl Marx: Selected Writings in Sociology and Social Philosophy*, New York: McGraw Hill.

Clark, Kenneth. (1965) *The Dark Ghetto,* New York: Harper & Row Publishers.

Clay, Phillip. (1981) "Housing and Neighborhoods," in *The State of Black America-1981,* New York: National Urban League.

Cox, Oliver C. (1970) *Caste, Class and Race,* New York: Monthly Review Press.

Cruse, Harold. (1967) *The Crisis of the Negro Intellectual,* New York: William Morrow.

_____ . (1968) *Rebellion or Revolution?,* New York: William Morrow.

Drake, St. Clair and Horace R. Cayton. (1962) *Black Metropolis,* New York: Harper & Row Publishers.

DuBois, W.E.B. (1969) *The Negro American Family,* New York: New American Library.

_____ . (1967) *The Philadelphia Negro,* New York: Schocken Books.

_____ . (1959) "The Talented Tenth," in *The Negro Problem,* (ed.) Ulysses Lee, New York: Arno Press and New York times, pp. 31-76.

DuBois, W.E.B. (1975) *W.E.B. DuBois on Sociology and the Black Community,* (eds.) Dan Green and Edwin Driver, Chicago: University of Chicago Press.

Ellison, Ralph. (1966) *Shadow and Act,* New York: New American Library.

Fanon, Frantz. (1968) *The Wretched of the Earth,* New York: Grove Press.

Frazier, E. Franklin. (1973) "The Failure of the Negro, Intellectual," in *The Death of White Sociology,* (ed.) Joyce A. Ladner, New York: Vintage Books, pp. 52-66.

_____. (1939) *The Negro Family in America*, Chicago: University of Chicago Press.

_____. (1957) *The Negro in the United States*, New York: Macmillan Company.

Gayle, Addison. (1971) *The Black Aesthetic*, New York: Doubleday & Co.

Glasgow, Douglas. (1981) *The Black Underclass*, New York: Vintage Books.

Glazer, Nathan and Daniel P. Moynihan. (1963) *Beyond the Melting Pot*, Cambridge: M.I.T. and Harvard University Press.

Hare, Nathan. (1965) "The Challenge of a Black Scholar," in *The Death of White Sociology*, (ed.) Joyce A. Ladner, New York: Vintage Books, pp. 67-78.

_____. (1976) "What Black Intellectuals Misunderstand About the Black Family," *Black World*, (March) 5-14.

Herkovits, M. (1941) *The Myth of the Negro Past*, New York: Harper & Row, Publishers.

Hill, Robert. (1972) *The Strengths of Black Families*, New York: Emerson Hall.

Jackson, Jacqueline. (1978) "But Where Are the Men?" in *The Black Family: Essays and Studies*, (ed.) Robert Staples, Belmont, Ca.: Wadsworth Publishing Company, pp. 110-117.

Karenga, Maulana. (1978a) *Beyond Connections: Liberation in Love and Struggle*, New Orleans: Ahidiana.

_____. (1978b) *Essays on Struggle: Position and Analysis*, San Diego: Kawaida Publications.

_____. (1980) *Kawaida Theory: An Introductory Outline*, Inglewood: Kawaida Publications.

_____. (1979) "On Wallace's Myths: Wading Thru Troubled Waters," *The Black Scholar*, 10, 8 (May/June) 36-39.

224   Black Social Organization

_____ . (1981) "The Problematic" Aspects of Pluralism: Ideological and Political Dimensions" in *Pluralism, Racism and Public Policy: The Search for Equality,* (eds.) Edwin G. Clausen and Jack Bermingham, Boston: G.K. Hall & Co., pp. 223-246.

_____ . (1967) *The Quotable Karenga,* (eds.) Clyde Halisi and James Mtume, Los Angeles: Saidi Publications.

_____ . (1982) "Society, Culture and the Problem of Self-Consciousness: A Kawaida Analysis," in *"Philosophy Born of Struggle: Anthology of Afro-American Philosophy From 1917,* (ed.) Leonard Harris, Dubuque, IA: Kendall/Hunt; pp. 212-228.

Ladner, Joyce.   (1973) *The Death of White Sociology,* New York: Vintage Books.

_____ . (1971) *Tomorrow's Tomorrow: The Black Women,* Garden City, N.Y.: Anchor Books.

Liebow, Elliot.   (1967) *Tally's Corner,* Boston: Little, Brown & Co.

Madhubuti, Haki.   (1980) "Not Allowed To Be Lovers," *Black Books Bulletin,* 6, 4, pp. 48-57, 71.

Mc Adoo, Harriette P.   (ed.)   (1981) *Black Families,* Beverly Hills: Sage Publications

Moynihan, Daniel.   (1965) *The Negro Family,* Washington, D.C.: Office of Planning and Research, U.S. Dept. of Labor.

Myrdal, Gunnar.   (1944) *An American Dilemma,* New York: Harper & Row, Publishers.

Nobles, Wade.   (1981) "African-American Family Life," in *An Instrument of Culture,* (ed.) Harriette P. McAdoo, Beverly Hills: Sage Publications.

_____ . (1978) "Africanity: Its Role in Black Families," in *The Black Family: Essays and Studies,* (ed.) Robert Staples, Belmont, Ca.: Wadsworth Publishing Co., pp. 19-25.

Reich, Michael. (1981) *Racial Inequality,* Princeton: Princeton University Press.

Rose, H.M. (1976) *Black Suburbanization,* Cambridge, Mass.: Ballinger.

Shange, Ntozake. (1977) *For Colored Girls,* New York: Emerson Hall.

Sowell, Thomas. (1981a) *Ethnic Minorities,* New York: Basic Books.

_____ . (1981b) *Markets and Minorities,* New York: Basic Books.

_____ . (1975) *Race and Economics,* New York: David McKay Company.

Spear, Allen H. (1967) *Black Chicago,* Chicago: University of Chicago Press.

Staples, Robert, (ed.) (1978) *The Black Family: Essays and Studies,* Belmont, Ca.: Wadsworth Publishing Company.

_____ . (1976) *Introduction to Black Sociology,* New York: McGraw Hill.

_____ . (1971) "Toward A Sociology of the Black Family: A Theoretical and Methodological Assessment," *Journal of Marriage and Family,* 33, 1 (February) 119-138.

Staples, Robert. (1973) "What is Black Sociology: Toward a Sociology of Black Liberation," in *The Death of White Sociology,* (ed.) Joyce A. Ladner, New York: Vintage Books, pp. 161-172.

_____ (1981) *The World of Black Singles,* Westport, Conn.: Conn.: Greenwood Press.

Sudarkasa, Niara. (1980) "African and Afro-American Family Structure: A Comparison," *The Black Scholar,* 11 (November/ December) 37-60.

_____ . (1981) "Interpreting the African Heritage in Afro-American Family Organization," in *Black Families,* (ed.) Harriette P. McAdoo, Beverly Hills: Sage Publications,

Toure, Sekou. (1959) *Toward Full Re-Africanization* Paris: Presence Africaine.

Turner, James. (1979) "The Political Sociology of Racism and Systematic Oppression: Internal Colonization as a Paradigm for Socio-Economic Analysis," *Studia Africana*, 1, 3 (Fall) 294-314.

Wallace, Michelle. (1979) *Black Macho and the Myth of the Superwoman*, New York: Dial Press.

Willie, Charles. (1979) *The Caste and Class Controversy*, New York: General Hall, Inc.

———. (1970) *The Family Life of Black People*, Columbus, Ohio: Charles Merrill.

Wilson, Franklin. (1979) *Residential Consumption, Economic Opportunity and Race*, New York: Academic Press.

Wilson, William J. (1978) *The Declining Significance of Race* Chicago: University of Chicago Press.

Woodson, Carter G. (1936) *The African Background Outlined*, Washington, D.C.: Assn. for the Study of Negro Life and History.

Young, Virginia. (1970) "*Family and Childhood in a Southern Negro Community*," *American Anthropologist*, 72:269-288.

V
BLACK POLITICS

INTRODUCTION

Politics can be defined as the art and process of gaining, maintaining and using *power*. Whether one uses system-oriented literature (Apter, 1977) or studies on revolutionary structures and processes (Gross, 1974), the focus is on power, the process of its acquisition, maintenance and utilization. Thus, the essence of politics is power which can be defined as the social capacity of a group to realize its will, even in opposition to others (Karenga, 1980:65). Social capacity is used here to stress both the *collective* and *structural* character of power as well as to indicate that power as a political concept and fact must be achieved in a societal context as opposed to a family or personal context.

Social capacity, then, is rooted in collective (group) capacity and is expressed in a group's structural capacity, i.e., its organizational and institutional ability to realize its will - even in opposition to others. Also, it is important at this point to make the distinction between influence and power which are often used interchangeably though technically they are very different. For whereas power is the capacity to act and achieve, influence is simply the ability to affect. It is having influence with people in power that often passes in Black leadership circles as having power itself.

It is in the context of these assumptions about the pervasiveness and centrality of power to politics that Jones (1972:8) defines Black politics as "a manifestation of one dimension or extension of the

227

universal struggle for power." This stress on power, then, is the beginning concept in establishing and developing a fundamental framework for the study of Black politics. However, there are other concepts key to a critical grasp of Black politics as both a study and a social process. These key concepts are *conflict, interests, change,* and *the state* which are also alternative related ways of defining and understanding politics and its central concept, power.

The stress on the struggle for power presupposes the real and continuing presence of conflict in society as another basic aspect of politics. As Walton (1972b:1) states, "Politics is born of societal conflict." This conflict is defined not only by the struggle for power but also, as Samuel D. Cook contended, for "values associated with and derived from the possession of power" (Walton, 1972b:xv). In other words, power, although the key social value in politics, is sought not simply for itself but for other key values or treasured things, which power can provide and protect, i.e., rights, resources, status, etc. The assumption here then, is that the presence of conflict in society is normal, rather than abnormal and that its most severe forms are rooted in the struggle for power and the values it provides and protects. Therefore, system theory which poses conflict as abnormal is not so much an analysis as it is a political projection and description of utopia (Parsons, 1951).

Another key concept of Black politics is interests. In fact, another way to define power is as a group's capacity to define, defend and develop its interests. To define them is to articulate and establish them; to defend them is to protect them against challenge and to develop them is to promote and expand them. Interests can be defined as social stakes, claims or concerns (Balbus, 1974). They may be subjective (simply perceived) or objective, i.e., existing independent of perception. In a society divided and defined by race and class, interests and the conflict around them assume a race and class character (Scott, 1980; Drake, 1971). Thus, another way of viewing social conflict is as the struggle between differing, competing and often antagonistic interests.

A fourth key concept in Black politics is social change which is linked to and rooted in social conflict. The assumption here is that the U.S. political system is defined by contradictory interests not simply by concensus as the pluralists (Apter, 1977;Dahl, 1967) contend. Consensus or universal agreement on values is clearly impossible in a society wracked by severe race and class division. Thus, constraint through coercion becomes a way to institutionalize and regulate interests and conflicts or suppress them. The political struggle to break through constraints and reorder society in a group's interests becomes the key impetus for social change.

Finally, it is important in understanding politics to realize that "power in society is *ultimately determined by a people's relationship to the state*" (Karenga, 1980:65). The state here is defined as "the totality of institutions which facilitate governance and insure social control." Within the general framework of these functions, two sets of institutions stand out as most definitive. These are the institutions of dominance, i.e., coercion (armed forces, police, courts, etc.) and political socialization (the educational system and other structures used to advance the ideas and values of those who rule). The instruments of political socialization represent the right and ability to define social reality and the instruments of domination represent the power of the state to make its definition stick. Given this awesome power of the state, and the fact that ultimately power is determined by a group's relationship to the state, an essential political question is how does one check, challenge, seize control of or effectively participate in the exercise of *state power?*

Walton (1972b: 2-4), however, is correct in his criticism of the exclusive or predominant emphasis on electoral politics in the study of Black politics. The political studies of Gosnell (1967) and Wilson (1960) in Chicago, Ladd's (1966) study of Black leadership in two North Carolina cities, and the readings on the Black electorate on the national level by Bailey (1967) all reflect this unbalanced focus on electoral politics. However, power and the struggle for it which are the essence of politics are much more multidimensional than electoral activity.

Essentially there are eight areas or bases of political power: 1) key positions in government; 2) voting strength; 3) community control; 4) economic capacity; 5) community organization; 6) possession of critical knowledge; 7) coalition and alliance; and 8) coercive capacity. Key positions in government at the national, state or local levels places a group in the position to determine or share in the determination of public policy. These positions may be appointed (cabinet members, advisors, bureaucratic positions) or elected (Congresspersons, mayors, council persons, etc.) Voting strength is key to electing one's own representatives or allies or in penalizing or threatening penalty. Community control is translated as command of and authority over the economic, political and cultural institutions and processes of the community as a result of community organization, institutional penetration and development. Economic capacity is transformed into political power through financing campaigns and lobbies, control of a city's economics, determining public opinion through control of the media, and buying votes and/or officials.

Community organization means a highly mobilized, organized political force which makes possible all the others. For if power is a collective and structural capacity, organization of the people itself is the *sine qua non* of this. Another source of power is the possession of critical knowledge, especially given the social tendency toward specialized knowledge. Possession of such knowledge whether in science, technology, finance or politics makes processes and structures dependent on the possessors and often puts the possessors at the very center of the social power process. Coalitions and alliances are also ways to create and augment power. Effective unity strengthens weak groups and increases the power of strong ones.

Finally, the ultimate power is coercive power, the capacity to impose one's interests, to physically factor out opposition under the cover of law, to raise class or race will and interest to the status of law and to establish authority through the strength of the gun. In the final analysis, the ultimate power is state power and state power is above all rooted in control of the coercive apparatus, i.e., army, police, etc. There is, however, the alternative power of violence, 'i.e., urban guerilla strikes, revolt and revolution against the state or social disruption in other forms.

Below is a discussion of three basic areas and expression of Black politics. Each represents Blacks' struggle to define, defend and develop their interests as a people in and outside of government. Hopefully, the discussion of these gives added meaning to Dymally's (1972:21) statement that:

> Because of the Black man's (and woman's) situation which is radical by any definition, and because of the nature of American politics, which is moderate to conservative by any definition, the Black man (and woman) in America has been condemned to seek radical ends within a political framework which was designed to prevent sudden and radical social and economical changes.

The radicalness of the situation is not always by choice, but by the fact that Blacks' social location - in terms of both race and class - is such that an effective end to their oppression must and will require the fundamental restructuring of society, i.e., its power and status relations. The history of Blacks in the U.S. offer ample proof of this contention and their future will indoubtedly reaffirm it.

PARTY POLITICS

RATIONALE

The rationale for party politics begins with the fact that a party is the key political structure in the acquisition and exercise of state power (Sorauf, 1976; Gross, 1974). By definition, a party, revolutionary or system-oriented, "is a political structure specifically designed to seize, control or effectively participate in state power" (Karenga, 1980:66). Within the framework of the party focus on the exercise of state power, Blacks, like other party members and/or supporters, seek to use the party to achieve their group and personal interests (Key, 1962). Among the perceived benefits of participation in Democratic and Republican party politics are: 1) a vital, even if tenuous, link to state power; 2) a vehicle through which one's interests are represented, i.e., advanced and protected; 3) a means of becoming one's own group representative, i.e., an elected or appointed official; 4) an opportunity to determine or help determine public policy; 5) a share of party patronage (appointments, jobs, funds, etc.)

In addition to participation in the two-party system, Blacks have also participated in non-Black Third parties such as the Socialist, Progressive, Communist, Populist, Liberty and the Peace and Freedom parties (Walton, 1969). Although these parties did not usually win and had little or no patronage to offer, Blacks supported them for various other reasons, as Walton (1972a) notes. These include: 1) dissatisfaction with the two dominant parties' level or lack of commitment to Black interests; 2) a sense of exclusion and alienation from the two major parties, as in Southern racist branches; 3) perception that opportunities to voice and fight for Black interests exist in alternative parties; 4) the ideological appeal of third parties; and 5) strong recruitment efforts by third parties.

Finally, Black parties have also emerged as an alternative to the two-party system (Walton, 1972a). Given the fact that Black parties are third parties, they tend to rise for similar reasons as other third parties. Frye (1980:5) states that "independent Black parties tend to rise when (1) Black participation in one or the other major party is denied," or (2) when "political leaders decide that aspects of their social, political and economical grievances cannot or will not be met by existing parties." He cites the founding of the Mississippi Freedom Democratic Party and the National Democratic Party of Alabama as examples of the first and the founding of the United Citizens Party in South Carolina and the Lowndes County Freedom Organization in Alabama as examples of the latter. In addition to these reasons for formation, Black parties also rise as a result of: 1) increased levels of Black consciousness; 2) the desire for an independent politics which not only wins a share of political power, but also makes a statement concerning their capacity for independent action; and 3) perception that party-building and electoral activities are ways of politically educating, mobilizing and organizing the masses of Blacks around vital issues.

THE REPUBLICAN PARTY EXPERIENCE

The first electoral activity of Blacks was in the context of the Republican party. During Reconstruction, Blacks joined the Republican party in great numbers and held various offices on the national, state and local levels. The reasons for the Black affiliation with the Republican were both by choice and the political situation in the U.S. at the time. First, Blacks joined and supported the Republican party because it was the party of Lincoln, Secondly, Republicans actively recruited Blacks in an effort to build a Black electorate in their struggle with the Democrats. Thirdly, they financed Black candidates for office. Finally, the Democratic party was closed to Blacks, thus, eliminating an alternative option. Morris

(1975:191) in discussing Republican motivation for involvement of Black cites three basic reasons: 1) their desire to solidify Republican control by developing a solid base of support among Blacks in the South; 2) their desire to punish the South by imposing a strong Black electorate on it; and 3) the struggle between the legislative and executive branches, with each needing to prove its predominance. In such a context, Morris concludes, Blacks and Republicans entered into a mutually beneficial relationship which, however, was short-lived

The decisive year was 1876 when Republican presidential candidate, Rutherford B. Hayes, agreed to withdraw federal troops and adopt a hands-off policy toward the South in exchange for Southern electoral votes needed to win the election. This "Compromise of 1877" led to massive violence against Blacks at the hands of white terrorist societies such as the KKK and to a division of the party into two factions, the lily-white Republicans and the Black and Tan Republicans (Walton, 1975). Thus, in their efforts to accommodate white racists, Republicans lost the Black electorate which began to transfer to the Democratic Party in 1932 with the election of Franklin D. Roosevelt.

Not until the late 70's did Republicans make a significant effort to challenge the Democratic monopoly on the Black vote and to reinvolve Blacks in the Republican party process (Karenga, 1978a). Their strategy had two basic aims: 1) to win a significant share of the Black vote in various elections and failing this; 2) to minimize the size and effect of the Democrats' share.

In 1978, it looked as though Republicans would at least make significant inroads in the Democratic monopoly on the Black vote, given the rise of a new middle class with interests which seemed to coincide with some Republican positions. As an indication of their seriousness in wooing Blacks, the GOP appropriated monies for recruitment and campaign finance for suitable Black candidates and invited leaders like Jesse Jackson of PUSH and Benjamin Hooks of the NAACP to open the dialogue on possible mutually-beneficial cooperation.

However, in 1980 with the election of Ronald Reagan, the push seemed to have been deemphasized. Blacks voted overwhelmingly Democratic in that election even when other ethnic and interest groups shifted (Williams and Morris, 1981). Reagan, being a model conservative and not exactly sensitive to or mindful of Black needs and interests, set about cutting the budget and advancing negative policy in areas most detrimental to Blacks, other Third World peoples and the poor. Given this, it was difficult for either Black or white Republicans to seriously suggest a reinvolvement of Blacks in the party.

Nevertheless, even if all this had transpired and Reagan had not turned out to exhibit so much of what is called now "social meanness" in his brutal attacks on social welfare programs, there still would have been formidable problems for the Republicans to overcome in their quest for Black support. Among these are: 1) the historical tendency of Blacks to vote Democratic regardless; 2) the ideological orientation of the Republican Party which stands for objectives and principles opposite to Black interests, i.e., it stands against social welfare, government intervention and African liberation movements; and 3) the conservative internal resistance to courting Blacks and making the kind of concessions this requires with no guarantee of positive results (Karenga, 1978a).

THE DEMOCRATIC PARTY EXPERIENCE

It was during the Roosevelt Administration beginning in 1932 that Black support for the Democratic party began. Before this, Blacks were repelled by the open racism advocated and practiced by the party. It not only opposed the vote for Blacks, but used terror and violence against them to discourage their voting. But during the New Deal era, the Roosevelt Administration drew Blacks to the party through economic initiatives which benefited Blacks and later through Roosevelt's anti-discrimination measures. Roosevelt also reinforced his position with Blacks by creating the "Black Cabinet", an advisory group of skilled Blacks, and by issuing Executive Order 8802 which created a Fair Employment Practice Commission and banned discrimination in industries with federal contracts.

Since the Roosevelt Administration, Blacks have maintained a steadfast loyalty to the Democratic party even though Roosevelt and subsequent presidents did not always live up to their commitments or even promise Blacks substantial gains. Walters (1975) has continuously called attention to this impolitic loyalty for the Democratic party, arguing that "there is no bargaining leverage in a situation where a Black vote for the Democratic party is *expected* and *delivered.*" Such a blind and impolitic loyalty is clearly disadvantageous to Blacks in the political arena and it becomes important to raise the question of why the persistence.

From available evidence, it seems that Blacks' party identification with the Democrats persists for several reasons. First, the Democrats have historically tended to be more favorable to socioeconomic issues facing Blacks. Secondly the party had been supportive of civil rights since the Roosevelt administration. Thirdly, the factor of group cohesiveness tends to reinforce existing patterns once they are established. Fourthly, socialization into a given party tends to persist. Finally, the Republican party offers no real alternative given its stand on socio-economic and civil rights issues (Morris, 1975; Barker and McCorry, 1976).

Although Morris (1975), Barker and McCorry (1976) and Williams (1979) see indicators of rising independent registration and voting, evidence does not suggest a substantial shift in party participation patterns. In fact, as late as the 1980 presidential election, Blacks gave 90% of their vote to Carter inspite of their severe criticism of him (Karenga, 1977) and inspite of shifts by Jews, labor and others to Reagan. Williams and Morris' (1981:227ff) suggest that the consequences of this vote might be an impetus to a more sophisticated and pragmatic approach to party politics. But again, as of this writing, there are no such indicators. This is not to say the shift will not come, but only to emphasize its difficulty and the need for a new and bolder politics than traditional approaches suggest (Strickland, 1972).

BLACK PARTY INITIATIVES

Black party initiatives have been on both the national and state levels, but the most successful efforts have been on the state level (Frye, 1980; Walton, 1972a). Moreover, these parties have been two basic types - parallel and independent parties (Walton, 1972a:80-81). Black party initiatives began as early as 1904 with the founding of the National Liberty Party. In that year delegates from 36 states met in a national convention in St. Louis and developed a platform dedicated to complete enfranchisement and the restoration of Black civil rights which were lost after the Compromise of 1877 (Walton, 1972a:51). This party, however, was short lived and in its place rose a series of non-partisan political organizations, beginning with the National Negro American Political League in 1908 and culminating in the National Negro Congress in 1936.

The 60's saw the rise of three independent Black parties: 1) the Afro-American Party in Alabama (1960); 2) the National Civil Rights Party (1963) and 3) the Freedom Now Party (1964). However, the electoral activity of these parties was also minimal and unsuccessful and they too eventually faded from the political scene. Although Walton considers the Peace and Freedom Party a Black party, its integrated character and predominant white membership contradict this classification. Moreover, even he (1972b:128) states that "it was a coalition of Black militants and white liberals," i.e., between the Panthers and their white allies, an arrangement which clearly pushes it outside any meaningful definition of Black.

Also, the 60's saw the rise of four major parallel Black parties: 1) the Mississippi Freedom Democractic Party (1964); 2) the Lowndes County Freedom Organization or the Black Panther Party of Alabama (1966); 3) the National Democratic Party of Alabama (1968); and 4) the United Citizen's Party of South Carolina (1969) (Walton, 1927a). The MFDP led the way and left valuable lessons for subsequent parallel parties. It taught the method and possibilities of challenge to the established parties at national conventions, the value of using elections to dramatize basic issues and politically educate the masses, and the possibilities and problems of being a parallel party (McLemore, 1971; Walton, 1972a: Chapter 3). The NDPA has clearly been the most successful Black party in terms of both votes received and offices won (Frye, 1980; Walton, 1972a:157). Although it declined in the late seventies, it too, by both its achievements and losses, left valuable lessons on the problems and possibilities of Black parties in the political arena.

The most recent example of the Black party thrust is the founding of the National Black Independent Political Party in 1980. The ideological origins of the party are rooted in the National Black Political Convention held in Gary in 1972 (Gilliam, 1975: chapter 6). Strickland (1972) who helped develop a National Black Political Agenda at Gary which set forth political goals for Blacks in the U.S., summed up the basic concerns for a new Black politics and a new party to initiate this process and give it an ongoing practical expression. He (1972:25-26) argued that the point was not to create just any party and certainly not the kind "that white folks have or talk about." Nor could it be one which is "simply an electoral party" or "simply a party that is dedicated to jobs and patronage or the election of individuals as a first concern." What was needed, Strickland posited, was a party which self-consciously strove to "advance the interests of the Black masses" and was fundamentally concerned with institutional-building and institutional control, the assumption of power and ultimately the shaping of the destiny and daily lives of Black people. Without such a bold and multidimensional approach, i.e., electoral *and* non-electoral politics, he concluded, the party would be neither new nor viable.

Thus although the Gary Convention did not produce a mandate for a new party, it did raise and thoroughly discuss the question. Moreover, it did produce a mandate for a new politics and a National Black Political Assembly. Daniels (1980:32) who served as chairman of NBPA and later of NBIPP posed the "principal role" of NBPA as "the shaping, projecting and institutionalization of an independent progressive Black politics of social transformation, economic democracy and self-determination." It is thus out of such a mandate, structure and political focus that the Black party merged (Elam, 1981a; Marable, 1980).

NBIPP has not assumed an electoral significance yet on the national or state level, but it has had some local victories, i.e., in northern California. Thus, its relevance resides not so much in its achievements, but in the multidimensionality and ambitiousness of its goals and the possibilities suggested by these. As all third parties, NBIPP has general and specific problems (Walton, 1969). Among these are: 1) building bases in local communities and a viable effective national structure; 2) developing a financial base; 3) developing non-material incentives in the absence of monies and patronage and in furtherance of a new politics; 4) building and maintaining an effective unity among the diverse tendencies in it, especially avoiding the disruptive struggles between nationalists and Marxists which has undermined so many other Black united efforts; and 5) making significant and ongoing gains which demonstrate its viability and possibilities.

Daniels (1971) poses both socio-psychological and structural constraints on Black party building. Among the former are Black "feelings of inferiority and of political inefficacy", a negative definition of politics, previous party identification and belief in integration. The structural constraints include the institutionalized cooptation process which absorbs real and potential Black challengers; single member districts which prohibit a numerical minority from winning; rigid built-in qualifying rules and gerrymandering of political districts. In addition and reinforcement of the above problems and constraint, I (1980:71) have also posed the following constraints: political underdevelopment of the Black community; ideological hegemony of the system which argues that only two parties are viable and realistic; fear of penalty, i.e., loss of benefits from the Democratic or Republican party; fear of failure; and lack of an historical model which worked well for a considerable time.

But inspite of these constraints and problems, Black party advocates still argue that the Black party is both possible and necessary. For if a party is impossible, they argue, then so is liberation and an effective relation to state power. In fact, Cruse (1974:10) has summed up their position quite well in his assertion that "if such a party is premature, then so is all talk of 'revolution' and "if an independent Black political party is unwise and unfeasible so is revolution unwise and unfeasible." In a word, if the party is key to state power, those without one can never hope to ever seize control or effectively participate in it.

BLACK ELECTED OFFICIALS

In the early seventies, a prevalent assumption rose that mass political struggle was somewhat passé and that electoral politics was the key to power and the future. In fact, Conyers and Wallace (1976:6) state that "...the presence of Blacks in elected government positions...is not only a manifestation of the Black community's political advance but a principal guarantee that advance will continue." Such faith is perhaps understandable but easily an overstatement. As Holden (1973:193) observed, "the electoral process is neither sufficient in itself nor has any politically sophisticated population regarded it as sufficient by itself." He states that "The basic rationale for electoral politics, insofar as policy is concerned, is that desirable policies will emerge when there is a clear identity between the interests and values of the elected and of those who elect them." But he notes, "This rationale also requires, of course, that those elected come into command of the appropriate public resources." Moreover, it presupposes a strong enough political force to assume command or at least share in it.

There have been many studies on the limitations of the electoral process and on the various constraints imposed on Black elected officials or BEO's. Speaking in general, Preston (1978:196-197) lists eight basic constraints: 1) lack of "permanent political machinery"; 2) lack of "tradition of power"; 3) "little economic clout"; 4) tendency of votes to be taken for granted by Democrats; 5) "lack (of) power to implement programs or policies"; 6) limited influence because of the structure of government and fragmentation; 7) reluctance of national policy makers "to deal with the issues of Blacks and the poor"; and 8) "minority status in a majority culture and the race variable." He notes that these eight constraints are in addition to the obvious fact of limited numbers and their inheriting long-term problems which have plagued the country for over two hundred years.

In his important study of Black politics in Gary and his subsequent study with Meranto on electing Black mayors in Gary, St. Louis and Cleveland, Nelson (1972; 1977) also found constraints on BEO's inside and outside the Black community. Among those internal are the low-level of political mobilization in the Black community, its position as an economic colony, its competition over resources, its "mosaic" of ideological positions and approaches, "social class tensions" and a pervasive distrust of Black leadership and alienation from the political system (Nelson and Meranto, 1977). In terms of political alienation, they advance Gamson's

(1971) theory of "stable unrepresentation" in which they argue that Blacks occupy a status essentially outside the area of political decision-making on a more or less permanent basis.

Moreover, Nelson and Meranto (1977:382) assert in their study that "the election of a Black mayor does not automatically mean that the colonized position of the Black community will be significantly changed." For "constraints placed on the administrative authority of Black mayors by a host of economic, political, social and psychological factors make it impossible for their administrations to effectively satisfy the quest for Black liberation," i.e., material, education and cultural benefits which "would encourage the development rather than the oppression of Black people." Among these constraints are: white racist resistance; bureaucratic obstruction, the political need to represent all the people; the tendency toward over-dependence on the federal government for the limited urban reform resources available, inability to successfully challenge the hold of the economic elite (especially corporations) on the decision-making process of the cities and finally, the "inability to attack the fundamental character of the economy and the political order" (Nelson and Meranto, 1977:385).

Inspite of all these constraints, there are studies which show the value of BEO's and of Black participation in the electoral process. Cole (1976), in his study of BEO's in New Jersey, found several important functions Black BEO's serve. First, they are able to formulate and influence the formulation of policies which affect Black life. This is, of course, more effective on the local level where voting blocs along racial lines are not often found. Secondly, Black BEO's are instrumental in the increasing number and level of Black appointments to governmental positions. Thirdly, they tend to influence white associates' sensitivity to Black issues and interests as well as demonstrate to whites their capacity to govern. Fourthly, Cole argues, Black BEO's provide a necessary link between government and Black citizens white BEO's could not possibly provide. And finally, he contends that Black BEO's serve an important function as a role model for the Black community demonstrating Black capacity to govern and challenging the concept of white superiority and their monopoly on government.

In sum then, as I (1980:76) have argued elsewhere, BEO's have the following positive functions: 1) introduce and advance Afro-American interests on the level of law, policy, appropriation, allocation, etc.; 2) expose contradictions and criticize the established order from a position of "legitimacy"; 3) create and propose alternatives to the existing order; 4) make appropriate alliances and coalitions; 5) serve as a symbol of the possibility of Black political power; 6) monitor use of social wealth and struggle for Blacks' just share; and finally 7) gain historical experience in electoral politics which could be transferred to building a Black party.

INTEREST GROUP POLITICS

As Barker and McCorry (1976:207) contend, "Interest groups are a dominant feature of American life." This is true and necessary because of the conflicting and competing interests which, as mentioned above, shape and define U.S. life. An interest group may be defined as a group organized to define, defend and advance common claims and/or stakes in society, i.e., common interests. Interest groups realize that "political organization and political power are inextricably intertwined" and that "An unorganized mass of people can have little impact on the governmental allocation of social and economic values" (Bailey, 1968:27). Moreover, interest groups tend to be aware that organizational power not only means the ability to help shape government policy, but also private policy, i.e., that of other groups and organizations, enterprises, institutions and persons. Finally, interest groups, in this case Black ones, embrace Prestage's (1968:460) contention that "any meaningful gains for Blacks will come as a result of *demands,* supported by evidence of Black willingness to cause great inconvenience to the community at large if these legitimate demands are ignored.''

Black interest groups use varying strategies and tactics to achieve their goals or policy objectives. Essentially, strategies are broad plans for the achievement of goals and tactics are specific methods of action used to carry out the strategy. Interest group tactics include electoral participation, i.e., voting, campaigning, donations, etc., influencing public opinion, verbal protests, lobbying governmental and non-governmental sources, negotiations, litigation, threats, mass action, i.e., strikes, demonstrations, marches, etc., disruption, violence and focus on internal development. Black interest group strategies can be categorized according to their goals and the methods used to achieve them. Given this, there are three major interest groups strategies among Blacks: liberal, conservative and radical.

LIBERAL STRATEGY

The liberal strategy is reflected in the leadership offered by such middle-class groups as the Urban League and NAACP, but it is prevalent among many sectors of Black people. This strategy like the leadership which proposes and pursues it is characterized by several factors. Among these are: 1) assumption that the system is flawed but salvagable; 2) stress on integration; 3) focus on goal pursuance through non-confrontational means where possible, i.e., litigation, elections, lobbying, etc.; 4) rejection of violence; 5) reliance on white political and financial support; 6) strong reliance on government intervention; 7) general confusion of influence with power, i.e., personal persuasion with structural capacity; and 8) focus on minimal goals rather than maximum goals, i.e., jobs vs. ownership, participation in major parties vs. building a Black one, etc. (Bailey, 1968; Thompson, 1963).

Out of these basic dimensions of liberal strategy, three seem to pose more problems than others. First is the over-emphasis on what Pinderhughes (1980) calls electoral lobbying, i.e., attempts to use the Black vote in sanction or support in order to affect decision-makers. Pinderhughes sees this as problematic in that the liberal interest groups do not yet have the ability to organize or direct the vote effectively. Thus, Stone's (1970) and others' suggestion to use the Black vote as a swing vote becomes impossible even if the election were close enough to allow it.

Moreover, such a heavy focus on electoral lobbying and the attendant posing of it almost as a panacea, has caused liberal Black interest groups to abandon the mass action tactics which served them so well in the past. In fact, the assumption developed is that these methods are passé and less than sophisticated. The expression used to advance this position is "Blacks must move from protest to politics." This seems to suggest protest and the pressure which accompanies it are not politics, but rather some unclassified or unsophisticated kind of action.

Secondly, liberal Black interest groups rely heavily on white philanthropic support and are thus vulnerable to its political pressure. In such a position, independence is also threatened by the belief that whites are indispensable for Black success as well as the patron-recipient relation which Hamilton (1979) rightly criticizes. Such positions clearly damage initiative and make self-determination highly problematic, if not impossible. Finally, liberal Black interest groups face the problem of over-reliance on governmental support. One can easily see the positive role government intervention has played in the Black struggle for rights and development during Reconstruction, and the Civil Rights era. But one can also see the vulnerability of over-reliance on government in the "benign neglect" of the Nixon Administration and the "social meanness" of the Reagan Administration or even the last years of the Carter Administration when it was clear that even a favorable

Administration might be unable to act in Black interests, if the political climate is against it and if interest groups who are more powerful oppose Black interests or simply push their own at Blacks' expense (Karenga, 1977; Robinson, 1982).

CONSERVATIVE STRATEGY

Although the liberal strategy was temporarily challenged by the Black Power Movement, it reigned unchallenged in the civil rights era and resurged in the early Seventies. However, it now faces a challenge from Black conservatism (Henry, 1982; Daniels, 1981, Willingham, 1981). Black conservative interest-group strategy is defined by: 1) opposition to government intervention and regulation on behalf of Blacks; 2) distaste for mass action tactics; 3) emphasis on individual self-reliance and achievement; 4) stress on group self-help; 5) tendency to blame Blacks for their social problems; and 6) a belief in the free-enterprise system as it was, i.e., without its current monopoly and with chances for Black and white miraculous success stories (Fairmont Papers, 1980; Sowell, 1981). Among the Black conservative strategists are Thomas Sowell, an economist at the Hoover Institute; Martin Kilson, a political scientist at Harvard; Walter Williams, an economist at George Mason University in Virginia; and J.A.Y. Parker, president of Lincoln Institute and the Educational Foundation in Washington.

The conservative strategy clearly mirrors the philosophy of Booker T. Washington who rejected Black protest, stressed economic developments as a temporary substitute for and path to political rights and power and argued the need for self-help. Likewise, the liberal counter to this adds the DuBoisian dimension to the debate with his emphasis on protest, political rights and the government's obligation to facilitate and insure the freedom, justice and equality for all. Although the conservatives do not have the historical record or structural capacity the liberals enjoy, the current conservative character of U.S. politics tends to give them an increased relevance they would otherwise lack.

As I (1982:18-19) have argued elsewhere, this increased relevance is based on several factors. First, Black conservatives are tied to the party in power - politically and/or philosophically - and will thus benefit in stature and influence from that position, i.e., in appointments, resource allocation and consultation. Secondly, Black conservatives will benefit from the country's shift to the right. In addition to patronage from the Administration, Congressional support is more likely as well as private support from "resource-rich white conservatives who have never been comfortable with the Black Civil Rights leadership" (Daniels, 1981:21). Thirdly, given their philosophical and political link with the Administration and the general rightward shift, they will probably be considered more "media worthy" and thus be given more time to introduce and argue their position. Fourthly, their relevance as an oppositional strategy to liberal strategy dominance will be more apparent the more they are used: to lessen the charge of racism by their inclusion at some level in policy decisions; to support and justify public policies negative to Black interests; and to break the monopoly on Black leadership which liberal interest groups usually enjoy. The irony of this is that liberal Administrations and other liberal whites used Black liberals for similar purposes, i.e., to push and justify their version of what the social order and social policy should be.

RADICAL STRATEGY

The radical interest-group strategy is basically nationalist although Pan-Africanist and socialist themes also inform it (Karenga, 1978b; Pinkney, 1976). Black nationalism is a social theory and practice organized around the concept and conviction that Blacks are a distinct historical personality and that they should therefore "unite in order to gain the structural capacity to define, defend and develop their interests (Karenga, 1980:15). It expresses itself in three basic ways. It is first a redefinition of reality, a redefining of the world in Black images and interests, i.e., from an Afro-centric perspective. Secondly, it is a social corrective, i.e., a thrust to build alternative structures, which check the deprivation and deformation of European institutions and house and advance Black aspirations and interests. Finally, nationalism is a collective vocation, a call and active commitment to liberate Black people, restore them to their traditional greatness and "make African presence both powerful and permanent thruout the world." It is this last aspect of collective vocation which points to the link between nationalism and Pan-Africanism.

There are two basic kinds of Pan-Africanism-continental and global. Continental Pan-Africanism is essentially thought and practice directed toward the liberation and unity of the African continent (Ajala, 1973; Padmore, 1971). Global Pan-Africanism is essentially thought and practice directed toward the liberation, unity and mutual support of African peoples throughout the world (Garvey, 1977; Chrisman and Hare, 1974). Afro-Americans are essentially global Pan-Africanists, but among them are two tendencies. The first tendency simply accepts and works within the general framework of the definition above and is represented by groups as diverse as TransAfrica, the Black lobby for Africa and the Caribbean, Ahidiana, the RNA and Us. The second tendency argues not only for the unity and liberation of Africa, but also the return of all Africans to the Continent. This tendency is represented most definitively by the All African People's Revolutionary Party which sees nationalism as a component part and a beginning level of Pan-Africanism (Carmichael, 1971).

Also, the radical strategy includes a socialist dimension, either as a separate thrust or as a component part of nationalism (Cruse, 1967; Allen, 1979). Moreover, some socialists see nationalism as a stage in socialist development (Boggs, 1974) and some nationalists see socialism as a contribution to nationalist development (Karenga, 1980). Given these qualifications, the radical interest-group strategy is defined by: 1) profound alienation from and what Barker and McCorry (1976:217) call "low-integration" into the established political system; 2) call and struggle for fundamental change in the economic and political structure of society; 3) willing-ness to use any means necessary to achieve ultimate goals; 4) preference for confrontational and mass action politics; 5) focus on the Black masses as the ultimate power with simultaneous stress on the role of a Black vanguard to organize, educate and lead them; 6) stress on power, self-development and self-determination; 7) emphasis on history, heritage and the distinctness this expresses; and 8) emulation of and solidarity with African and other Third World peoples and struggles.

The radical interest groups include among others the RNA, All African People's Revolutionary Party (AAPRP), the East, Ahidiana, the NOI, Us, Council for Independent Black Institutions (CIBI), and Institute of Positive Education (IPE). Once SNCC, CORE and the Panthers were included in this category, but these groups have either disbanded or been transformed into less than radical mod-els. For a review of these and other radical group ideologies, tactics and achievements, see Civil Rights and Revolts in Chapter 2. The problems radical interest groups face are many. First, they face the severe and sustained hostility of the system reserved for those who challenge its legitimacy. Secondly, they are actively opposed by the established liberal and conservative interest groups who consider their strategy rhetoric, irrational and negative to their and Black interests. Thirdly, except for possibly the NOI, they lack the financial resources available to the liberal and the conservative groups. Fourthly, they have less institutional bases than the liberals and conservatives. Fifthly, they are upstaged by the liberals in their thrust for mass leadership. However, in crisis and with the continu-ing failure of the liberals to produce resources or viable plans, they get the opportunity to advance alternatives and win greater respect. Finally, the radical interest groups have not yet firmly established the kind of viable working alliance that the liberals had in the Sixties with its Big Six leadership grouping, i.e., SNCC, CORE, SCLC, NUL, NAACP and NALC (Barker and McCorry, 1976:216ff) and now have in the National Black Leadership Forum.

The radical interest groups have, however, begun to build such a group, the National Black United Front. Given the essentiality of such a structure of combined strength and resources and collective planning, it can be safely argued that their success or failure in building it will certainly help determine their success or failure in achieving the objectives they have set for themselves. Also, key to their success will be the development of an intellectual vanguard which can give both a critical and substantive theoretical and practical dimension to their strategy with both rooted in the social reality of U.S. society (Strickland, 1975; Cruse, 1967). Without such a theoretical and practical rootedness in U.S. social reality, their throught and practice will be less effective and the alternative strategies will reign unchecked and unchallenged. Even worse, the alternative to building internally and calling on Blacks to develop and use their own resources instead of depending on external sources will be reduced by critics to rhetoric and denied its deserved status as a viable and critical alternative.

THE PROBLEM OF COALITIONS

Another key concern and problem of Black politics is the problem of coalition. Central to the problem is the definition, character and results of those coalitions. As Carmichael and Hamilton (1967:59-60) noted, "all too frequently, coalitions involving Black people have been only at the leadership level, dictated by terms set by others, and for objectives not calculated to bring major improvements in the lives of the Black masses." Historically, Black middle class leadership, i.e., the liberal interest group leadership, has depended on white coalition partners -Jewish and Gentile - for financial, legal and political support. In fact, there is or seems to be a basic assumption among this leadership that Blacks would not have come as far as they have, if it were not for whites of goodwill. Such a conception is problematic on at least three levels and speaks to the crisis which currently plagues Black middle class leadership. First, it has been an underlying theme for misconceptions created about Black/white coalitions. Secondly, it has led to a confusion of patronage with coalition. And thirdly, it has tended to encourage denial and reductive translation of Blacks' contribution to their own struggle.

Two of the coalitions on which Blacks have relied on heavily are the Jewish and Democratic coalitions. These coalitions have produced their share of misconceptions and at the same time revealed the nature of the problem of coalitions faced by Blacks, especially the Black middle class leadership. The misconceptions which surround coalitions are many. Carmichael and Hamilton (1967:58ff) have cited three myths of coalitions which are important to understanding their weakness and unworkability. Agreeing with and incorporating some of their contentions, I have developed five misconceptions of coalitions which clearly create a problem for the coalitions in which Black middle class leadership involves itself.

First, there is a clear misconception that the basis of coalition is long-term common interests and priciples rather than short-term specific goals. This is a confusion between alliance and coalition. Alliance is a long-term ongoing unity based on common interests and common basic principles, whereas a coalition is a short-term working association based on specific short-term goals. Failure to make and observe this basic distinction has created situations in which Blacks have assumed too much about their relationship with their more powerful coalition partners and left themselves vulnerable to joint actions not mutually beneficial and to withdrawal of expected support at crucial times. The Andrew Young affair with the Jews and Carter's poor performance in behalf of Blacks are good examples (Fuller, 1979; Karenga, 1977).

A second misconception is that common goals on one level or in one area is a bases for unity in the other. For example, Jews might support Blacks against one kind of racism (neo-Nazi or KKK attacks) but oppose them in correctives for racism (affirmative action). Thirdly, there is a misconception that moral unity - assumed or real - is a substitute for unity around concrete goals and self-interests. This is clear in the case of the assumed Black/Jewish unity based on common or similar suffering. But no unity is automatic, neither political nor personal; each must be built around concrete goals and interests which change or disappear and therefore, must be reinforced and renewed or replaced by others.

A fourth misconception is that a genuine coalition between the powerful and the powerless (or clearly less powerful) is always possible, rather than always problematic and often pure patronage politics. In fact, one of the problems of the Jewish and Democratic coalitions is that they often deteriorate into patronage politics, i.e., dependence by Blacks on Jewish and Democratic patrons who may be unable or unwilling at various times, to give the largesse or support Blacks request or need (Hamilton, 1979). And the problem is that Blacks cannot effectively penalize or reward these partners in any significant way to compel compliance. The Jewish withdrawal of support from SNCC and CORE as they transformed into Black power structures and their opposition to affirmative action are examples of the disenchantment and disengagement without penalty from coalition partners. So are the Democratic Party's unwillingness to support fully Black social justice and social welfare goals under Carter and their unwillingness and inability to produce under Reagan.

In such a coalition, the less powerful partner can lessen or eliminate such politically unhealthy arrangements in three basic ways. It can: (1) unite with other less powerful partners in the coalition to increase its power; (2) build other coalitions to offset negative effects of the problematic one; and (3) shelter no misconception about the problems of coalitions between the powerful and clearly less powerful. Black middle class leadership does not seem to have achieved any of these alternatives options.

A final misconception about coalitions is that coalition action is a substitute for a people's or group's own initiative. Such a misconception leaves a group hopelessly and slavishly dependent on forces outside its control and often beyond its influence. There is, in fact, no substitute for the structural capacity to define, defend and develop one's interests. For regardless how numerous or sincere one's allies are, a people that cannot save itself is lost forever.

The Black/Jewish coalition is a classic study in the problems of coalitions. Not only does it reflect commitment to the misconceptions which characterize coalitions in general, it also carries its own particular myths or misconceptions held mainly by its Black members. Among these are first, the myth that Jews are not white inspite of visual reality, self-definition and social acceptance of this fact. A second myth is that the Jews are Blacks' best friend, a myth which Cruse (1967:467) argues is misphrased. It would be far more accurate to say, he states, that "certain Jews have been best friends of certain (Blacks) which in any case is nothing unusual." Thirdly, there is a myth of moral affinity between Blacks and Jews based on similar suffering - historical and current.

These myths suggest or seek to foster a unity and commonality of interests that do not exist and thus produce a political practice and thought based on false premises problematic to Black interests. The first myth seeks to redefine Jews into the Third World to achieve unity through a contrived similarity. The second makes a claim more true for the Black middle class leadership than the Black masses and the third assumes an automatic unity and commonality of interest and implies that moral affinity, if it exists, can substitute for concrete interests and goals as a basis for a viable coalition.

As Isaacs (1974:160-181) and Weisbord and Stein (1970) point out, concrete differences of interests and goals not only separate Blacks and Jews, but also often place them in active opposition to each other. The Andrew Young Affair; affirmative action; the 1966 New York City referendum on a civilian review board; the fight over the Forest Hills housing project in Queens, New York; and the struggle for Black community control in Brooklyn's Ocean-Hill Brownsville School district, all clearly reflect this. This is due to the fact that Jewish power, wealth, social achievement and status and white skin privilege objectively give them a different set of priorities and interests than Blacks whose race and general class character assigns them a marginal and subordinate role and status in the social process (Shorris, 1982).

Since Roosevelt's New Deal in the 30's, Blacks have aligned themselves with the Democratic Party. But the alliance was never of equals or semi-equals. On the contrary, like the other alliances, it was essentially a question of patronage, an alignment based on influence not power and, thus, subject to the interests and aspirations of the patrons who control it. The Party, as a political structure, after all is out to win votes and to do so will no doubt cater to the cutback, cut-off and trim-down attitudes dominant now among white voters. Black middle class leadership finds itself, then, locked into the Democratic Party, with no structural or financial ability to significantly reward or punish it to induce it into compliance with the demands of Black interests. Moreover, it has developed no party alternative either with the Republican Party or through the building of a national Black independent party.

As mentioned above, there was talk in 1978 of Blacks moving in significant numbers to the Republican Party as a way of increasing their bargaining power and political options, but as also noted above, nothing serious has come of it. There is no current strategy to enter or construct, conduct or benefit from the proposed relation with the Republicans, to pressure the Democracts or demand and get from each party a minimum set of legislative and financial concessions. It could well be that both will decide Blacks are dispensable, that given their overall structural incapacity to reward or punish with organized, self- conscious voting or financial and campaign labor contributions, they are neither needed nor worthy of serious consideration. This obviously presents a practical problem for Black middle class leadership which counts so much on the Democratic coalition and talked so much about the Republican option.

The question of alliances also must be answered. And although coalition and alliance are used interchangeably in most political science literature, I would like to maintain the difference. Essentially, alliances are internal first and then among others whose long term goals and principles coincide or mesh with those of Afro-Americans. These are usually other Third World people. Two examples of internal alliance are the Black Leadership Forum among the liberal middle class leadership and the National Black United Front among the radical leadership.

The Black Leadership Forum, formed in 1977, is a national coalition of 16 Black civil rights groups and leaders. The Forum focuses on political and economic issues vital to Blacks and tries to influence public policy in support of Black interests. To achieve this, members meet and lobby with presidents and Congresspersons and make joint position statements. However, it is not well-known or visably active in the daily problems confronting Blacks as was the Big Six.

The National Black United Front, as noted in Chapter II, was founded in 1980 and has regional and local networks. Unlike the BLF, NBUF is visably involved in the daily struggles of Black people. Like NBIPP, it is dedicated to "defense of social service programs and civil rights laws; the fight against the upsurge in racist violence, and opposition to the imperialist war danger" (Elam, 1981b:5). It is also engaging in political education, mass rallies, demonstrations, strikes, and boycotts as well as various expressions of support for continental African and Third World liberation struggles.

The second kind of alliance has been established at various times with various Third World peoples, most notably Puerto Ricans in the East and Mexicans in the Southwest. In late 1978, Blacks and Hispanics formed a coalition called "Working Committee on Concerns of Hispanics and Blacks" to ensure that the two constituencies "not bear the brunt of a restrictive economic, social and political climate" (Williams, 1979:74). Participating in the formation of this coalition were Black, Puerto Rican, Mexican and Cuban organizations.

As I (Karenga, 1980:77) have argued elsewhere, there are concrete bases for alliances among Third World peoples growing out of their situational similarity in that they are oppressed and exploited on the bases of race and class. In order for such alliances to work, however, clear principles of unity must be established and observed. Among these should be: 1) mutual respect for each people's political, economic and cultural interests; 2) non-interference in each other's internal affairs; 3) a clear conception of each other's interests; 4) independent power bases; 5) a clear conception of possibilities and problems in unity; 6) clear and concrete goals around which to unify; 7) a clear statement and agreement on principles of cooperation; and 8) a clear statement and agreement on methods of cooperation and struggle" (Karenga, 1980:77-78). Although acceptance and agreement on these principles will not eliminate all obstacles and problems to Third World alliances, it will lay a necessary basis for them.

Henry (1980:230) notes that although there are admittedly obstacles confronting such alliances, they nevertheless "appear to be less formidable than those facing Black-white coalitions..." Moreover, given the existence of over 50 million Blacks and Hispanics in the U.S., the importance of exploring and building such an alliance is clear and compelling. For if the essence of politics is power and power rests in structural capacity, an alliance becomes a way not only to increase one's own strength, but to deprive the opposition of an ally. This is especially true in an oppressive and conflict-laden society where competing sides seek allies constantly and neutrality is objectively supportive of the established order. For it deprives smaller power blocs of possible added strength and spares the established order a united challenge from the oppressed. Black politics, then, as argued at the beginning, has been and must remain multidimensional in both theory and practice. Afterall, given the multidimensional character of the problem of liberation and a higher level of human life, anything less would certainly be unsucessful.

STUDY QUESTIONS

1. What is politics? Discuss some of its core concepts.
2. What are eight areas of power?
3. What is the rationale for party politics?
4. Discuss the Democratic party experience.
5. Discuss the Republican party experience.
6. Discuss Black party initiatives in terms of problems and possibilities.
7. Cite and discuss constraints on BEO's.
8. What are some of the valuable functions BEO's serve inspite of constraints?
9. What is an interest group and what are three basic Black interest group strategies?
10. What are some misconceptions about coalitions?

11. Discuss two basic coalitions Blacks have been in and the problems of each.

12. Discuss two kinds of alliances giving examples of each.

REFERENCES

Ajala, Adekunle. (1973) *Pan-Africanism: Evolution, Progress and Prospects,* New York: St. Martin's Press.

Allen, Robert. (1970) *Black Awakening in Capitalist America,* Garden City, New York: Doubleday.

Apter, David. (1977) *Introduction to Political Analysis,* Cambridge, MA: Winhtrop Publishers, Inc.

Bailey, Harry, Jr. (1968) "Negro Interest Group Strategies," *Urban Affairs Quarterly,* 4, 1 (September).

_____. (ed.) (1967) *Negro Politics in America,* Columbus, OH: Charles Merrill Books.

Balbus, Isaac. (1974) "The Concept of Interest in Pluralist and Marxian Analysis," *Politics and Society,* (eds.) Ira Katznelson, et al, N.Y.: David McKay Co., Inc., pp. 278-304.

Barker, Lucius and Jesse McCorry, Jr. (1976) *Black Americans and the Political System,* Cambridge, MA: Winhtrop Publishers, Inc.

Boggs, James. (1974) *Revolution and Evolution in the Twentieth Century,* New York: Monthly Review Press.

Carmichael, Stokely. (1971) *Stokely Speaks,* New York: Vintage Books.

Chrisman, Robert and Nathan Hare. (1974) *Pan-Africanism,* Indianapolis, N.Y.: Bobbs-Merrill Co., Inc.

Cole, Leonard. (1976) *Blacks in Power,* Princeton, N.J.: Princeton University Press.

Conyers, James and Walter Wallace. (1976) *Black Elected Officials*, New York: Russell Sage Foundation.

Cruse, Harold. (1967) *Crisis of the Negro Intellectual*, New York: William Morrow.

Cruse, Harold. . (1974) "The National Black Convention at Little Rock," *Black World*, 24, 1 (November) 4-21.

Dahl, Robert. (1967) *Pluralist Democracy in America*, Chicago: Rand McNally.

Daniels, Johnnie. (1971) "The Development of an Independent Black Political Party," *Afro-American Studies*, 2, pp. 95-105.

Daniels, Lee A. (1981) "The New Black Conservatives," *New York Times Magazine* (October 4) Section 6:20, 54, 58.

Daniels, Ron. (1980) "The National Black Political Assembly: *The Black Scholar*, 11, 4 (March/April) 32-42.

Drake, St. Clair. (1971) "The Social and Economic Status of the Negro in the United States," in Edward Greenberg et al (eds.) *Black Politics*, New York: Holt, Rinehard and Winston.

Dymally, Mervyn. (1972) "The Black Man's Role in American Politics," (ed.) Lenneal Henderson, Jr., *Black Political Life in the United States*, San Francisco: Chandler Publishing Company.

Elam, Frank. (1981a) "NBIPP: Problems and Prospects," *Guardian*, (October) 7ff.

_____ . (1981b) "NBUF Action Plan Targets Budget Cuts, Racism, War," *Guardian*, (July 15) 5.

The Fairmont Papers, Black Alternatives Conference. (1980) San Francisco: Institute for Contemporary Studies (December).

Frye, Hardy. (1980) *Black Parties and Political Power*, Boston: G.K. Hall & Co.

Fuller, Hoyt. (1969) "Black Leadership and the Black-Jewish Debacle," *First World*, 2, 3.

Gamson, William. (1971) "Stable Unrepresentation in American Society," in *Black Politics*, Edward S. Greenberg, et al (eds.) New York: Holt: Rinehart and Winston.

Garvey, Marcus. (1977) *Philosophy and Opinions of Marcus Garvey, I & II,* New York: Atheneum.

Gilliam, Reginald, Jr. (1975) *Black Political Development*, Port Washington, N.Y.: Dunellen Publishing Company, Inc.

Gosnell, Harold (1967) *Negro Politicians: The Rise of Negro Politics in Chicago,* Chicago: University of Chicago Press.

Hamilton, Charles. (1979) "The Patron-Recipient Relationship and Minority Politics in New York City," *Political Science Quarterly*, 95, 2, pp. 211-227.

Henry, Charles. (1980) "Black-Chicano Coalitions: Possibilities and Problems," *The Western Journal of Black Studies*, 4, 4 (Winter) 222-231.

_____. (1982) "Black Neo-Conservatism," a paper presented at the Annual Meeting of the National Conference of Black Political Scientists, New Orleans, L.A., (April 21-24).

Holden, Matthew, Jr. (1973) *The Politics of the Black Nation*, New York: Chandler Publishing Company.

Isaac, Stephen. (1974) *Jews and American Politics*, Garden City, N.Y.: Doubleday.

Jones, Mack. (1972) "A Frame of Reference for Black Politics," in Lenneal Henderson Jr. (ed.) *Black Political Life in the United States*, San Francisco: Chandler Publishing Co. 7-20.

Karenga, Maulana. (1978a) "Blacks and the GOP: The Newest Deal From the Same Deck," *In These Times*, (October 11-17) 16.

Karenga, Maulana. (1977) "Carter and His Black Critics: The Dialogue and Its Lessons," *The Black Scholar*, 9, 3 (November) 52-54.

_____. (1982) "The Crisis of Black Middle-Class Leadership," The Black Scholar, 13,6 (Fall) 16-36.

Karenga, Maulana. . (1978b) *Essays on Struggle: Position and Analysis*, Inglewood, CA: Kawaida Publications.

_____. (1980) *Kawaida Theory: An Introductory Outline*, Inglewood, CA: Kawaida Publications.

Key, V.O. Jr. (1962) *Politics, Parties and Pressure Groups*, New York: Thomas Y. Crowell Company.

Ladd, Everett. (1969) *Negro Political Leadership in the South*, New York: Atheneum.

Marable, Manning. (1980) *From the Grassroots*, Boston: Southend Press.

McLemore, Leslie B. (1971) "Mississippi Freedom Democratic Party," *The Black Politician*, 3, 2 (October) 19-22.

Morris, Milton. (1975) *The Politics of Black America*, New York: Harper & Row Publishers, Inc.

Nelson, William Jr. (1972) *Black Politics in Gary: Problems and Prospects*, Washington: Joint Center for Political Studies.

Nelson, William and Philip Meranto. (1977) *Electing Black Mayors*, Columbus, OH: Ohio State University Press.

Padmore, George. (1971) *Pan-Africanism or Communism*, Garden City, N.Y.: Doubleday.

Parsons, Talcott. (1951) *The Social System*, New York: Fress Press.

Pinderhughes, Dianne. (1980) "The Limits of Electoral Lobbying," a paper presented at the Annual Meeting of the National Conference of Black Political Scientists, Atlanta, Ga. (March 19).

Pinkney, Alphonso. (1976) *Red, Black and Green: Black Nationalism in the United States*, New York: Cambridge University Press.

Prestage, Jewel. (1968) "Black Politics and the Kerner Report: Concerns and Directions," *Social Science Quarterly,* 49, 3 (December) 453-464.

Preston, Michael. (1978) "Black Elected Officials and Public Policy," *Policy Studies Journal,* (Winter) 196-201.

Robinson, Pearl T. (1982) "Black Political Power - Upward or Downward," in *The State of Black America* (ed.) James Williams, New York: National Urban League.

Scott, Joseph W. (1980) "Capitalism, Socialism and Libertarianism: Race, Class and Power in the Black American Experience," *Western Journal of Black Studies,* 4,2 (Summer) 78-83.

Shorris, Earl. (1982) "The Jews of the New Right," *The Nation,* 234, 18 (May 8) 543, 557-561.

Sorauf, Frank. (1976) *Party Politics in America,* Boston: Little, Brown & Company.

Sowell, Thomas. (1981) *Ethnic Minorities,* New York: Basic Books.

Stone, Chuck. (1970) *Black Political Power in America,* New York: Dell Publishing Company.

Strickland, William. (1975) "Black Intellectuals and the American Social Scene," *Black World,* 25, 1 (November) 4-10.

_____. (1972) "The Gary Convention and the Crisis of American Politics," *Black World,* 21, 12 (October) 18-26.

Thompson, Daniel. (1963) *The Negro Leadership Class,* Englewood Cliffs, N.J.: Prentice Hall, Inc.

Walters, Ron. (1980) "Black Presidential Politics in 1980: Bargaining or Begging? *The Black Scholar,* 11, 4 (March/April) 22-31.

_____. (1975) "Strategy for 1976: A Black Political Party," *The Black Scholar,* 7 (October).

Walton, Hanes, Jr.   (1972a) *Black Political Parties*, New York: Free Press.

_____. (1972b) *Black Politics,* Philadelphia: J.B. Lippincott Co.

_____. (1975) *Black Republicans,* Metuchen, N.J.: The Scarecrow Press.

_____. (1969) *The Negro in Third Party Politics*, Philadelphia: Dorrance & Co.

Weisbord, Robert and Arthur Stein.   (1970) *Bittersweet Encounter: The Afro-American and the American Jew*, Westport, Conn.: Negro Universities Press.

Williams, Eddie.   (1979) "Black Political Participation in 1978," *The State of Black America*, New York: National Urban League.

Williams, Eddie and Milton Morris, (1981) "The Black Vote in a Presidential Election Year," *The State of Black America*, New York: National Urban League.

Willingham, Alex.   (1981) "The Place of the New Black Conservatives in Black Social Thought: Groundwork for the Full Critique," unpublished paper, Philadelphia, PA., (October).

Wilson, James Q. (1960) *Negro Politics*, New York: Free Press.

VI
BLACK ECONOMICS

INTRODUCTION

Economics is generally defined as the study and process of producing, distributing (or exchanging) and consuming goods and services. Such a definition, however, in part hides the fact of how economics penetrates every aspect of social life. Whether one talks of poverty, income, jobs, housing, class, racial discrimination, education, religion, the arts or social status, all at one level imply and necessitate a concern with economics. Even the major ideologies and social systems of today which compete for the minds of peoples i.e., capitalism, socialism, nationalism, etc., have been shaped in significant part by important economists of the past, i.e., Adam Smith, Karl Marx, and John Maynard Keynes, etc. (Heilbroner, 1972; Fusfeld, 1977).

Moreover, it would be relatively impossible and certainly unwise and irregular for national leaders to make political decisions without economic considerations. In fact, politics and economics are unavoidably linked on several levels. First, wealth and power are mutually engendering and supportive. The possession of one implies and leads to the possession of the other. Likewise, the lack of one implies the lack of the other. Secondly, those with power and wealth tend to strive to monopolize both. Thirdly, those with wealth and power tend to shape society in their own image and interests at the expense of those without it, especially Blacks and other Third World peoples whose relative possession of both wealth and power are at low levels. It is thus difficult to imagine corporations not having political power, i.e., significant and greater control and influence over public policy, especially as it relates to their own interests. Finally, the struggle for distributive justice or an egalitarian distribution of social wealth is both an economic and a political struggle. In fact, the decision of who gets what and how much is both an economic and political decision, made by those whose wealth and political power enable them to control directly or indirectly the decision-making process.

It is this interrelatedness of politics and economics which prompts some Black and radical economists to insist that the science of economics is best categorized as *political economy*. As the staff of the *Review of Black Political Economy* explained in their inaugural issue (Spring/Summer, 1970), the term seems a more accurate one. For it "includes within its scope the political realities of economic relations" and thus describes "the necessary focus of Black economic development." Moreover, given the political dimension of economics, "for Black people to affect any significant alteration in their economic position, they will first be obliged to develop a sound political strategy."

Political economy, then, can be defined as the study of the interrelationship between politics and economics and the power relations they express and produce. It focuses not simply on the economic process, but also on economic policy and the race and class interests and value judgments this suggests. Thus, the study of Black economics of necessity includes a study of the politics which shape economics in both positive and negative ways. This will become clear as the problems and solutions posed are discussed.

PROBLEMS

POLITICAL ECONOMIC STATUS

The ghettoization of the Black community is both an economic and political reality as argued in Chapter IV. The general state of political and economic subordination is obvious and unarguable. The only question is the character and process of the subordination. The race and class character and process of the exploitation and oppression of the ghetto has been summed up by many as domestic colonialism. As early as 1962, in an article reprinted in a later book, Cruse (1968) used the category "domestic colonialism" to discuss Black-white relations in U.S. society. He (1968:77) argued that "from the beginning (the Afro-American) has existed as a colonial being...The only factor which differentiates the (Afro-American's) status from that of a pure colonial status is that his position is maintained in the 'home country' in close proximity to the dominant racial group." Clark (1964) argued the colony analogy two years later using the political, economic and social structure of Harlem to demonstrate it. Although, he (1965) did not pursue the analogy in *Dark Ghetto,* he used the category and most of his analysis pointed to the same conclusion.

Two years later, Carmichael and Hamilton (1967:6ff) advanced the internal colony analogy in their book on Black Power. Admitting that "the analogy is not perfect," they argued that regardless of the differences between the classical colony and the ghetto, there are still enough significant similarities to justify calling the ghetto an internal colony. Among these similarities were: 1) economic exploitation of the colony as a cheap supply of labor and a captive market; 2) external control of the colony by the ruling country, usually by indirect rule through political puppets; and 3) the socio-psychological results of racist humiliation and assignment of Blacks to "subordinate, inferior status in society." Allen (1970) also discussed the Black community in terms of the internal colony analogy. He (1970:7ff) maintained that "Black communities are victims of white imperialism and colonial exploitation." Colonialism, he suggested, can be defined as direct and overall subordination, administration, economic exploitation and cultural destruction of a nation, people or country by another whose power is enshrined in law and backed by coercive bodies, i.e., armies and police. Thus, he concludes, the status of the Black population in the United States shows a striking similarity to this colonial situation.

Allowing for limitations of the analogy, one still is unavoidably struck by the political oppression and economic exploitation which stand at the heart of any form of colonialism. The ghetto economy stands out at the center of urban poverty. Its unemployment is so high that if it occurred in the overall economy, it would be defined as symptomatic of a depression. Its labor is superexploited in both racial and class terms, being employed mainly in the low-wage sector of the economy. And although Blacks who comprise 11.3% of all employed workers are 14.1% of all union members, they are ruled in the unions by whites whose interests and ideas of what is possible and political often diverge from those of Blacks (Harris, 1982).

Moreover, the ghetto economy is marked by a continuous drain of financial, physical and human resources. The savings are placed in financial institutions whose loans are primarily made to enterprises outside the ghetto. The approximately $150 billion annual purchasing power is spent mainly outside the ghetto. Brimmer (1982:30) notes that Black firms are continuously losing ground in growing competition by white firms for Black consumer dollars. "In 1969 receipts of Black firms were equal to 13.5 percent of total Black income. By 1980 the share was down to 8.9 percent, and it may decline to 7% by 1990." Furthermore, products sold in the ghetto and outside it are made outside the ghetto, most of the businessmen live outside the ghetto, and the enterprises which service the retail business, i.e., wholesale, shipping, advertising, etc., also are located outside the ghetto (Browne, 1971).

In addition, Blacks pay 36-60% of their income on rent compared to 25-30% by others and most of that is to outside owners. Given that 70-80% of Blacks rent instead of own, the outflow of money involved here is clearly substantial (Fusfeld, 1970). Finally, there is a low level of repairs and renewal of physical plants in the ghetto, and better educated Blacks with higher salaries tend to move out, thus, depriving the ghetto of persons whose education, income, and initiative would be valuable to its revitalization and organized efforts to free itself. It is in such context of oppression, exploitation and relative powerlessness, that the colonial analogy seems to be a definitive one (Tabb, 1970).

THE RACE/CLASS QUESTION AGAIN

The race and class question serves as a problem for Black economics on two levels. First, both race and class are the bases of Black exploitation and oppression. And secondly, the development of sharp class divisions among Blacks tend to impede an overall solution to the problem of Black economic development (Turner, 1976). In fact, the interpretation of the source of and solution to Black oppression can in fact end up as a class focused interpretation rather than an overall Black one.

For example, one could take the interpretations of Sowell (1975, 1981a, 1981b). Sowell essentially argues that race is not as important a factor as often suggested and that the attitudes and skills of Blacks may be as important to social achievement and social status as racism. Moreover, he maintains that demographics rather than racism explain differences in income among ethnic groups. Thus, the sources of Blacks' differential income can be found for example in the fact of age, i.e., they are disproportionately younger and still climbing the income ladder, and in the fact of residence, i.e., they live more often in the South where wages are usually lower. He also rejects affirmative action as insulting special treatment and gratuitous government intervention in an admittedly flawed though essentially workable system. Finally, Sowell argues that racism, where it exists, can be explained by economic motivations and interests and that once racism becomes economically unprofitable, racists will no longer practice it. Therefore, he argues that market forces are much more effective mediators of racial inequities than non-market forces like collective Black struggle and government intervention.

Much of the criticism of Sowell has been ad hominem and unworthy of repetition. But his argument tends to support and dovetail Wilson's ideas which will be covered below. Thus, criticism of Wilson's contentions will for the most part answer Sowell's. However, it is important to note that Sowell, like Wilson, tends to blame the victim, overlook or minimize the active force and results of racism, and while blaming Blacks for defective attitudes and habits, seems reluctant to indict racist attitudes and practices of whites. Moreover, his contention that racism ends when it is no longer profitable is not always true. Reich (1981:311-312) in a recent work discovered that although "racism works against most whites' economic interests, it is being reinforced today" by a series of social, cultural and personal factors.

Certainly, one of the most provocative works in recent sociological literature is Wilson's (1978) *The Declining Significance of Race*. Wilson's work while attempting to de-emphasize the significance of race also points to the problem of uneven development among Blacks and the accompanying class divisions. Essentially, Wilson argues that race has declined in significance and been replaced by class as the key determinant affecting life-chances and institutional access in U.S. society. He contends that this shift on the basis of social stratification is due to government intervention and support, the current predominance of service industries (transportation, government and social service, public utilities, finance, social welfare, etc.), over productive industries (manufacturing, mining, etc.), and the substitution of class characteristics for racial ones as criteria for employment. Moreover, he maintains that this declining significance of race has created a new middle class insensitive to "lower" class Black needs and is increasingly used by the whites to control Blacks in the working class and underclass. Furthermore, he (1978:152) argues that "the traditional racial struggles for power and privilege have shifted away from the economic sector and are now concentrated in the sociopolitical order."

The arguments against Wilson's thesis are numerous and cogent (Willie, 1979). First, Wilson's use of the advancing middle class as an index of the declining significance of race is impoverished data, showing not that race has declined, but suggesting that racism against the middle class has declined. Furthermore, Black and white middle class income are not the same still and evidence of "catching up" does not eliminate the fact that significant differences still exist. Also, there are not enough Blacks in these new positions or in significant power positions to claim such a momentous event as the decline of the significance of race. They are not in ownership positions or significantly represented in high level management. Finally, it could be argued that allowing certain sectors of the Black middle class access to new status is also based on race and a political calculation. For it tends to legitimize and reinforce the system and win it new Black allies which, even Wilson admits, can and may be used against the interests of the Black masses.

Secondly, he concentrated only on the narrow data of income increase to prove his thesis as if income increase were an inclusive category of the various forms of racism. A modicum of acquaintance with the various open and covert expressions of racism tends to disprove such a contention. Thirdly, he commits a gross conceptual error by attempting to separate the economic arena from the socio-political one. A holistic conception of society shows that all areas of society interact, and policies in one area tend to affect and often determine conditions and behavior in others. Affirmative action legislation had impact on the economic and educational spheres. And the Supreme Court decision outlawing segregation, *Brown vs. Board of Education,* affected virtually every area of social life.

Fourthly, Wilson's contention that the discrimination against the Black poor is only because of their low level of education and few marketable skills, overlooks the fact that it is racism which imposed this condition on them and continues to exclude them. Thus, a system which is responsible for inadequate acquisition of education and skills by Blacks and other Third World peoples cannot escape the charge of racism simply by saying that their lack of qualifications is the reason for their occupational rejection. Finally, Wilson's position suggests that now Blacks are responsible for their non-access and non-achievement, as if wealth and power were equitably distributed and equally available. This personalization of blame for social evils could be and perhaps already is being used as a justification for an end to public and private policies and programs designed to end racist and socio-economic inequities in U.S. society.

Regardless of Wilson's flawed interpretation of the declining significance of race, his charge of increasing class division and middle class insensitivity to the interests of the Black masses requires discussion. For if he and others are correct, then rather than being a resource for Black liberation and economic development, the Black middle class will serve the opposite function of retarding development and the social struggle for a higher level of social life. The problem of the middle class was first raised extensively in Frazier's (1962) classic work, *Black Bourgeoisie.* In it, he posed the middle class as essentially living in a world characterized by make-believe, self-hate, conspicuous consumption, rejection of the Black masses and the fruitless and frustrating quest for white status and acceptance.

Hare (1965), a student of Frazier, reinforced Fraziers' view of the middle class in his book, *Black Anglo Saxons,* which posed "aping of the white man as their overriding concern." Cruse (1967:312) in his seminal work on the Black intellectual also reinforced Frazier's stress on the theme of personal self-interest of the middle class, arguing that "No matter how you view it, the integration movement is run by the middle class who, even when they are militant and sometimes radical, twist the meaning of integration to suit their own aspirations." If these assessments are correct, then, the problem of class division and distance become not simply a problem of economics, but also a problem of politics. For if middle class interests are pushed at the expense of the masses of Blacks, then, rather than being a resource in terms of capital and leadership for economic development, the middle class will become an obstacle in both the political and economic sense.

The above claims do not go without challenge. There is evidence to suggest that the claims of a growing middle class are exaggerated and must be seen in the light of several related facts. First, although "professionals and managers" is the standard census category for middle class, it also includes modest status jobs as dental technicians and night managers, along with doctors, lawyers and other traditional professionals. Moreover, growth in the professional occupations is concentrated at the lower end of the income scale with technicians, counselors and health technologists. Secondly, Anderson (1982:7) notes that many of these occupational gains were in the public sector in social welfare. This public sector concentration makes the Black middle class highly vulnerable to the current administration's reduction-in-force policy which calls for heavy layoffs at social service agencies which employ large numbers of Blacks.

In addition, Hill (1978) argues that the advocates of the new middle class are confusing "middle income" with "middle class." "Income only indicates how much money a person has, while class helps determine *how* that money is spent." In a word, a class is not simply defined by income but by wealth, status, "styles of life, living standards, values, beliefs." Also Hill (1980:40) contends that although middle class classifications usually include all persons holding white collar jobs or moving into higher status jobs, movement in higher status jobs do not necessarily mean higher paying jobs. In fact, he (1980:37) states, "only a small minority of Black white collar workers have middle class incomes." He concludes that instead of a spectacular growth of the Black middle class, one has statistics that show 25% of Blacks belong to the middle class as compared to 50% of whites.

Finally, in terms of middle class insensitivity, the argument can be made that leadership of the civil rights movement and their constant struggle to maintain gains of the 60's contradict the insensitivity and selfishness suggested by Frazier and reinforced by those after him. Moreover, it can be argued that a distinction must be made between the radical or socially-conscious and active segment of the middle class and the "tomish" sector. The former, it can be said, led the struggles, and the latter served the traditional role of buffer between the masses and the rulers of society. The radical, Cabral (1969) argues, has committed "class suicide" and identified with the aspirations of the masses whereas the toms have thrown their lot in with society's rulers. The problem, then, becomes one of how to initiate and sustain the process which radicalizes a significant sector of the middle class and causes them to assume the "Talented Tenth" role of leadership which DuBois (1969) and others posed for them.

THE EMPLOYMENT SITUATION

Unemployment is another major problem of vast proportions. In late 1981, almost 13 million Blacks were in the labor force comprising 12.1% of the labor force. Of this number, 11 million were employed and two million unemployed with an unemployment rate of 15.5%. At this writing, the Black unemployment rate is approximately 19%. Among Black youth, it is approximately 50% with the likelihood it will rise higher given the fact they will "comprise an increasing proportion of the youth population; and probably will continue to be concentrated in areas of limited job opportunities" (Anderson, 1982:5). Furthermore, Black youth unemployment will be more difficult to reduce due to increased competition for jobs and the problem of preparation.

It is these unemployed youth which form a significant part of the underclass. Although there is continuing debate on the character and reality of this class, Glasgow (1981:3,5) in his book, *The Black Underclass*, defines this underclass as "a permanently entrapped population of poor persons, unused and unwanted... unemployed, welfare dependent and without sufficient income to secure a descent quality of life." Such an entrapped sector of the population, Glasgow maintains, not only poses a threat to the broader social order, but more importantly to the safety and survival of the Black community. For what this situation creates is not only the potential for violence turned inward and crime, but also a waste of Black youth and thus, a limitation on Black future, since Black youth are indeed Black future.

There are several reasons offered for Black unemployment: low-educational levels and lack of job skills (Sowell, 1981, Wilson, 1979); unwillingness to take menial jobs; displacement, the move of industry from the central city; shutdowns in industries where Blacks are in heavy numbers; periodic recessions and above all, continuing discrimination. In his analysis of racism, Alexis (1980) challenges Becker's (1957) often quoted study on discrimination. He (1980:338) argues that Becker's focus on personal discrimination fails to see that "discrimination is against Blacks as a group, not as individuals" and that hiring or not hiring is a political decision as well as an economic one. In what he calls the "malice-envy approach", the economic discriminator (employer, employee, government or consumer) interprets the relative well-being of Blacks as a decrease in his/her own welfare. Blacks are thus viewed as opponents and under such competitive conditions, the white employer "might be willing to reduce (his/her) own welfare, if by doing so, (he/she) could reduce the welfare of (his/her) competitor by more." Given this political aspect of economic discrimination, Alexis maintains that the "remedy to the economic plight of Blacks is not to be found in economic activity alone." Thus, "until and unless Blacks achieve some degree of effective power, (i.e., command over institutions -public and private - that establish the rules of the game and determine the payoffs) they will continue to suffer from second-class economic citizenship."

The problem of preparation remains a problem of employ-ment. Brimmer (1982:32) notes that science and technology with heavy reliance on computers will be the area of the fastest growing occupations. Thus, he states, "if Blacks are to get a fair share of the new jobs, they will have to accelerate and upgrade their basic preparation in mathematics and communication skills." Secondly, the private sector will expand more rapidly than the public sector. By 1990, Brimmer estimates that this decline will cost Blacks jobs given their large share of public jobs, i.e., in 1980 22.5% compared to whites 15.2 percent.

Not only will most of the jobs be in the private sector, but they will demand a high degree of skill. In fact, Brimmer states that corporate requirements for entry and promotion are the typical skills needed. And many of these professional and managerial positions will be in production, marketing, distribution and finan-cial controls (i.e., accounting). Clearly, Black preparation is neces-sary to be eligible for these positions. But whether they will get them depends upon not only on their availability, but also the willingness of firms to hire Blacks. Without a concern for the prob-lems of the economy and the problems of discrimination in it, job possibilities are so much self-delusion.

THE PROBLEM OF BUSINESS

The problem of economic development is also tied to the problems of Black businesses. Although Frazier's (1962) contention that Black business was a "social myth" was extremely harsh, one cannot disagree that it has certainly found itself fragile and marginal to the larger economy (Coles, 1975; Tabb, 1970). First, among the problems of Black businesses is undercapitalization which insures smallness and inefficiency, prevents acquisition of managerial competence and often leads to failure. It is estimated that Black firms had receipts of only $11.1 billion in 1980 which equals to 0.17 percent of the total in U.S.

Secondly, Black businesses inspite of some diversification are essentially concentrated in personal services as in the past. Even Black Enterprises 1982 Top 100 Black Businesses report (June, 1982) reaffirms this. Thus, the essential process of production escapes them and is not a fundamental part of government or private proposals for Black economic development. Thirdly, as mentioned above, Black businesses are losing in the grossly unequal competition for Black consumer dollars, receiving only 8.9% of total Black income in 1980. Fourthly, low-level of managerial competence continues to plague Black businesses. Most are self-owned and too small to hire any other employees, let alone skilled managers which could insure correct business decisions.

Fifthly, Black businesses essentially operate in a restricted market which is marked by small savings, high debt, low income, high unemployment and an environment shunned by possible large investors. Finally, the shift in the politics and economics of the country to the right with a focus on the rich at the expense of the poor and stress on less government assistance to the Black community in general and Black businesses in particular bodes ill for Black business. For government assistance had been an important source not only of loans but also of support for affirmative action contracts for Black business and hiring.

Still, the Black Enterprise's Board of Economists predicts marginal gains for Black businesses in the next decade, especially in the high growth technology sector (Lee, 1982). In order to sustain growth and avoid following on the fatality list, Black businesses will have to, among other things: 1) acquire increased amounts of capital from other sources than the government; 2) diversify and work to get a greater share of the approximately $150 billion annual income of Blacks; 3) locate in industries such as telecommunications, cable, high technology and manufacturing; 4) engage in collective community planning; and 5) participate in building political bases among Blacks through service, donation and investment which come back in higher levels of Black support as consumers, investors and partners in political and economic development of the Black community.

SOLUTIONS

INTRODUCTION

Given the severity of the political-economic problems of the ghetto, the question of what is to be done and who is to do it are necessarily raised. Three basic resource structures are identified as fundamental to reversing the tendency and fact of ghettoization: 1) government; 2) the private sector; and 3) the Black community itself (Barnett and Hefner, 1976; Williams, 1982; Karenga, 1980). Governmental intervention and assistance are proposed for four basic reasons. First, the problems are of dimensions beyond the means of any one or combination of community structures. Secondly, the problems are socially-rooted and the result of racist discrimination and the government is obligated to assist in providing necessary correctives for these problems. Thirdly, Blacks helped create the social wealth of America and deserve an equitable share of it, not in the sense of sympathetic welfare, but in the sense of *distributive justice*, i.e., that share which is rightly theirs by their contribution and by just reasoning. Finally, it is objectively in the interest of the whole of society to solve these problems, for as long as they are unsolved, their negative effect will impact on the larger society also. For example, acquisition crime, generational poverty, socially incompetent members of society, and violently aggressive alienation all merit societal attention.

Secondly, the private sector is proposed because: 1) there is a sense that businesses, especially large corporations have drained and exploited the community and thus, owe it support in its revitalization efforts; 2) that businesses will benefit in tax credits, public relations, and even make a profit on their investment in the ghetto; and 3) they too should be concerned about the negative impact of unsolved ghetto problems on the larger society.

Undoubtedly the most important resource structure, however, in solving Black problems is the Black community itself. Regardless of external goodwill, a people must initiate and lead the struggle for its own liberation. However, this necessitates the structural capacity - an institutional and organizational network - to wage such a struggle. As noted above, one of the greatest, if not the greatest, problems Black face is structural incapacity to define, defend and develop their interests. This, therefore, must be a priority. Each year in its *State of Black America*, the National Urban League gives recommendations for the struggle for Black freedom, justice and equality, placing heavy emphasis on governmental intervention and assistance. However, the tasks proposed and the struggle to be waged presupposes and necessitates a self-conscious organized people to execute them. Afterall, one cannot expect the government to respond simply because recommendations are published or verbally proposed yearly. The government is a political structure, organized around the holding, using and respect of power. Thus, Blacks must politically educate and organize themselves and become a self-conscious social power with which to reckon.

Often, it is pointed out that the problems of the ghetto are too large and deep-rooted for Blacks to solve and that talk of community self-help is utopian. There are several things wrong with this "reasoning" which are immediately observable. First, no one offers such a position to Jewish or Gentile communities or any other Third World communities except the Afro-American community. Secondly, as noted above, resources from the government or others still require organization, knowledge of policy, collective strategy and the power to have an impact on policy. Thirdly, given Black structural incapacity, the government and the private sector are not likely to run to the rescue with the immediately necessary resources, as history as shown. Moreover, given the shift to the right in and out of government, the unlikelihood of this is even greater. Fourthly, given the above reality, it would seem sensible and contributive to survival and development if Blacks developed structures which even on a limited scale helped improve conditions of the ghetto.

Finally, Blacks have already built structures to deal with their deprivations imposed by discrimination; the point then would be how to expand and strengthen them. And here again, the Sixties provide a model, as I have argued in Chapter II. For not only were structures built to provide services, politically educate and organize the community, pressure was also put on the system to produce legislation, judicial decisions and programs which improved conditions in a significant way. The problem often faced is the one of dismissing Black strategies that do not produce the maximum goals or results and making alternative suggestions that theoretically produce maximum gains, but practically are less than effective or realistic. It is obvious that the three resource structures must be tapped and utilized for whatever gains are possible. But it is equally obvious that without a *structural base* of its own, the Black community will not only be unable to effectively demand from government and the private sector what is rightfully theirs, but will also be unable to provide for itself what is possible in the meantime. Black history is full of examples of Black self-help and struggle to win their rightful share of social wealth and social space. Not to honor this history by continuing it, seems not only an avoidable loss, but also an irrational and self-defeating position.

In terms of proposals for each resource structure, several recommendations for government and the private sector (businesses) are most often quoted (Barnett and Hefner, 1976; Williams, 1982). Economically, recommendations for the state and federal governments are: 1) continued and reinforced employment training programs; 2) more federal government revenue for domestic programs and less for an inflated defense budget; 3) less layoffs of government workers which affect Blacks, other Third World people and women disproportionately; 4) perception of federal Third World business program as economic programs rather than social welfare programs and improvement of delivery services to them; 5) encouragement of majority-owned and operated business to assist and use services of Third world businesses; 6) encouragement of employment and training of Blacks by private industry and small and medium businesses through tax incentives, wage subsidies, work study, etc.; 7) rejection of altered minimum wage for youth; 8) serious efforts toward full employment; 9) a reduction of budget cuts which affect monies and services vital to Blacks, other Third World peoples and the poor; and 10) continued application and support of Affirmative Action. Recommendations for the private sector are: 1) location of plants in the ghetto; 2) job training and employment for Blacks; 3) use of Black business services and products; and 4) provision of resources to insure expansion of alternative educational programs.

Politically, government, especially federal, is asked to: 1) resume and reinforce its traditional defense of civil rights; 2) monitor white terrorist and racist organizations like the Klan and neo-nazi groups; 3) appoint qualified Blacks in the government structure; 4) support the Voting Rights Act; and 5) oppose reapportionment schemes that dilute Black voting power or dissolve districts represented by Blacks. Educationally, government should: 1) oppose the voucher education system which is detrimental to public education; 2) increase support for historically Black colleges; 3) continue federal resources for quality education for the disadvantaged; and 4) insist that post-secondary institutions receiving federal monies maintain effective affirmative action programs for faculty and students.

In terms of the Black community, it is clear as stated above, that their primary focus must be on building a *structural capacity* to define, defend and develop their interests. This essentially means building an organizational, institutional and enterprise network that not only provides social services, but politically organizes and educates the community to its interests and possibilities. This requires strengthening existing structures and building new ones, building economic enterprises on the individual and cooperative level, alternative educational institutions, Black united fronts for collective planning and actions, and eventually, a Black political party which is dedicated exclusively to organizing Blacks for political power and effectively participating in the exercise of state power.

BROAD STRATEGIES

There are obviously several eclectic approaches to Black economic development which are initiated and controlled by Blacks (Coles, 1975; Cash and Oliver, 1975; Browne, 1976; America, 1977). But approaches can also be defined by their rootedness in or advocacy of three broad development strategies: capitalism, socialism and cooperative economics. Although it is theoretically possible to combine these developmental strategies, advocates of each usually tend to praise one and condemn or severely question the others. However, cooperative economic and socialist strategies are often linked and capitalist advocates have been known to tolerate parallel cooperative strategies. The discussion below seeks to give the basic contentions of each of these strategies with explanatory comments where warranted.

BLACK CAPITALISM. Black capitalism which gained popularity as a strategy during the Nixon Administration attempted to reduce the "perceived cycle of Black dependency" on governmental intervention. The alternative was to expand Black ownership which would stress private efforts, profit pursuit and free marketism for Blacks using the model of capitalism on a societal level (Cross, 1969). Black capitalism as a strategy contains several basic principles which define it and also lay the basis for its criticism.

First, it argues that increase in Black private ownership and control will enhance Black independence and pride, employ Blacks and help ease unemployment, increase the availability of services for the community and expand the wealth in the community. Secondly, Black capitalism argues for market protectionism that would shield Black enterprises from competition with larger more competitive outside enterprises. Thirdly, it advocates Black self-help and solidarity which would support Black business and benefit from its expansion. Fourthly, Black capitalism demands subsidization from the dominant society, i.e., government and the private sector. Subsidization may take the form of loans, grants, property, equipment or training and is seen as a contribution to capital formation as well as a moral and economic debt U.S. society owes Blacks for long-term discrimination and deprivation.

Criticism of Black capitalism is severe and from many quarters. First, Boggs (1970) argues that it is an irrational strategy which poses itself as a collective strategy, but is in fact a class strategy to further enrich a few at the expense of the many. Secondly, Allen (1970) and Zweig (1972) argue that the political economy of subsidization is negative to Black self-determination and will mean creation of a manipulated class still dependent on outside sources. Thirdly, Ofari (1970) calls attention to the fact that the strategy is overweighted toward service rather than *production,* the key process in economics. And finally, Brimmer and Terrell (1971), as well as Ofari, point to its nonviability given the small amount of capital available to Black enterprises, their low expansion possibility, low efficiency, marginal existence, high mortality rate, and restricted and problematic market, i.e., the ghetto economy.

SOCIALISM. Black advocates of socialism see Black capitalism as a myth and hindrance to serious Black economic development and political emancipation (Ofari, 1970; Allen, 1971). Their focus is essentially on Black labor rather than Black capital. As Harris (1978:141) argues, "Blacks cannot be adequately understood except as an integral part of the capital labor relation as a whole in U.S. capitalism." Given the fact that the Black working class is approximately 90% of the Black population, a strategy which does not focus on problems and possibilities of Black labor is both deficient and self-deluding.

Secondly, Black socialists argue that regardless of the temporary and partial measures that Blacks institute for economic betterment, a real and full solution depends on the transformation of society from capitalism to socialism. Given this reality, Black socialists argue for greater stress on the political dimensions of the economic process, and stress the need for organizing Black workers and the Black community into a self-conscious political force which challenges and transforms the established order (Alkalimat and Nelson, 1974).

Fourthly, the Black socialist strategy involves seizure of power and institution of: 1) collective ownership and control of the productive apparatus; 2) an egalitarian distribution of wealth; 3) a planned economy; 4) a political and economic democracy; and 5) an end to class, race and sexual alienation (Karenga, 1980:61-62).

Essentially this is seen as a long-range strategy, and the organization of the Black workers (and the Black community) as a fighting force for democratic rights, higher wages, better work and living conditions and greater participation in political and economic decision-making are posed as immediate goals.

This stress on the working class, especially by orthodox Marxists, however, often poses a problem for a specifically Black solution. For not only does it tend to play down racism as a simple function of capitalism (Harris, 1978), but it also ends up with no ethnic-specific program for Blacks - only for workers in general. Thus, as Browne (1976:153) contends, given Marx's and Lenin's failure to "directly address the unique situation in which American Blacks find themselves...there are very real limits on the extent to which that analysis speaks to our racial situation, irrespective of how eloquently it may dissect our economic dilemma."

COOPERATIVE ECONOMICS. As Ofari (1970:89) states, the theory and practice of cooperative economics has an early history in the mutual aid societies in northern Black communities which pooled resources and dedicated themselves to social service and community development. The idea, however, was eventually submerged with the emergence of a Black elite which developed a capitalist merchant class orientation (Harris, 1936). But in 1940, DuBois (1968) proposed a comprehensive theoretical framework and rationale for cooperative economics as a viable and necessary alternative to capitalism.

He (1968:216-219) stressed the need for a communal, Black-focused solution which would emphasize and establish: 1) social ownership; 2) strong family and group ties; 3) consumer unions; 4) economic planning; 5) socialized medicine; 6) cooperative organization of Black professionals for social service; 7) the elimination of private profit; 8) a Black controlled educational system; and 9) the essentiality of collective self-reliance. This solution he called "a cooperative commonwealth," a communal social system which built new relations among Blacks and gave them the internal strength to resist the corrupting influence of capitalism and the collective values necessary for cooperative community development.

Although DuBois' program was never implemented, it did yield an important model and since the 60's cooperatives have been posed as an important mode of Black economic development, especially in the South (Marshall and Godwin, 1971). Over one hundred were formed during the 60's in the South and ninety of those were organized in the Federation of Southern Cooperatives. Although they have been resisted by hostile forces, they nevertheless have provided food, jobs, and capital otherwise unobtainable and have thus helped raise the overall standard of living among the rural population.

Ofari (1970:89), though a socialist, admits that inspite of its problems, the Black cooperative proposal is "by far the most positive proposal that has been offered." Likewise, Allen (1970) who is also socialist, concedes the limitations of cooperative economics, but maintains that given the distance of the socialist revolution and the problems of integrating into a capitalist economy, a transitional program of cooperative economics is necessary." Led by an independent Black party, this transitional program, he (1970:278) states, should involve "a struggle to create an all encompassing, planned communal social system on a national scale and with strong international ties."

Finally, as I (1980:62-64) argued elsewhere, cooperative economics proves its validity in that it: 1) aids in increasing capital capacity, necessary for economic development; 2) increases the beneficiaries, unlike Black capitalism; 3) teaches the value for shared social wealth, egalitarianism, collective work and decision-making, the priority of the person over profit and the centrality of the community; and 4) establishes cooperative thought and practice which can be transferred to other areas, i.e., political struggle and social construction. Again, then, it is clear that politics and economics are unavoidably linked and any strategy for one must have as a major focus concern for the other.

STUDY QUESTIONS

1. Define economics.
2. Discuss the relation between politics and economics and why political economy is a more accurate word for economics.
3. Discuss the political economic status of the ghetto as an internal colony.
4. Discuss Sowell's and Wilson's contentions and arguments against them.
5. Why is the middle class both a resource and problem in Black economic development and political emancipation?
6. Discuss the employment problem of the Black community.
7. What are some basic problems of Black business?
8. Discuss the three basic resource bases for Black economic development and the rationale for each.
9. What are the basic principles and criticisms of Black capitalism?
10. What are the basic contentions and objectives of socialism?
11. What were DuBois' cooperative economic proposals?
12. What are the arguments for cooperative economics?

REFERENCES

Alexis, Marcus.   (1980) "Race and Social Organization: An

Economic Perspective,'' *The Review of Black Political Economy*, 10, 4 (Summer) 334-353.

Alkalimat, Abdul H. and Nelson Johnson. (1974) ''Toward the Ideological Unity of the African Liberation Support Committee,'' a position paper, South Carolina (June-July).

Allen, Robert L. (1970) *Black Awakening in Capitalist America*, Garden City, N.Y.: Anchor Books.

America, Richard. (1977) Developing the Afro-American Economy, Lexington, Mass.: Lexington Books.

Anderson, Bernard C. (1982) ''Economic Patterns in Black America,'' (ed.) James D. Williams, *The State of Black America, 1982*, New York: National Urban League, pp. 1-32.

Barnett, Marguerite and James Hefner. (1976) *Public Policy for the Black Community*, New York: Alfred Publishing Company.

Becker, Gary. (1957) *The Economics of Discrimination*, Chicago: University of Chicago Press.

Boggs, James. (1970) ''The Myth and Irrationclity of Capitalism,'' *The Review of Black Political Economy*, 1, 1 (Spring/Summer) 27-35.

Brimmer, Andrew. (1982) ''Economic Growth and Job Opportunities: The Long-Term Outlook,'' *Black Enterprise*, 12, 7 (February) 32.

Brimmer, Andrew and Henry S. Terrell. (1971) ''The Economic Potential of Black Capitalism,'' *The Black Politician*, 2, 4 (April) 19-23, 78-88.

Browne, Robert S. (1976) ''The Black Community and Contemporary Economic Dynamics,'' *The Review of Black Political Economy*, 6, 2 (Winter) 145-160.

_____. (1971) "Cash Flow in a Ghetto Economy," *The Review of Black Political Economy*, (Winter/Spring).

Cabral, Amilcar.   (1969) *Revolution in Guinea*, New York: Monthly Review Press.

Carmichael, Stokely and Charles Hamilton. (1967) *Black Power*, New York: Random House.

Cash, William L., Jr. and Lucy R. Oliver (eds.).   (1975) *Black Economic Development*, Ann Arbor: The University of Michigan Press.

Clark, Kenneth. (1965) *Dark Ghetto*, New York: Harper & Row.

_____. (1964) *Youth in the Ghetto*, New York: Haryou Associates.

Coles, Flournoy A.   (1975) *Black Economic Development*, Chicago: Nelson Hall.

Cross, Theodore L.   (1969) *Black Capitalism*, New York: Atheneum.

Cruse, Harold.   (1967) *The Crisis of the Negro Intellectual*, New York: William Morrow & Co.

_____.   (1968) *Rebellion or Revolution*, New York: William Morrow & Co.

DuBois, W.E.B.   (1968) *Dusk of Dawn*, New York: Schocken Books.

_____.   (1969) "The Talented Tenth," (ed.) Ulysses Lee, *The Negro Problem*, New York: Arno Press and the New York Times, pp. 31-76.

Frazier, E. Franklin.   (1962) *Black Bourgeoisie*, New York: Collier Books.

Fusfeld, Daniel.   (1977) *The Age of the Economist*, Chicago: Scott, Foreman and Co.

_____.   (1970) "The Basic Economics of the Urban and Racial Crisis," *The Review of Black Political Economy*, 1, 1 (Spring/Summer) 58-83.

Glasgow, Douglas.   (1981) *The Black Underclass,* New York: Vintage Books.

Hare, Nathan.   (1965) *The Black Anglo-Saxons,* New York: Marzani and Munsell, Inc.

Harris, Abram.   (1936) *The Negro as Capitalist,* Philadelphia: American Academy of Political Science.

Harris, Donald J.   (1978) "Capitalist Exploitation and Black Labor: Some Conceptual Issues," *The Review of Black Political Economy,* 8, 2 (Winter) 134-151.

Harris, William H.   (1982) *The Harder We Run,* New York: Oxford University Press.

Heilbroner, Robert.   (1972) *The Worldly Philosophers,* New York: Simon and Schuster.

Hill, Robert B.   (1980) "Black Families in the 70's," (ed.) James D. Williams, *The State of Black America, 1980,* New York: National Urban League, Inc., pp. 29-58.

_____.   (1981) "The Economic Status of Black Americans," (ed.) James D. Williams, *The State of Black America, 1981,* New York: National Urban League, Inc.

_____ .   (1978) *The Illusion of Black Progress,* Washington, D.C.: National Urban League Research Department.

Karenga, Maulana.   (1980) *Kawaida Theory: An Introductory Outline,* Inglewood, CA: Kawaida Publications.

Lee, Elliot.   (1982) "The BE Board of Economics Look at the Future," *Black Enterprise,* 12, 11 (June) 191-200.

Marshall, Ray and Lamond Godwin.   (1971) *Cooperatives and Rural Poverty in the South,* Baltimore: The John Hopkins Press.

Ofari, Earl.   (1970) *The Myth of Black Capitalism,* New York: Monthly Review Press.

Reich, Michael.   (1981) *Racial Inequality,* Princeton, N.J.: Princeton University Press.

Sowell, Thomas. (1981a) *Ethnic Minorities,* New York: Basic Books.

———. (1981b) *Markets and Minorities,* New York: Basic Books.

———. (1975) *Race and Economics,* New York: David McKay.

Tabb, William K. (1970) *The Political Economy of the Black Ghetto,* New York: W.W. Norton and Company.

Turner, James. (1976) "Implications of Class Conflict and Racial Cleavage for the U.S. Black Community," *The Review of Black Political Economy,* 6, 2 (Winter) 133-144.

Williams, James D. (ed.) (1982) *The State of Black America, 1982,* New York: National Urban League, Inc.

Willie, Charles. (1979) *The Caste and Class Controversy,* New York: General Hall, Inc.

Wilson, William J. (1978) *The Declining Significance of Race,* Chicago: University of Chicago Press.

Zweig, Michael. (1972) "The Dialectics of Black Capitalism," *The Review of Black Political Economy,* 2 (Spring) 25-37.

VII
BLACK CREATIVE PRODUCTION

INTRODUCTION

Although the category, creative production, can be used more generally to include various other forms of creative work, it will focus in this chapter of Black Art, Music and Literature. These are definitive of Black aesthetic creations and can, for the purpose of this chapter, be categorized as Black Arts or Art in the general sense. By Art, I mean "cultural production informed by standards of creativity and beauty and inspired by and reflective of a people's life-experiences and life-aspirations" (Karenga, 1980:80). The focus here is on the collective base of art, for as Evans (1979:37) contends concerning Black art, "...it is Black art because it is satu-rated in the experiences and behavior patterns of the people for whom it is created and because its substance is functional."

DuBois (1925) also stressed the collective source of Black art in his discussion of its social origins. He (1925:53) stated that even though Black art has both a personal and universal aspect, these are "combined with a certain group compulsion...meaning that the wishes, thoughts and experiences of thousands of individuals influ-ence consciously and unconsciously the message of the one who speaks for all." This "social compulsion", DuBois continues, was shaped by Black experiences in slavery and emancipation, and the struggle Blacks waged to liberate themselves and strive upward.

It is this struggle for freedom, dignity and self-definition in a hostile and challenge-filled world, then, that shaped Black art and gave it its relevance and reality. Black art, therefore, "as an expression of Black life experienes and aspirations, is the conscious and unconscious aesthetic contribution of Black people to their struggle to rescue and reconstruct their history and humanity in their own image and interests" (Karenga, 1980:80). Thus, Locke (1969:266), a key figure in the Harlem Renaissance of the 1920's, argued for the development of an African-American mode of artistic expression which spoke directly to the Black need for self-expression in their own terms. "We ought and must have a school of (Black) art," he asserted, "a local and racially representative tradition." The impetus and inspiration for this, he maintained, would come from Blacks' recognition, respect and use of their African heritage.

Although this question was raised and debated during the Harlem Renaissance and after, it received its most critical and enthusiastic attention during the Sixties in the debate revolving around the Black aesthetic (Gayle, 1971). The Black aesthetic had two distinct but interrelated meanings. First, it was used to mean a distinctive mode of aesthetic expression by which Black art could be identified. Secondly, it meant a criteria by which Black art could not only be judged in terms of its creativity and beauty, but also in terms of its social relevance.

If one combines these two interrelated definitions, the Black aesthetic can be defined as a distinctive mode of artistic expression and a distinctive standard by which Black art can be identified and judged in terms of its creativity and beauty as well as its social relevance. From the debate around this question which continues even now, two schools evolved, the detached-art school and the committed-art school. Writers such as Ellison (1966) and Redding (1966) argued the primacy of art rather than race or politics, suggesting art was universal and personal but not Black. They asserted that the artist does a disservice to himself/herself and his/her profession by being overly concerned with race and politics.

Langston Hughes, Richard Wright and the creative artists and critics of the 60's all argued against such a view. Hughes (1970:262) stated that he was "ashamed for the Black poet who says 'I want to be a poet not a (Black) poet', as though his own racial world were not as interesting as any world." Also, he expressed shame for the Black artist who paints sunsets instead of Black faces "because he fears the strange un-whiteness of his own features." Wright, as Gayle (1970:xiii) notes, "argued, in essence, that conditions in America had not changed to the degree that the (Afro-American) could desert the race question, engage in an art for art's sake endeavor or wander free in the sunny utopia of abstraction in attempt to desert the harsh reality of being Black in the twentieth century."

In the 60's Hoyt Fuller, Larry Neal, Mari Evans, Haki Madhubuti (Don L. Lee), Carolyn Rodgers, Rhonda Davis, Addison Gayle, Amiri Baraka, Sonia Sanchez, Woodie King, Ron Milner, Dudley Randall, this author and others contributed to the discussion and definition of the Black aesthetic (Gayle 1971). Neal (1971:272) posited essential contentions of the committed-art school when he rejected "any concept of the artist that alienates him from the community," posed Black art as "the aesthetic sister of the Black Power concept" and argued that the Black artist's primary duty is to speak to the spiritual and cultural needs of Black people." Moreover, the Negro Digest (later named the Black World) under the editorship of Hoyt Fuller (1971) who helped establish it in 1967, ran over a year of continuous commentary and discussion on the Black aesthetic from September 1968 through November 1969. In the January 1968 issue, a wide spectrum of views was presented on the question of the Black aesthetic. Most of these commentaries reaffirmed the need for Blacks to create and employ an aestheic in their own image and interest.

In the 70's, the discussion continued. Catlett (1975:13) reaffirmed the need for art being linked to Black struggle, stating that

"Only the liberation of Black people will make the real development of Black art possible. Therefore, it is to our advantage as
artists as well as Blacks to lend all our strength to the struggle." She
notes that art "...will not create authentic social change, but it can
provoke thought and prepare us for change, even helping in its
achievement. For art can tell us what we do not see consciously,
what we may not realize, and that there are other ways of seeing
things-maybe opposite ways."

Killens (1975:46) also reemphasized that culture and literature
were weapons for liberation and "words are the writer's ammuni-
tion." And Madhubuti (Lee) (1972:39) continued his stress on the
social role of art and the artist, and the need to develop a people-
focused art stating that "To be able to define one's self from a
historically and culturally accurate base and to follow through in
your work; keeping the best interest of your history and culture in
mind is to-actually-give direction to the coming generations." In
addition, Evans (1979:37) reaffirmed the political character and
role of Black art, contending that "It is political since its intent is to
speak to the Black community about the quality of life in that
community and the ramifications of individual responsibility for the
community both within and outside the systems of the larger
society."

Finally, Everett (1975:34,35) reasserts the need for respect of
Black tradition. For any art "which denies tradition removes the
necessary cultural cohesion of the form, sensibilities and integrity"
of the art itself. Artists, he continues, "enrich themselves and their
works when they bring to themselves and to their writing a clear
perspective of and appreciation for the cultural and historical
tradition of Black life and (art)." The need, then, is to "advance the
best of this tradition and 'standing on the shoulders of our forefathers' set our rainbow in the sky!"

It is in the context and support of the commitment-art school,
that I (1971, 1980:34ff) offered suggestions for a Black aesthetic,

first in the *Black World* series of commentaries and afterward in an outline of *Kawaida Theory*. Essentially, I (1980:84ff) argued that "for Black Art to truly be in the image and interest of Black people to whom it owes its existence and inner thrust, it must be informed, inspired and judged by social criteria as well as an aesthetic criteria." This social criteria which evolved within the framework of Kawaida theory was based on: 1) the traditional role of art in African society; 2) the discussions by advocates of the commitment-art school during and before the 60's; and 3) a Kawaida perception of the demands of Black life and struggle (Ransaw, 1979).

Thus, I (1980:84ff) contended that Black art to be real and relevant had to have three basic characteristics, i.e., it had to be functional, collective and committing. For art to be functional is to be useful. For if art is not useful, it is by definition, useless. Thus, to be functional, art must self-consciously have and urge social purpose, inform, instruct and inspire the people and be an unashamed partisan for them. "In a word, to be functional, Black art must be an aesthetic translation of our will and struggle for liberation and a higher level of life," searching for and creating new forms and styles to speak our truth and possibilities. To be collective, Black art must be done for all, drawn and synthesized from all, and rooted in a life-based language and imagery rich in everyday relevance. It must be understandable without being vulgarly simplistic, i.e., so pedestrian and impoverished that it does damage to art as a discipline and to the social message it attempts to advance.

Finally, Black art must be committing, i.e., not simply inform and inspire Blacks, but also commit them to the historical project of liberation and a higher level of human life. To do this, "It must demand and urge willing and conscious involvement in struggle and building of a new world and new men, women and children to inhabit it." And it must move beyond protest and teach possibilities, beyond victimization and teach Blacks to dare victory. Art, then, "must commit us to what we can become and are becoming and inspire us to dare the positive in a world defined and deformed by the negative.

Moreover, "Committing art is nationally self-conscious art, i.e., consciously a fundamental contribution to the definition, defense and development of the national Black community." This is not to deny art's human character, but to endow it with a concrete human reality by giving it a people-specific expression. For "our art, like our lives, are great not because it's defined as more human than Black, but because we have explored the richness of our own life experience and aspirations and discovered and offer life-lessons from which the whole world can benefit — not only aesthetically, but culturally in the wide sense of the word." It is in the framework of these assumptions that the following summaries of Black artistic achievement are offered and explained. This also maintains the stated thrust of this text to present a proactive and positive view of Black life and struggle in its current and historical unfolding.

BLACK ART

Afro-American art has its origins in Africa where art and artistic production, like religion, manifested itself in all aspects of communal life. African art was functional as well as aesthetic, being created for and used in various religious and social activities (Porter, 1970). African artists were carvers in wood, ivory and bone, sculptors in stone, clay, bronze, gold and iron, and created one of the oldest and most skilled traditions of functional and aesthetic art in the history of humankind (Locke, 1936; Butcher, 1956). Although there is continuing controversy over how much of the African artistic tradition was transferred to the U.S., the fact cannot be denied that there are clear evidences of the African motif in early Afro-American art (Porter, 1943; Dover, 1960).

Even though slaveholders often condemned and destroyed Black art to destroy Black communication and culture, enslaved Africans nevertheless produced impressive works of art (Driskell, 1976:14-15). These included not only personc | art objects but public works as Lewis (1978:9ff) asserts. Among the personal art objects, Thompson (1969) lists ceramics, basketry, earthenware, grave decorations, woodcarvings and weavings. Examples of these are in Fine (1973:12ff) and Driskell (1976:12ff). Porter (1943) contends that the Janson House, built on the Hudson River in 1712 for a Dutch patroon, exhibits a clear African motif in its construction and ornamentation, i.e., hand-forged hinges and detailed-work fireplace. He also cites their art work in silver, gold and iron. Driskell (1976:22ff) shows remarkable similarities between African and Afro-American art and architecture, among which are wrought iron balconies in New Orleans, plantation houses in African motif, a cylindrical quarter for enslaved Africans in Virginia which resemble Tembu houses in South Africa, and carved mantels with an African mask motif in North Carolina.

In addition, there is impressive evidence of African building and masonry skill in the Chapel of Cross in Chapell Hill, N.C., the Virginia State Capital building, the Torrence House of Mecklingburg County, the Harvey Castle near New Orleans, St. Andrew's Episcopal Church in Prairieville, Ala., and the famous Melrose plantation, near Natchitoches, La. (Dozier, 1974; Newton, 1977). Newton concludes that there were at least 90 different areas of arts and crafts in which Afro-Americans exhibited skillful workmanship.

Lewis (1978:12-13) marks the emergence of the professional artist before Emancipation with painters Scipio Moorhead and G.W. Hobbs in the 1770's, and Josua Johnston who "was the first artist of Black ancestry to gain public recognition in the United States as a portrait painter." After these were Julien Hudson (active 1830-40); Robert Douglass (1809-87); an abolitionist and painter, Patrick Henry Reason (1917-50); an engraver, William Simpson (active 1854-72); and later Robert Duncanson, Edward Bannister, Grafton Brown and Nelson Primus.

Edmonia Lewis (1843-1900) was the first Black woman in the U.S. to gain widespread recognition as an artist and the first Black to gain national reputation as a sculptor. Her *Forever Free,* a Black couple looking upward with broken chains, is in Howard University's Gallery of Art. Also, one of the most impressive early Black artists is Henry O. Tanner (1859-37), famous for his oil on canvas pieces such as *Banjo Lesson* and *The Thankful Poor.* However, having suffered much from racism, Tanner went to Paris and although he helped young Black artists who came to Paris, he refused to return to the U.S. and establish the Black Art School Locke advocated.

The Harlem Renaissance produced race and socially conscious artists who reached back to Africa and to the Black masses for a distinctive Black motif. As mentioned above, Locke (1968:267) had challenged Black artists to turn to their "ancestral arts of Africa" in order to develop a race art. He argued that if African art had influenced Pablo Picasso, Modigliani, Matisse and other white artists, it was surely "not too much to expect... its influence upon the culturally awakened (Black) artist of the present generations." Three artists in particular — Palmer Hayden, Archibald Motley, Jr. and Aaron Douglass — focused on developing styles that reflected the Black aesthetic.

Hayden in his Fetiche et Fleurs (Fetish and Flowers) used and African head and African print to emphasize Africanness and later painted subject matter which stressed the life and custom of the Black masses as in *John Henry on the Right, Steam Drill on the Left* and *The Janitor Who Paints.* Motley also used African and Afro-American themes. His *Old Snuff Dipper, The Barbecue* and *Chicken Shack* are clear examples of his focus on Black life. Douglass was a "pioneer Africanist", using the ancestral legacy to develop an original style which "combined modernism and Africanism in an astonishing (and original) synthesis'' (Driskell, 1976:62). Focusing on the beauty and strength of Black life, he employed geometric figures reflecting an African motif in his illustrations for Locke's (1968) *The New Negro* and James Weldon Johnson's *God's Trombones* and in his major work, a series of murals for the Countee Cullen Branch of the New York Library which portrayed the history of Afro-Americans.

Hale Woodruff also reflected a race and social consciousness in his art. In 1939, he painted a series of three socially conscious oil on canvas pieces entitled *The Amistad Murals* in honor of the Amistad Mutiny. This creation for Talladega College in Alabama, reflects the influence of socially-conscious Mexican muralists Jose C. Orozco, Diego Rivera, and David Siqueiros had on him and other Black artists during the 30's and 40's (Lewis, 1978:67-68). Richmond Barthe (b. 1901) is clearly one of Afro-America's leading sculptors. His sculptural figures are technically immaculate and graceful and focus on Black life, strength and dignity. Among these are *Blackberry Woman, Wetta, African Dancer,* and *The Negro Looks Ahead.* He also produced two marble reliefs, *Exodus* and *Dance.*

The 40's continued the tradition of race and socially conscious art, and mural art stood out as a major mode of expression. This, as mentioned before, was influenced by the Mexican muralists Rivera, Orozco and Siqueiros, but also as Lewis (1978:110) notes, "mural art is a major aspect of African architectural tradition". Charles Alston was one of the most important Black muralists during this time. Using a cubist style, his mural, *Magic and Medicine* for the Harlem Hospital in 1937 depicts a contrast between African and American life, the former being nature-oriented and warm, and the latter, mechanical and cold. Alston also produced with Hale Woodruff a joint mural documenting Black contributions to the founding of California for Golden State Mutual Life Insurance

Company of Los Angeles. Alston's panel is *Exploration and Coloni-zation* (1537-1850) and Woodruff's is *Settlement and Development* (1850-1949).

Charles White is by all estimations one of the most gifted race and socially conscious Black artists. Early in his art he announced that he was interested in the social role and function of art and sought to express it in his own. He showed Black people in various roles in history as worker, soldier, mother, father, scientist, civic leader, and musician. Drawing from the muralist school, his works are monumental, bold and defiant. Some of his most famous murals are *Five Great American Negroes* and *The Contribution of the Negro to American Democracy*. His lithographs, *Frederick Doug-lass* and *Harriet Tubman*, and his crayon *Mother and Child* are also impressive pieces.

James Porter, who wrote *Modern Negro Art*, and was appointed head of Howard University's art department and art gallery in 1953, also painted. Essentially between 1954 and 1964, he painted African and Afro-American themes and as an art critic and art historian, he like Alain Locke, played a vital role in the early establishment and development of Black art (Lewis, 1978:102).

Lois Mailou Jones and Elizabeth Catlett were two important Black women artists during this period. Although Jones at first painted the French countryside in an earlier period, she evolved into a self-conscious Black artist, visited 11 African countries and incorporated African imagery in her subsequent painting. Her *Moon Mask* from her African series reflect this consciousness. Catlett, a sculptor and printmaker, was involved in the Civil Rights Movement as a student and teacher, and assigned art a social role in the struggle against oppression. Some of her strongest works are *Black Unity*, in honor of Pan-Africanism; her lithograph *Negro Es Bello* (Black is Beautiful), a gentle rendition of the profile of a Black child; and *Malcolm Speaks For Us*, a strong linocut in her series on Black heroes.

The Sixties and Seventies saw an impressive growth of race conscious and socially conscious art. The Black Art Movement of the 60's which demanded that art serve Black people and their struggle recruited many artists who reflected in their art not only a commitment to their heritage but also a commitment to use their medium to support and achieve Black liberation. Murals again became a way to make art serve and express the people. Among these are *Mural at Massachusetts* in Boston by Dana Chandler and Gary Rickson, Eugene Eda's *Howard University Mural,* John Outterbridge's *Something From Nothing* in Compton, California, Dana Chandler's *Knowledge is Power: Stay in School* in Boston, and in Chicago, William Walker's *Peace and Salvation Wall,* Mitchell Caton's *Universal Alley Wall* and *Wall of Respect* by Eugene Eda, William Walker, Jeff Donaldson and other members of the Organization of Black American Culture, a group of artists and community workers dedicated to bringing art to Black people.

Paintings with Black themes of struggle, repression and daily life are also found in the works of David Hammonds, Cliff Joseph, Faith Ringgold, Alvin Hollingsworth, Benny Andrews, Milton Johnson, Joe Overstreet, Daniel Johnson, Ben Jones, Murray De Pillars, Malcolm Bailey, Ernest Trove, Lovett Thompson, Ernie Barnes and Mikelle Fletcher. Herman Kofi Bailey's *Unity,* Varnette Honeywood's *Gossip in the Sanctuary,* David Driskell's *Shango Gone,* John Bigger's *The Time of Ede, Nigeria* and *Web of Life "Ananse",* Jacob Lawrence's *The Worker,* Vernell DeSilva's *Chicago Pool Hall* and *Harriett Tubman;* and Murray De Pillars' *People of the Sun* are definitive period pieces also.

Mixed media assemblages include Noah Purifoy's *Sir Watts,* Betye Saar's *Nine Mojo Secrets,* John Outterbridge's *Shoeshine Box,* and Kay Brown's *Take It Now.* In sculpture, Margaret Burrough's *Head* and Doyle Foreman's *Corner* with their African projections stand out. And in graphic processes, Ruth Waddy's *The Key,* Jeff Donaldson's *Victory in the Valley of Eshu,* and Carol

Ward's *Foloyan* are strong examples of African and Afro-American focus. Examples of these and all others listed above can be found in Lewis (1978), Driskell (1976) and Fine (1973).

BLACK MUSIC

The African origins and character of Black music are well-documented (Southern, 1971; Meadows, 1979; Maultsby, 1979). Not only did Africans bring songs and dances but also brought and reconstructed musical instruments played in Africa such as the banjo, the balafo (xylophone), the musical bow, flutes, the elephant tusk horn, a kind of bagpipe, types of clarinets (dududen), trumpets made of wood and ivory, gongs, rattles, castanets, the quill or panpipes, the sansa or thumb piano and, of course, the drum. Courlander (1963) gives a detailed discussion of Africa-derived instruments played by African Americans. Moreover, as Meadows (1979:185) notes "the performance practices, melodies, rhythms, and aesthetic musical practices of today's Black Americans are only a mirror of the practices of their African forefathers and mothers."

None of this means that Africans in the U.S. did not borrow from their new environment for they did (Levine, 1977). But as Maultsby (1979:200-21) states, "these elements were recycled through the concepts and aesthetic principles that defined the musical tradition of the Africans." For example, melodies, rhythms, texts, and tempos were changed and shouts, calls, words, clapping, footstomping, and body movements were added to give them an African character.

The first music Black sang in the U.S. were songs from Africa. These included war songs and holiday songs in their own languages. However, fearing rebellions and plots, the slaveholders moved to prohibit both African songs and languages as well as instruments like drums which could be used for communication.

Following African tradition, early Afro-Americans distinguished many different types among their songs according to how they were used (Southern, 1971:175). Given the religiousness of Africans, the largest number of songs in the ante-bellum or pre-Civil War period were religious songs or spirituals. DuBois (1969) in 1903 was the first scholar to pay deserved attention to the beauty and significance of the spirituals. He saw these "sorrow songs" of enslaved and disappointed Africans as a message to the world in their expression of "faith in the ultimate justice in the world."

There are three basic approaches to the interpretation of the spirituals, i.e., that they are: 1) essentially social; 2) essentially religious; and 3) a synthesis of both the social and religious. Lovell (1969) and Fisher (1953) see them as essentially expressions of social strivings and struggle whose themes are: 1) the desire for freedom, justice and penalty for the oppressor; 2) criticism of the existing order; and 3) coded messages of escape, meetings and struggle. "Go Down Moses," "Swing Low Sweet Chariot," "Oh Freedom, Oh Freedom," (Before I'd Be A Slave I'd Be Buried In My Grave), "If I Had My Way I'd Tear This Building Down," "Oh Mary Don't You Weep, Don't You Mourn," "My Lord Delivered Daniel," and "No More Auction Block For Me," etc. are examples of these.

Secondly, Thurman (1947) and Mays (1968) saw the spirituals as essentially religious. Thurman (1947:12) contended that "The clue to the meaning of the spirituals is to be found in religious experience and spiritual discernment." He saw them as a religious expression of the enslaved African's struggle to maintain his/her dignity, personality and human spirit and transcend the context dedicated to their destruction. Mays (1968:21) argues that the spirituals are rooted in the "compensatory idea, that God will bring His own out victoriously in the end." The compensatory aspect, then, is rooted in a religious force and outcome, not social ones.

Finally, Cone (1972) sees the need for a synthesis of the two interpretations. He (1972:20) contends that "no theological inter- pretation of the Black spirituals can be valid that ignores the cultural environment that created them." The enslaved African found him/herself in a violent and brutal and dehumanizing envi- ronment and he/she offered both social and religious resistance. Spirituals, then, Cone concludes are a religious expression of resist- ance. It is reinforcement of identity and dignity, an expression of the use of religion as a "source of strength in a time of trouble" and "a vibrant affirmation of life and its possibilities in an appropriate aesthetic form" (Cone, 1972:32-33).

Work songs, as Southern (1971:177) notes, grew out of work activity in the fields, in prison, on roads, on the waterfront, on railroads, and other worksites. Essentially, this was not only psychic relief from tedium, but also depicted graphically the worker's situation and built a sense of shared responsibility and fate (Roberts, 1974:140ff). Especially relevant were heroic work songs like "John Henry" which showed Blacks defeating "white society on its own terms "by smashing its expectations and the stereotypes, by insisting that their lives transcend the traditional models and roles established for them and their people by the white majority" (Levine, 1977:420).

Southern (1971:182) also lists dance songs and play songs often called "fiddle songs," "devil songs," etc. As the names suggests, these were recreational songs. In addition, there were also narra- tive songs, satirical songs and field and street cries. All these reflected Blacks' aesthetic expression created in the midst of giving beauty and color to a hostile and challenge-filled world.

It is important to stress here how each kind of Black music, both religious and secular, reaffirms and reinforces the functional, col- lective and committing character of Black art forms. All truly Afri- can art was/is rooted in and reflective of life-situations, aspirations and possibilities. Thus, Black music, as an art form, expresses these characteristics also. This is clear also in Blues which began to take form in the late nineteenth century and "by the twentieth century had become a major form of Black expression" Maultsby (1979:203).

Cone (1972:112) argues that the Blues are secular spirituals; secular in their focus on this world and the body and spiritual in that "they are impelled by the same search for the truth of the Black experience." Jones (1963:18) argues that "the immediate predecessors of blues were the Afro-American...work songs which had their origins in West Africa." Maultsby contends that Blues is rooted in both secular and religious musical traditions, citing the training Blues singers had in church, their singing of both hymns and Blues, the tendency to call on the Lord while expressing deep sorrow, etc.

Blues, then, is rooted in the totality of the Black experience in the U.S. and the historical and social burden of being Black in a racist society which this implied, i.e., exploitation and oppression, loss of love, "hard rows to hoe," bad news and worse dreams, drinking and loving hard, resignation, reaffirmation and above all *durability*. In my (1971) earlier article on Black art, I criticized Blues as being essentially focused on resignation, but as my critics have rightly observed, Blues is much more multidimensional than that (Neal, 1972).

Thus, Blues speaks of: Black beauty; woman so good looking "make a bulldog break his chain and a snail catch a train;" being down and out, "sometimes I feel like nothing, somethin' th'owed away, Then I get my g'itar and play the blues all day;" defiant dignity, "I'd rather drink muddy water, sleep in a hollow log, Dan stay in this town and be treated like a dirty dog;" sexual betrayal, "went out this morning left my gate unlatched, come back home, found that boy in my potato patch;" plea bargaining, "come back baby please don't go, cuz the way I love you baby, you'll never know;" and social criticism, "Uncle Sam ain't no woman, but he sure can take yo' man, Boys dey got'em in the service, doin something I cain't understand."

Some of the more important names in Blues are William C. Handy, considered the "Father of the Blues," who first published "Memphis Blues" in 1912 and in 1914, "St. Louis Blues" which made Blues a household word around the world; Ma Rainey, the first professional Blues singer; John Lee Hooker; Leadbelly; Muddy Waters; Blind Lemon Jefferson; B.B. King; Bobby Blue Bland; Lightin Hopkins; Aaron T-Bone Walker; "Sonny Boy" Williamson; Bessie Smith; Alberta Hunter; Josh White and Ray Charles.

Ragtime, like Blues and spirituals, was another early manifestation of distinct Black music. Because it was associated primarily with the piano, it evolved after slavery when Blacks had access to the instrument. It was especially designed for Black consumption and was played by Black musicians anonymously and known in eating places, saloons, riverside dives, honky tonk spots and later clubs. Ragtime composers were many. Among the earliest were Irving Jones and Cris Smith. Others were Scott Joplin, the "King of Ragtime," whose music was made popular in the 70's by the movie *Sting*; Thomas Turpin, "Father of St. Louis Ragtime," Joe Jordan; Eubie Blake; James Scott; Scott Hayden and Louis Chauvin.

Gospel music rose out of the late 19th century and early 20th century folk church as opposed to the 20th century middle class church (Williams-Jones, 1975; Heilbut, 1975). Essentially, it is created in a context of individual and collective spontaneity, improvisation for church service and are thus called "church songs." Methodist minister, Charles Albert Tindley, the pioneer Gospel song creator, wrote his first songs in the early 1900's. And Thomas Dorsey, another pioneer, contributed to the Gospel idiom "a ragtime, boogie woogie piano style, his blues-based melodies, harmonies and an interest in religious spirit and faith (Maultsby, 1979:204). From this instrumentation, chants, calls, handclapping and footstomping were added in the free creativity and expression characteristic of folk environments. Some of the most notable Gospel singers are Mahalia Jackson, James Cleveland, Clara Ward, Marion Williams, Sis. Rosetta Thorpe, Sallie Martin, Mother Smith, Bessie Griffin, Golden Gate Quartet, the Sensational Nightingales the Dixie Humming Birds, Ruth David and the Staple Singers.)

Southern (1971:374) states that "the fusion of blues and ragtime with brass band and syncopated dance music resulted in a music called Jazz, a music with its own characteristics." Jazz started in New Orleans with pioneers like King Oliver and his Creole Band; Jelly Roll Morton and his Red Hot Peppers, Louis Satchmo Armstrong with his Hot Five and Hot Seven and clarinetist Johnny Dodds. From New Orleans, Jazz moved in the 20's to the Chicago Southside. In addition, big bands like those of Chuck Webb, Jimmie Lunceford, Cab Calloway, Erskine Hawkins, Lionel Hampton, Count Basie and Duke Ellington also emerged in the 20's.

With Jazz several styles developed among which were: *swing* in the 30's associated with Duke Ellington and big bands; *bop* in the early 40's which evolved into *hardbop* or *soul jazz* in the 50's represented by Dizzy Gillespie, Theolonius Monk, Kenny Clark, Charlie Christian, Lester Young, Jimmy Blanton, Charlie Parker, Bud Powell, Miles Davis, Earl Hines, Max Roach, Art Blakey, Horace Silver, Nat and Cannonball Adderly, Sonny Rollins, *avant garde* in the late 50's exemplified by Ornette Colman, John Coltrane, Cecil Taylor, Charles Mingus and Eric Dolphy. In addition, Sun Ra, Pharoah Saunders, Albert Ayler, Don Ayler, Marian Brown and Archie Shepp have shown impressive originality.

There are obviously too many Black musicians to be listed in this short overview, but it is important to mention musical greats like jazz singers Ella Fitzgerald, Billie Holiday, King Pleasure, Joe Williams, Sara Vaughn, Arthur Prysock and pianists Fats Wallar, Errol Garner, Hazel Scott and trumpeter Donald Byrd.

Rhythm and Blues emerged during the 40's and 50's, but reached its height in the 60's. Essentially an urban product, it reflected a self-conscious identity, cohesiveness and pride, combining elements of pop, gospel and blues traditions. In the 60's Rhythm and Blues became "Soul" music, a further indication of its identification with the Black Power thrust of the 60's. Stress was placed on distinctiveness from white music, Black pride and consciousness. This is by far the most popular music among Blacks although it is constantly challenged by white attempts to absorb and dilute it and deprive it of its distinctiveness as in the case of disco.

Some of the notable names in the 60's were James Brown (I'm Black and I'm Proud), Mr. Soul; Aretha Franklin (Respect), Ms. Soul: Ottis Redding (Sitting on the Dock of the Bay); Chuck Berry; The Four Tops; Curtis Mayfield; The Impressions (We're A Winner); Marvin Gaye and Tammy Terrell (Ain't No Mountain High Enough); The Supremes (Love Is Like An Itchin In My Heart); Gladys Knight and the Pips; The Temptations (My Girl; Message From A Black Man); Al Green (Let's Stay Together); Sam Cooke (Change Gon' Come); Smokey Robinson (I'll Try Something New); Nina Simone (Young, Gifted and Black); Ray Charles; Les McCann and others. (Current artists are assumed to be familiar to the student so there is little need to list them.)

Given the influence music has on Black life, there is a continuous discussion on how to make it better serve the interests of Blacks. This question becomes especially urgent in terms of Rhythm and Blues which is the most popular music among Blacks, and which has not only lost its social consciousness for the most part but is losing its distinctiveness as Black music. One cannot help but notice the contrast between the race and socially conscious quality music of the 60's and the insipid, socially irresponsible, raw sex-focused rhythm and blues music of today. What one is witnessing, as disco most vividly showed, is the merciless drive of the music industry to make money, reducing all music to a homogenized packageable sound, regardless of its effect on social life, aesthetics or a rich Black heritage (Byrd, 1978). In the early 20's, Locke (1969:45) had argued Black music had become "tarnished with commercialism and the dust of the market place," and that Black musicians were "in commercial slavery to the Schylocks of Tin Pan Alley and in artistic bondage to the cash of...dance halls and vaudeville stages." If this were true then, it is obviously even more so now (Byrd, 1978; Ashborne, 1977).

Few artists are strong or politically conscious enough to oppose the tide of commercialism and create the race-and socially-conscious model and music which so marked the 60's. Paul Robeson stands as a model in the past of the socially conscious artist who excelled aesthetically and refused to compromise politically (Dent, 1976). Currently, Terry Callier "Be A Believer;" "African Violet" and "Martin Street Martin", and especially Gil Scott-Heron stand out as models of artists who have a high level of aesthetic achievement and social consciousness. As Salaam (1982:12) states, "Scott-Heron represents the most socially conscious element of (the message-music) tradition." His hits, among which are "The Revolution Will Not Be Televised," "The Bottle," an attack on alcoholism, "We Almost Lost Detroit," a criticism of nuclear power, and "Angel Dust," an appeal to youth to avoid it, all demonstrate a commendable aesthetic and socially conscious quality.

The need then is for the *cultivation* and *support* of more Calliers and Scott-Herons in every area of Black music, but especially in rhythm and blues. For in the final analysis, a people saves itself from social danger and disintegration or there is no hope for it. Moreover, Blacks are for the most part Black artists' main customers and have the capacity to give or withhold support. Thus, if the records and concerts of negative artists were not bought or attended, raw sex, labelling Black women superfreaks, the reductive translations of love and other negatives could not survive. And in place of the current music which has neither socially or aestheti-

cally redeeming value, a music marked by race and social consciousness and solid aesthetic quality can and will reemerge, and a
rich distinctive Black heritage will be preserved and expanded. The
success of such a project, however, will depend upon the success of
the revival of the cultural and political development and struggles
which characterized the Sixties. For without a cultural struggle to
transform consciousness and the political struggle to acquire control of Black destiny and daily life, neither Black music nor their lives
will be shaped in their own image and interests.

BLACK LITERATURE

Black literature does not begin with written aesthetic expressions but with oral ones. Although some African literature was
written, much of it was not and still none of what was written was
brought by enslaved Africans when they came. Debate still rages
on how much oral literature survived from Africa but every serious
writer concedes a significant amount of African survivals (Courlander, 1976; Dorson, 1965). Moreover, as Bontemps and Hughes
(1958) noted, in addition to Africanization, there was a parallel
process of Americanization which translated as modifying charac-
ters and themes to reflect more accurately their new experience in
the U.S. Thus, the African animals jackal, hare, tortoise and hyena
are translated in an American environment as the fox, rabbit, turtle
or terrapin and wolf.

Afro-American folklore is often associated with animal stories
like Ber Rabbit, made familiar to American audiences through Joel
Chandler Harris' collection and publication of them in his *Uncle
Remus: His Songs and Sayings* and Walt Disney who made them
into a movie, "Song of the South." But as Brown (1970) contends, it
is important to note that there are much more kinds of folklore than
the animal stories. Zora Neale Hurston (1935) in her collection,
Mules and Men, Charles Chestnut in the *Conjure Woman* (1889),

Arthur Huff Fauset, Thomas Talley, J. Mason Brewer, all give an idea of the rich variousness of Black folklore.

From the above, several kinds of folklore emerge: 1) animal stories; 2) legendary hero stories; 3) human trickster stories; 4) exaggeration stories; 5) why stories; and 6) tales of satire. In animal stories, is the theme of weakness overcoming strength through intelligence and cunning. Ber Rabbit, Ber Squirrel and other small animals outwit the larger slower ones. In legendary men stories, like those of Stagolee, Blacks are posed as defiant and rebellious or in colloquial terms "a bad, crazy nigger that don' take no shit from nobody, Black or white." In the ones like John Henry, they are posed as beating the white man at his own game, breaking stereotypes and winning against all odds. The human trickster is ol' John that outwits the white man playing on his ego — saying," I went on the red light cuz the whites were going on the green and I knew then it wasn't for me." The exaggeration stories in Hurston's collections have mosquitos sing like alligators, eat up the cow and then ring the bell for the calf or a man so fast he shoots at a deer, runs and catches the deer and holds him til the bullet hits him. Why stories give explanations of the origin of the world, races, division of labor, etc. And tales of satire lampoon the slaveholder and white man in general who figure with a crooked pencil, that "ought's a ought, figger's a figger, all for de white man, none for de nigger."

Although blues, spirituals and work songs can be considered folklore also, their treatment in the music section will be considered sufficient. It is important to note here that folklore though originally oral, took on a written form in the works of Charlie Chestnutt, Paul Lawrence Dunbar, Earl Gaines, George Henderson, Langston Hughes, Zora Neal Hurston, Claude McKay, Jean Toomer, Margaret Walker and Sarah Wright.

A second early period of Black literature began in 1746 with Lucy Terry's (1730-1821) writing a poem on a Massachusetts Indian raid which was the first known piece of literature by an Afro-

American (Whitlow, 1974:15). After her, Jupiter Hammond, poet and essayist and Phillis Wheatley, a poetess came. Slave narratives by Briton Hamon in 1760 and Gustavus Vassa in 1789 followed with Vassa's being the most popular and detailed on life in Africa and in slavery. These early writings are marked by a "redeemed Christian" mentality which is racially self-effacing and apologetic for slavery, seeing it as God's way of rescuing them from savagery.

The 1800's marks a third period, i.e., the rise of what is commonly called "protest" literature, i.e., the speaking out strongly against the established state of things — slavery, oppression, exploitation, racism. It is set in the midst of the slave revolts and other forms of resistance like abolitionism. Thus, almost all Black writers who published during this period wrote in the spirit of protest (Whitlow, 1974:29). George Moses Horton's (1797-1883) *Hope of Liberty,* James Whitefield's *America and Other Poems* and Frances Harper's *Poems on Miscellaneous Subjects* all indict the slave system for its injustice and brutality. In this period also autobiographies were written by Frederick Douglass (1917-1895), *Life and Times,* a brilliant well-written autobiography with strong political content and by William Wells Brown, *The Narrative of William Wells Brown.* Also, Brown wrote three novels and three plays. The first novel *Clotel: or the President's Daughter* was written in 1853 and was the first Black novel. Other novelists were Frank Webb, *The Garies and Their Friends,* and Martin Delaney, *Blake.* Delaney also wrote a major political work, *The Condition, Elevation, Emigration and Destiny of the Colored People of the United States.*

The pre-Harlem Renaissance period begins with publication of poetry by one of Afro-America's most gifted poets, Paul Laurence Dunbar. Dunbar is well-known for his poetry in Afro-American idiom like when "Malindy Sings," the Antebellum Sermon" and "Keep A Plugging Away." But he also wrote short stories and a novel. His works were, however, consciously unpolitical to accommodate the fact that his main audience was white. For the Black middle class was embarrassed by his use of folk language instead of standard English.

Charles Chestnut is known for his the *Conjure Woman and Other Tales*, based on folklore heard in North Carolina and narrated by Uncle Julius, a shrewd ex-enslaved African who manipulates his employer with these tales. However, he wrote short stories and three novels. James Weldon Johnson spans two main periods in Afro-American literature. He wrote his novel, *Autobiography of An Ex-Colored Man* in 1912, *God's Trombones, Seven Negro Sermons* in verse in 1927, *Black Manhattan,* an excellent study of Black culture in 1930 and his autobiography *Along This Way* in 1933. His sermon "The Creation" is considered a classic. Also Johnson wrote the Black National Anthem, "Lift Every Voice and Sing" in 1900. W.E.B. DuBois wrote in this period also. In addition to his social and political writings, he wrote two novels. His most known piece during this period was his *Souls of Black Folk* in 1903.

The Harlem Renaissance was one of Black writers' most prolific periods (Huggins, 1979). It was a time when Harlem became the capital of Black America; Blacks looked to their African roots for revitalization; Garvey issued the call for Black pride and power and the rescue and reconstruction of Africa (Garvey, 1977), and Alain Locke (1969), the main interpreter of the Renaissance, announced the coming into being of the "New Negro." In fact, Garvey's and Locke's influence on the Harlem Renaissance cannot be overestimated. Garvey's ideological and political push for respect, African heritage and race pride, coincided with Locke's stress on the need for examination and use of the African ancestral legacy. And although Garvey was misunderstood and often maligned by the Black writers of this period, it is safe to assume he and his movement are significantly responsible for their stress on Black culture and consciousness.

Locke's *The New Negro is a classic and his most known work, but he wrote and edited other works on Black culture, i.e., Four*

Negro Poets, The Negro in Art, and The Negro and His Music. Claude McKay was one of the most militant writers of the Renaissance. His "If We Must Die" in 1917 which calls for Blacks not to die like dogs but fight the "murderous cowardly pack" is definitive and is considered by some to be the beginning of the Renaissance. His Home to Harlem is also well-known. Jean Toomer's Cane, a collection of prose and poems; Countee Cullen's collection of poems, Copper Sun; Nella Larsen's novel Quick-sand; and Langston Hughes classic poem, "The Negro Speaks of Rivers," his dozen books of poetry and two autobiographies, The Big Sea and I Wonder as I Wander, stand out as definitive of the period.

The Depression of 1929 marked the slowing of the prolific writing of the Renaissance. New writers emerged such as Zora Neal Hurston, Mules and Men (folktales), three novels and a satire on America race relations; and Arna Bontemps, three novels, Black Thunder, Drums at Dusk and God Sends Sunday.

In the period of 1940-1960, Richard Wright stands out as a giant with his classic novel, Native Son, and his autobiography Black Boy. He established a school of writing called Urban Realism, a rough unadorned exposure and critical depiction of urban Black life. Among the writers who were included in this school were Chester Hines, If He Hollers Let Him Go, and Ann Petry, The Street Ralph Ellison's work Invisible Man (1952), is another Black classic in which he poses Black as invisible in a racist society and in search of a solid identity. James Baldwin is a multitalented essayist, novellist and playwright. Among his works are the novel, Go Tell It On The Mountain (1953); an essay, The Fire Next Time (1963); a play, The Amen Corner (1967); and his latest novel Just Above My Head (1982).

Gwen Brooks is obviously one of the most gifted poets in the U.S. She won the Pulitzer Prize for Poetry and her collection Annie Allen 1949, the first Black to receive the award. She continues to write, lectures around the country and aids young aspiring poets.

Margaret Walker is known for her classic poem "For My People" and her novel, *Jubilee*. Her poem written in free verse is a praise poem to the life, struggle, adaptive vitality, durability, strength and achievement of Blacks. It is also a call for struggle and a new social order. Robert Hayden has published five volumes of poems, among which are *A Ballad of Remembrance* and *Words in the Mourning Time*. Lorraine Hansberry's play, "A Raisin in the Sun," was a successful Broadway production and marked a high point in critical achievement and recognition for Black drama.

The Sixties is considered by many a *Second Black Renaissance* (Bigsby, 1979). It produced and was produced by both literary and political diversity and multiplicity. It was, as argued in chapter II, Blacks' most significant decade in terms of self-conscious goals and achievements. The Harlem Renaissance was in part fostered by white patrons and declined with their withdrawal after the Crash of '29. But the Sixties was self-generating, self-determining and self-sustaining. Its literary personalities are often known in political as well as literary circles. For the decade demanded a merging of the political and the literary. Larry Neal, Askia M. Toure, Ishmael Reed, Amiri Baraka, Sonia Sanchez, Nikki Giovanni, Mari Evans, Etheridge Knight, A.B. Spellman, Johari Amini, June Jordan, Quincy Troupe, Lucille Clifton, Stanley Crouch, Joe Goncalves (Dingaan), Carolyn Rodgers, Yusef Iman, Ed Bullins, James Randall, Stephany, Conrad Rivers, Eugene Redmond, Haki Madhubuti and Kalamu ya Salaam are but a few examples of Black socially conscious writing (Randall, 1971). Many of the above wrote poetry, drama and prose.

Definitive of this period are Sonia Sanchez's *We a BaddDDD People*; Amiri Baraka's *Black Magic Poetry 1961-67* and *Four Revolutionary Plays*; Johari Amini's *Black Essence*; Haki Madhubuti's *We Walk The Way of the New World*; June Jordan's *Who Look At Me*; Ishmael Reed's *Yellow Back Radio Broke-Down*; Ed Bullins *New Plays From the Black Theatre*; Larry Neal's and Leroi Jones' (Baraka) *Black Fire*, Mari Evans' *I'm A Black Woman*; Etheridge Knight

Poems From Prison; Nikki Giovanni's *Black Feeling Black Talk;* and John Williams' *The Man Who Cried I Am.*

The Seventies saw the emergence of Alice Walker whose credits include novels, *Meridian,* poetry, *Revolutionary Petunia* and short stories, *In Love and In Struggle;* novelist Toni Morrison who has written four novels and whose *Song of Solomon* won the Best Novel of the Year Award in 1977; and a long list of Black poetesses and poets which have published in the Black Literature issues of the *Black Scholar,* '71, '75, '78 and '81. Notable also are the new poetry of Sonia Sanchez, *I've Been A Woman;* Mari Evan's, *Night Star;* Bell's, Parker's and Guy-Shefall's, *Sturdy Black Bridges: Visions of Black Women in Literature;* Gwen Brooks anthology of new Chicago poets, *Jump Bad,* Maya Angelou's *I Know Why the Caged Bird Sings,* Kalamu ya Salaam's *Revolutinary Love,* and Eugene Redmond's *Drum Voices: The Mission of Afro-American Poetry.*

Although these writings do not have the self-conscious urgency and fire of the 60's, they, nevertheless, like the literature of the 60's and other periods, speak the truth of Black people, i.e., their hopes, aspirations, love and constant struggle to have a full and free life. Thus, by teaching beauty in the midst of ugliness and strength and durability under stress and strain, they inspire and teach possibilities which, as argued at the outset, is the fundamental function of Black literature.

STUDY QUESTIONS

1. What is art?

2. What is the Black aesthetic and what are the two schools which developed around the issue? Discuss their views.

3. What is the Kawaida social criteria for art? Discuss the three criteria.

4. Give examples of African art survivals.

5. Discuss the artists of the Harlem Renaissance period and of the 40's.

6. Discuss some of the main Black women artists.

7. What were the main themes of Black art in the 60's and 70's?

8. What are three basic approaches to interpretations of the spirituals?

9. Discuss the multidimensionality of the Blues as a reflection of the Black experience.

10. Discuss the origin of Gospel and Ragtime and some of the pioneers.

11. Discuss the evolution of Jazz and the different styles.

12. What are the origins of Rhythm and Blues and the problems it poses?

13. What are the several forms of Black folklore?

14. Discuss the evolution of Black literature from narratives through the 70's including themes and focus.

REFERENCES

Ashburne, Michael R. (1977) Black Music: A Financial Perspective," *Western Journal of Black Studies,* 1, 4 (December) 263-269.

Bigsby, C.W.E. (1980) *The Second Black Renaissance,* Westport, Conn: Greenwood Press.

Bontemps, Arna and Langston Hughes. (1958) *The Book of Negro Folklore,* New York: Dodd, Mead.

Brown, Sterling A. (1970) 'Negro Folk Expression'' in *Black Expression,* (ed.) Addison Gayle, Jr., New York: Weybright and Talley.

Butcher, Margaret J.. (1956) *The Negro in American Culture,* New York: Knopf.

Byrd, Donald. (1978) "Music Without Aesthetics: How Some Non-Musical Forces and Institutions Influence Change in Black Music," *The Black Scholar,* (July-August) 2-5.

Catlett, Elizabeth. (1975) "The Role of the Black Artist," *The Black Scholar,* 6, 9 (June) 10-14.

Cone, James. (1972) *The Spirituals and the Blues,* New York: The Seabury Press.

Courlander, Harold. (1963) *Negro Folk Music, U.S.A.* New York: Columbia University Press.

Courlander, Harold. (1976) *A Treasury of American Folklore,* New York: Crown Publishers, Inc.

Dent, Roberta Y (ed.) (1976) *Paul Robeson Tributes and Selected Writings,* New York: Paul Robeson Archives, Inc.

Dorson, Richard M. (1965) *American Negro Folktales,* Greenwich, Conn.: Fawcett.

Dover, Cedric. (1960) *American Negro Art,* Connecticut: New York Graphic Society.

Dozier, Richard K. (1974) "Black Architects and Craftsmen," *Black World,* (May) 5-7.

Driskell, David C. (1976) *Two Centuries of Black American Art,* New York: Los Angeles County Museum of Art and Alfred A. Knopf.

DuBois, W.E.B. (1925) "The Social Origins of American Negro Art," *Modern Quarterly,* 3, 1 (October-December) 53-55.

––––––– . (1969) *The Souls of Black Folk,* New York: The New American Library.

Ellison, Ralph. (1966) *Shadow and Act,* New York: Signet Books.
Evans, Mari. (1979) "Political Writing as Device," *First World,* 2,3:34-39.

Everett, Chestyn. (1975) "Tradition in Afro-American Literature," *Black World*, 25, 2 (December) 20-35.

Fine, Elsa H. (1973) *The Afro-American Artist*, New York: Holt, Rinehart and Winston.

Fisher, Mark M. (1953) *Negro Slave Songs in the United States*, New York: Citadel Press.

Fuller, Hoyt W. (1971) "Introduction: Towards a Black Aesthetic," in *The Black Aesthetic*, (ed.) Addison Gayle, Jr., Garden City: Doubleday.

Garvey, Marcus. (1977) *Philosophy & Opinions*, New York: Atheneum.

Gayle, Addison, Jr. (ed.) (1971) *The Black Aesthetic*, Garden City: Doubleday.

_____ . (1970) *Black Expression*, New York: Weybright and Talley.

Heilbut, Tony. (1975) *The Gospel Sound*, Garden City: Anchor Books.

Huggins, Nathan I. (1979) *Harlem Renaissance*, New York: Oxford University Press.

Hughes, Langston. (1970) "The Negro Artist and the Racial Mountain," in *Black Expression*, (ed.) Addison Gayle Jr., New York: Weybright and Talley.

Jones, LeRoi (Amiri Baraka). (1963) *Blues People*, New York: William Morrow:

Karenga, Maulana. (1971) "Black Cultural Nationalism," in *The Black Aesthetic*, (ed.) Addison Gayle, Jr., Garden City: Doubleday.

_____ . (1980) *Kawaida Theory: An Introductory Outline*, Inglewood, Ca.: Kawaida Publications.

Killens, John O. (1975) "The Image of Black Folk in American Literature," *The Black Scholar,* 6, 9 (June) 45-52.

Levine, Lawrence W. (1977) *Black Culture and Black Consciousness,* New York: Oxford University Press.

Lewis, Samella. (1978) *Art: African American,* New York: Harcourt Brace Jovanovich.

Locke, Alain. (1969) *The Negro and His Music,* New York: Arno Press/New York Times.

_____ . (1936) *Negro Art,* Washington, D.C.: Association in Negro Folk Education.

_____ . (1968) *The New Negro,* New York: Atheneum.

Lovell, John. (1969) "The Social Implications of the Negro Spiritual," in *The Social Implications of Early Negro Music in the United States,* (ed.) Bernard Katz, New York: Arno Press.

Madhubuti, Haki (Don L. Lee). (1972) "The Achievement of Gwendolyn Brooks," *The Black Scholar,* 3, 10 (Summer) 32-41.

Maultsby, Portia K. (1979) "Influences and Retentions of West African Musical Concepts in U.S. Black Music," *Western Journal of Black Studies,* 3, 3 (Fall) 197-215.

Mays, Benjamin. (1968) *The Negro's God,* New York: Atheneum.

Meadows, Eddie S. (1979) "African Retentions in Blues and Jazz," *Western Journal of Black Studies,* 3, 3 (Fall) 180-185.

Neal, Larry. (1972) "The Ethos of the Blues," *The Black Scholar,* 3, 10 (Summer) 42-48.

_____ . (1971) "Some Reflections on the Black Aesthetic," in *The Black Aesthetic,* (ed.) Addison Gayle, Jr., Garden City: Doubleday.

Newton, James E. (1977) "Slave Artisans and Craftsmen: The Roots of Afro-American Art," *The Black Scholar,* 9, 3 (November) 35-44.

Porter, James. (1970) "African Art From Prehistory to Present," in *The Negro Impact on Western Civilization*, (eds.) Joseph S. Roucek and Thomas Kiernam, New York: Philosophical Library, pp. 467-487.

_____. (1943) *Modern Negro Art*, New York: Dryden Press. Randall, Dudley. (1971) *The Black Poets*, New York: Bantam Books.

Ransaw, Lee A. (1979) "The Changing Relationship of the Black Visual Artist to His Community," *Black Art*, 3,3: 44-56.

Redding, J. Saunders. (1966) "The Negro Writer and American Literature," in *Anger and Beyond*, (ed.) Herbert Hill, New York: Harper & Row.

Roberts, John Storm. (1974) *Black Music of Two Worlds*, New York: William Morrow.

Salaam, Kalamu ya. (1982) "Hit Records in an Old Tradition," *In These Times*, (May 19-25) 21.

Southern, Eileen. (1971) *The Music of Black Americans*, New York: W.W. Norton.

Thompson, Robert F. (1969) "African Influences on the Art of the United States," in *Black Studies in the University*, (eds.) A.L. Robinson, etc., Connecticut: Yale University Press, 122-70.

Thurman, Howard. (1947) *The Negro Spiritual Speaks of Life and Death*, New York: Harper & Row.

Whitlow, Roger. (1974) *Black American Literature*, Totwa, J.J.: Littlefield, Adams & Co.

Williams-Jones, Pearl. (1975) "Afro-American Gospel Music: A Crystallization of the Black Aesthetic," *Journal of the Society for Ethnomusicology*, XIX (September.)

VIII
BLACK PSYCHOLOGY

INTRODUCTION

Psychology is essentially the science that systematically studies human behavior in its relationship to the complexity of mental, emotional, physical and environmental factors which shape it. Although there is a tendency to include the study of animal behavior as part of the definition, of psychology (Kagan and Haveman, 1976), I have purposely omitted it in order to maintain focus on the human personality as the core and motive force of psychological study. In fact, even the study of animal behavior in psychology is only relevant in its use to deepen and expand understanding of human behavior. Otherwise, such study of animals is better defined as zoology rather than psychology.

Furthermore, all science is ultimately systematic study and knowledge to enhance human grasp of and effective encounter with themselves and their environment. Psychology, then, as a person-focused discipline, stands out as a key science in this historical project of overall human understanding of self, society and the world. For at its most relevant level, it not only focuses on the structure and functioning of the human personality, but equally important, points to the possibilities of its unlimited expansion and thus the realization of a higher level of human life on the personal and social level (Karenga, 1978).

The concerns of Black psychology revolve around the development of a discipline which not only studies the behavior of Black persons, but seeks to transform them into self-conscious agents of their own mental and political liberation. This is achieved through: 1) a severe critique and rejection of white psychology, in terms of its methodology, conclusions and the ideological premises on which it rests; 2) provision of Afro-centric models of study and therapy; and 3) self-conscious intervention in the social struggle for a more Black and human environment (Jones, 1980; Jackson, 1982).

Black psychology has its origins in the 1920's when Francis Sumner became the first Black Ph.D. in psychology in 1920, and subsequently Blacks began to publish research to disprove racist charges of Black inferiority, to push for stronger departments of psychology in Black schools, and to attempt to provide better psychological services to the Black community (Guthrie, 1976). It gained greater strength as an educational thrust when in 1938 Herman Canady of West Virginia State College began to organize Black professionals interested in psychology. Although he was unable then to organize an independent Black psychologist association, he did establish a Black psychologists' caucus within the American Teachers Association, the main professional structure for Black educators. Among the goals they set for themselves were: 1) to promote the teaching and application of psychology, especially in Black schools; 2) to stimulate study, research and exchange; and 3) to set up qualifications for teachers of psychology and assist Black institutions in training and selecting psychologists (Guthrie, 1976:115ff).

However, it was not until the 60's as Jackson (1979:271) notes, "that Afro-American psychologists made a concerted and sustained effort to expand their concerns into a distinct system of thought and not until the 70's that publications appeared in the form of a Black Psychology." In the 60's, the resurgence of Black nationalism, and its Black Power expression, encouraged and demanded Black caucuses within traditionally white-controlled and white-oriented professional organizations as well as independent Black organizations. In 1968 the Association of Black Psychologists (ABP) was founded in the midst criticism of the American Psychological Association (APA) for its limited vision and conscious and unconscious support of the racist character of American society.

Pledging themselves "to the realization that they are Black people first and psychologists second," the ABP vowed not to "ignore the exploitation of the Black community" and expressed urgent concern "about its role and that of the APA in Black people's struggle for dignity and equality in this country" (Williams, 1974:11-12). The suggestion that the APA had a role in the Black struggle and the subsequent 10-point program for correctives of the APA's thought and practice shows that Black psychologists were still in transition toward an Afro-centric psychology. However, in 1974 when Williams wrote a brief history of the ABP, it was his assessment that traditional psychology was out and Black psychology coming into being. "Black psychologists, he (1974:24) asserted, "have finally broken the symbiotic relationship with white psychology." Black psychology must now, he continued, "be about the business of setting forth new definitions, conceptual models, test theories, normative behavior, all of which must come from the heart of the Black experience."

The history of the Black Psychologists Association reflects the consolidation and development of distinct but overlapping schools of Black psychology. These are the traditional, reformist and radical schools. Although these approximate Jackson's (1979) reactive, inventive and innovative categories of Black psychology components, I find the categories "inventive" and "innovative" close enough in definition to warrant alternative categories. Thus, I have offered "reformist" and "radical" as alternative categories. It is important to state here that I suggest no pejorative meaning to reform or the reformist school. I recognize it as a transitional and middle posture between the traditional and the radical schools and as having exhibited necessary and significant development from the traditional school. Moreover, the reformist school not only often borrows from the radical school, but also often leads to the assumption of a radical posture.

The traditional school is defined by: 1) its defensive and/or reactive posture; 2) its lack of concern for the development of a Black psychology and its continued support of the Eurocentric model with minor changes; 3) its concern with changing white attitudes, and 4) its being essentially critical without offering substantive correctives. (Guthrie, 1970).

The reformist school represents a period of historical evolution as well as a current posture. It maintains some of the concern for white attitudes and behavior, but focuses more on change in public policy than on simply attitudinal change. Furthermore, this school begins to advocate an Afro-centric psychology but still combines it with traditional focus on appeal for change that would ostensibly benefit Blacks and whites and thus U.S. society (Thomas, 1971; Cross, 1971).

The radical school makes no appeal to whites and directs their attention instead to Black people in terms of analysis, treatment and transformation. Moreover, they insist on and are developing a psychology that has its roots in the African worldview which is opposite of and opposed to the European worldview (Jackson, 1982; King, et al, 1976). Moreover, the members of this school are socially conscious theorists and practitioners who advocate self-conscious participation of Black psychologists and Black people in the transformation of social reality through cultural and political struggle. This, of course, is in the Fanonian tradition which influenced many of them (Fanon, 1968, 1967).

PERSPECTIVES

THE TRADITIONAL SCHOOL

KENNETH CLARK. Clark who is the first and only Black to be president of the APA, early established himself with the citation of his work on the damaging effects of segregation by the U.S. Supreme Court in its historical *Brown vs. Board of Education* (1954) decision. The author of several books and articles, his work, *The Dark Ghetto: Dilemma of Social Power* (1965) stands out as a seminal work on the sociology and psychology of the ghetto. In chapter IV of his book, entitled the "Psychology of the Ghetto," he essentially gives a "traditional" analysis of segregation. He (1965:63) argues that "racial segregation, like all other forms of cruelty and tyranny, debases all human beings-those who are its victims, those who victimize, and in quite subtle ways those who are merely accessories."

The victims, Blacks, are essentially portrayed with little or no strengths, i.e., as fantasy-oriented, sexually excessive, matriarchal, irresponsible, etc. However, Clark does not attribute these negatives to Black inferiority, but to an insensitive and brutally segregated society which imposes these patterns of thought and behavior on Blacks. Clark argues that social (white) insensitivity is "a protective device" and criticizes some of its "primitive examples," i.e., labelling of Blacks as inferior and "subhuman persons who cause and perpetuate their own difficulties" (1965:75-76).

In addition, he criticizes those social scientists whose "preoccupation with trivia...leads to the irrelevance of much of social science research, and "detached professionalism," which, in reality is a false objectivity and masked insensitivity. And finally, he (1965:77, 80) criticizes the "professional perspective which constricts social vision to the impulses, strengths and weaknesses of the individual 'client' as if these can be isolated from the injustices and pathologies of his life,..." Such a detached and alleged objectivity, he concludes, serves "not to enlarge truth but to constrict it."

WILLIAM GRIER AND PRICE COBBS. Grier and Cobbs are best known for their work, _Black Rage_. Although it was written in a popular style, it nevertheless reflects some of the basic contentions of the traditionalist school. Like Clark, Grier and Cobbs are concerned with whites knowing what they are doing to Blacks in order to change their attitudes and behavior. Concerned with the implication of the mutual racial hostility, they (1968:2) assert that "if racist hostility is to subside and if we are to avoid conflict on a nationwide scale, information is the most desperate commodity of our time." And, they continue, "of all the things worth knowing, none is more important than that all Blacks are angry," - in a word enraged.

Having established the fact of Black rage, Grier and Cobbs then set out to explain its origins and expressions. They establish the effects of what they call the shadows of the past, i.e., slavery, arguing that through this oppression and its sequel, "The psyche of Black men has been distorted." But, they assert "their genius is that they have survived" through adaptations of both positive and negative dimensions (1968:31). Unwilling and/or unable to see significant distinctness in Black life, they (1968:29) contend that "the psychological principles first understood in the study of white men are true, no matter what the man's color." And they (1968:86) maintain that "all that is uniquely (Black) found its origins on these shores, and provides a living document of Black history in America."

In what seems to be a contradiction to the denial of Black uniqueness, Grier and Cobbs then set down some principles of a "Black norm" which they claim distinguishes black psychological postures from others but which are essentially a list of unsubstantiated and self-indicting negatives (1968:149ff). Among these are: 1) Blacks' understandable and necessary cultural paranoia; 2) their cultural depression and cultural masochism rising out of "sadness and intimacy with misery;" and 3) cultural anti-socialism, i.e., disrespect for white laws which are designed to protect whites not Blacks. They (1968:124) conclude that their "dismal tone is deliberate" in an attempt to stir the feelings of the reader to the "depression and hopelessness" Blacks feel daily.

ALVIN POUSSAINT. Poussaint's major work is his *Why Blacks Kill Blacks*. In this work, he covers a series of topics including Black Power, Black suicide, Black sexuality, and suggestions to white parents on how to raise their children free of prejudice. Criticizing the racial and socio-economic bias of traditional white psychiatry, Poussaint (1972:49ff) shows sensitivity to Black "suspicion of its concepts and practice" and their tendency to label it the "white man's psychology." He (1972:51) states that not only have white psychiatrists preferred to treat members of their own race and class, but their "short-sighted training...has made it impossible for them to distinguish deviant behavior from what is in fact *different* behavior." In this regard, he (1972:54) argues for "understanding special cultural adaptations or interests" of Blacks, if white psychiatrists are to be effective clinicians. For he (1972:55) believes that "despite obvious handicaps, some white psychiatrists are sensitive to the Black experience and have helped all types of Black patients."

In his chapter on "Why Blacks Kill Blacks," Poussaint (1972: 69-70) beings by criticizing deficient modeling of Blacks as "culturally deprived" and "socially disadvantaged" and "culturally paranoid." These labels would fit the racist more than the Black, he argues. Likewise, the "creation of self-serving theories by some white academicians" about how Blacks hate themselves is not only exaggerated, but "another subtle attempt to maintain the oppressor's false sense of superiority." In fact, "it is likely," he maintains, "that whites have more self-hate and insecurity than we do, since they need racism to maintain a sense of self."

Recognizing, however, that there are negatives among Blacks and that crime and violence by Blacks against each other is a

serious problem, he posits several reasons for it. Among these are:
1) the American cultural experience that teaches "crime and violence as a way to success and manhood;" 2) the fact that "Americans respect violence and often will not respond to just demand except through violence" as with the revolts; 3) the sense of power violence gives the oppressed; and 4) dehumanizing transformation in incarceration which perpetuates the cycle of violence. Poussaint, however, rushes to say, that regardless of the blame white society must shoulder for the Black condition, Blacks, in the final analysis, must move to intervene in and transform their own lives and life-conditions. This essentially means development of community programs which check the negatives and the development of "deep self-love that ends the self-defeating behavior among ourselves."

THE REFORMIST SCHOOL

CHARLES THOMAS. Thomas is one of the founders and first co-chairpersons of the ABP and was instrumental in shaping the early moves of Black psychology from the negatives of the traditional school. He and others of the school stand as bridges between the traditional and radical schools, attempting a synthesis of the social and discipline criticism of the traditional school and the demands for and development of new models and professional engagement from the radical schools. Thomas' book, *Boys No More*, and subsequent articles represent this attempt toward synthesis.

Thomas (1979, 1971) begins by assigning Black psychologists the fundamental task of "instructive intervention" which leads to change in Black attitudes, self-mastery, social competence and personal fulfillment. He asserts that social scientists have an ethical responsibility for changing the Black condition "by defining, defending and developing information systems that will give Blacks increased socio-political power" (1979:7). Thus, he rejects the simple treatment-centered therapy and urges community engagement for the psychology.

Secondly, Thomas (1974) argues the significance of the Ethnocentrism factor. By ethnocentrism or ethicity, he means, focus on and pride in one's bio-social identity - in this case, one's Blackness. For Thomas, ethnicity not only provides the "frame of reference-...for the development of countervailing social forces and institutions it encourages self-activiated behavior and breaks down patterns of self-hate and self-denial. Thomas contends that within the context of Black oppression four major social roles were generated to meet it: "hybrid or bad niggers, conformists or good negroes, marginalists or white middle class negroes and rebels or Black 'militants.' " Each group not only represents a search for identity but except for the last one, they also represent "modes of escape which are ineffective." This is so for the flight from oneself essentially means a flight from one's humanity. Ethnicity as a proactive alternative, then, poses and cultivates "the renewed thrust toward self-esteem, environmental mastery, definition of self in terms of potential and a variety of other concerns around intervention or prevention of pathological cognition..."

Also, Thomas (1978:11ff) is concerned about the damage done by white or other social scientists who "have confused knowledge *about* a people with knowledge *of a people*." The first is superficial learning from without and imposing a conceptual framework; the latter is learning from within the group and sharing its conceptual framework. The bio-asocialists who deny cultural differences, the cultural pathologists who are "preoccupied with the victim of oppression rather than with oppressive institutions," and the integrationists which limit social options on the assumption that Blacks "ought to be white or placed in situations where they can be treated as if white," all fit in this category of deficient and damaging social science.

Finally, Thomas (1978, 1971) poses deficient-deficit modeling as a major problem of Black psychology as well as for Blacks in terms of its implications for public policy and self-actualization.

Examples of this are terms such as minority, and all its variations, i.e., minority status, culture, etc., disadvantaged, culturally deprived negro, etc. He (1978:21-22) states that "if 'Blackness' came into existence as a healthy support state, it cannot be logically used as a symptomatology of maladaptive behavior." The need, then, is for imaginative cross cultural conceptual models which press for para-cultural (equal rather than sub-cultural) frames of reference.

JOSEPH WHITE. Although White has written other articles, his "Toward A Black Psychology," written in 1970, is seen as an important piece of literature in the early criticism of and move from the traditional school of psychology. In fact, he (1980:5) begins his article, arguing that "it is very difficult, if not impossible to understand the life styles of Black people using the traditional theories developed by white psychologists to explain white people." Furthermore, "when these traditional theories are applied to the lives of Black folks, many incorrect, weakness-dominated, and inferiority-oriented conclusions come about."

White maintains that traditional psychology's use of "an Anglo middle-class frame of reference" gives it a distorted view of the adaptive vitality of Black children and the Black family. Instead of a correct and positive view, hypotheses of cultural deprivation and matriarchal families are advanced. His contention is that a Black frame of reference is necessary which will enable Black psychologists and others "to come up with a more accurate and comprehensive explanations" of Black life, as well as enable them "to build the kinds or programs within the Black world which capitalize on the strengths of Black people" (White, 1980:8).

He also argues "that not all traditional white psychological theory is useless." The existentialists' stress on pain and struggle as unavoidable and the self-theorists' stress on understanding one's experiential background to understand a person are examples of useful theories. The need, then, in building a Black psychology is to incorporate what is useful and reject the rest. Finally, White (1970:11) argues the value of Black/white dialogue and exchange in encounter groups, suggesting they give whites a better chance to experience Blackness "outside the protective group setting."

WILLIAM CROSS. Concerned with the prevalence and negatives of Western thought and science, and the need for "psychological liberation under conditions of oppression," Cross (1971:13) offered a model suggesting the stages persons go through in the process of the "Negro-to-Black conversion." In a subsequent article, comparing this model to one Thomas developed, he (1980) terms these models of "nigrescence," i.e., the process of becoming Black. The first stage of nigrescence is the *pre-encounter* (or prediscovery) stage in which the person is out of touch with himself/herself racially and "the person's worldview is dominated by Euro-American determinants" causing him/her to act in manners which degrade and deny Blackness (Cross, 1971:15ff).

The second or *encounter* (discovery) stage involves a shocking personal or social event which pushes the person past his/her old conceptions of Black and Black conditions to an intense search for Black identity. The third stage is one of immersion-emersion. In the first phase, there is an intense involvement in being and demonstrating Blackness and rejection and condemnation of white people and culture. In the second phase, there is a levelling off and emergence from either/or and racist positions and the oversimplified aspects of Blackness, as well as acceptance of white humanity. Stage four is one of *internalization,* a sense of security, receptivity to discussion, and action and resolution of the conflict between the old and the new. The final state is *internalization-commitment* in which one "becomes the new identity and pro-Black attitudes become more expansive, open and less-defensive."

In focusing in on and criticizing Blacks for high levels of racial identity and severe rejection of whites and white values in the immersion phase, Cross seems to demonstrate again the reformist school's concern for relations with whites. This is not to say or imply that this represents servility, but to make the point that this is clearly an issue the radical school would neither raise, be concerned with, nor agree with. On the contrary, the radical school would see questioning of white humanity and total rejection of their values as positives.

THE RADICAL SCHOOL

NA'IM AKBAR. Akbar's (1981, 1976, 1974) critique of the traditional psychology model begins with the historical fact that African-Americans have been victims of intellectual as well as physical oppression. "Intellectual oppression," he asserts (1981:18), "involves the abusive use of ideas, labels and concepts geared toward the mental degradation of a people." And, he states, "there is no area in which mental or intellectual oppression is more clearly illustrated than...the area of mental health judgement." In such a context not only are white oppressors' sanity not questioned, but Black mental health is not linked with the social conditions which shaped it.

The white oppressor, Akbar, (1981:18, 49) states, uncertain as to "what constituted a normal human being" established a kind of "democratic sanity" model of mental health. This was a kind of "majority rule application to mental health judgment, i.e., insane behavior was determined "on the basis of the degree to which it deviated from the majority's behavior in a given context." This approach had the tragic consequence of judging sane and competent "entire communities of raving inhuman lunatics...because the majority of people in that particular context either participated in the questionable behavior or refused to question (it)." It is, Akbar maintains, clearly necessary to raise questions about the mental health standards and mental competence of a people who enslaved, terrorized and murdered numerous non-hostile peoples throughout the world.

Secondly, Akbar (1981:20) criticizes white scientists for "acquiring great scholarly renown for documenting deficits of Afro-Americans," a pathology perspective based on the norm and context of the people who uphold the "democratic sanity" standard. Thirdly, he (1981:20) criticizes Black traditionalists like Clark and Grier and Cobbs for "following the lead of Caucasian scholars in both conceptualizing and analyzing problems." He especially critizes Grier and Cobbs for their "guide to the neurotic Negro," *Black Rage,* and their overgeneralization and use of the pathology model in it. Moreover, he concludes that the traditional school: 1) equates mental health with imitation of white middle class behavior; 2) assumes similarity of sources of Black and white behavior; and 3) assumes "democratic sanity" standards are "reflective of human standards documented by thousands of years of human history."

Fourthly, he argues that these and other traditional psychologists fail to take into consideration "two essential variables in determining the adequacy of human behavior:" 1) the historical antecedents, or determinants of the behavior; and 2) the effects of inhuman conditions on the human being. As a result of these failures, there are attempts to eliminate or diminish many behaviors in African Americans "which are essential to their survival and development."

Having critiqued the traditional school, Akbar defines mental health in proactive terms as a state "reflected in those behaviors which foster mental growth and awareness (i.e., mental life)." Mental illness, then, is posed as reflected in "ideas and forces within the mind that threaten awareness and mental growth. It also can mean from an extended self concept, disorders reflected in "behaviors or ideas which threaten the survival of the collective self," i.e., one's people. Given these definitions, one can understand the reasoning of an insane parasitic people which justifies domination as a mode of survival and the reasoning of the dominated people which poses liberation as a mode of survival and development.

Finally, within the framework of his definitions, Akbar (1981) poses four kinds of disorders which threaten Black life and development, i.e., "anti-life forces." These are the alien-self disorder, a socialization to be other than oneself on a race, class and sex level; the anti-self disorder, which expresses "overt and covert hostility towards the groups of one's origin and thus one's self;" the self-destructive disorder, a destructive retreat from reality, i.e., drugs, etc.; and organic disorders, physiological, neurological or bio-chemical malfunctions. He (1982:25) concludes noting that these four disorders, it must be remembered, all emanate from "a psychopatic society typified by oppression and racism," a situation which must be changed for Blacks to "realize the full power of their human potential."

JOSEPH BALDWIN. Within the context of his contribution to Black psychology, Baldwin (1980, 1976) focuses in on the function of definitional systems in liberation and oppression. Definitional systems are key, he (1980:96) posits, for they "determine how we experience (perceive and respond to) the various phenomena that characterize the ongoing process of everyday existence." Moreover, the definitional system or worldview represents the ideological or philosophical base of a social system or a people and thus determine the meanings or values a people attach to their experience including their experience of themselves and how they will react.

The problem, however, arises, Baldwin argues, when an alien worldview is imposed on and/or accepted by a people, leaving that people at the mercy of definitions negative to their image and interests. Such is the case of Blacks under white domination.

According to Baldwin, race, i.e., biogenetic commonality, "constitutes the principal binding condition underlying the evolution of definitional system which "in their most basic fundamental nature have a 'racial character.' "

Given this, what passes and is pushed as a universal worldview turns out to be nothing more than a European definitional system. This system is not only diametrically opposed to Black interests, but reinforces a distorted reality in the image and interests of the Europeans. Thus, African Americans "operate in a space dominated primarily by a definitional framework which does not and cannot give legitimacy to our African social reality" (1980:108). Complicating resistance to this state of things, Baldwin (1980:101) contends is that the "Europeans control the formal process of social reinforcements," i.e., economics and political power. This gives them power to impose their "definitions and the experiential confirmations on the experiences of Black people in society."

Although there has been some Black resistance to this imposition, it has "not necessarily been of a highly conscious form," that is to say, "it has not generally taken the form of a carefully planned or necessarily intentional collective resistance" (1980:106) Thus, if Blacks are to liberate themselves and validate and expand their own African definitional system and social reality, "*conscious, collective resistance* is ultimately required." This of necessity requires a "clear frame of reference from which to ultimately examine the psychological nature of (Black) oppression" (1980:107). This in turn demands a Black psychology, Baldwin concludes, which not only explain the "ongoing process of psychological genocide," but contributes to a critical understanding of Euro-American society by which African people can "ultimately achieve the fullness of psychological and physical liberation from it."

WADE NOBLES. Clearly Nobles (1980, 1976) is the pioneer and most quoted in the area of using African philosophy as a foundation for Black psychology. In his seminal essay on the subject, Nobles (1980:23) begins by arguing that black psychology is more the psychology of the underprivileged, the ghettoized or the enslaved and more than the 'darker' dimension of general psychology. In a word, "Its unique status," "is derived not from the negative aspects of being Black in white America," he argues, "but rather from the positive features of basic African philosophy which dictates the values, customs, attitudes and behavior of Africans in Africa and the New World."

Nobles argues that what we have here is a commonality of consciousness based on guiding beliefs, an ethos which is at the core of African philosophy. This ethos determines two operational orders - the notions of oneness with nature and of the survival of one's people. Given its distinctiveness from the white ethos and its place at the center of African philosophy, African philosophy easily and effectively serves as the foundation for Black psychology. A study of African philosophy shows several fundamental themes which not only explain African philosophy, but also African (Black) psychology.

First, one sees the rootedness of philosophy in religion. Religion, in turn, was life-practice, not sect or church or Sunday or proselytizing. "Traditional Africans made no distinction between the act and the belief" (1980:25). Secondly, the notion of unity of humans with God and the whole universe is key to African philosophy. A third key concept is the concept of time which is/was essentialy "a composition of events" in two dimensions, the past and present, which are experienced rather than calculated. A fourth fundamental concept is that of death and immortality through recognition and remembrance. A final concept is one of kinship or collective unity which created a sense of collective identity, i.e., an extended self.

What this explanation of African philosophical themes does is demonstrate a distinctiveness of philosophy and psychology. The point now, Nobles (1980:31) contends is to " 'prove' that Africans living the Western world and in contemporary times still have or maintain an African philosophical definition." Thus, there is a need for demonstration of links and ways Black express and African perception of reality. Nobles argues that several Africanisms did survive slavery and contemporary times. The first is the stress on the survival of the people which expressed itself in a mentality and structures like benevolent societies and the church. Also the idea of a man being inseparable, one with nature and the community is a surviving Africanism. Oral tradition in the form of folktales, the dozens, rappin, etc., have also survived. Finally, the concept of time as phenomenal, potential and flexible rather than mathematical as expressed in CP time is also a surviving Africanism. These, Nobles (1980:35) states, are some examples which demonstrate a distinctiveness of Black consciousness rooted in and reflective of African philosophy. "The task of Black psychology, (then), is to offer an understanding of the behavioral definitions of African philosophy and to document what if any, modifications it has undergone during particular experiential periods" in the U.S.

FRANCES CRESS WELSING. Welsing, (1970, 1980) a noted psychiatrist, advances one of the most controversial and discussed theories in the area of Black psychology, "The Cress Theory of Color-Confrontation and Racism (White Supremacy)." Welsing builds on the contentions of Neeley Fuller in his *Textbook for Victims of White Supremacy* (1969). Fuller essentially argued that: 1) white supremacy was the only functional racism; 2) all Third World peoples are victims of it; 3) racism is not merely an individual or institutional phenomena, but a universal system of domination; and 4) that European theories and systems of political and economic organization are designed to establish, insure and expand white domination.

Having accepted these essential contentions, Welsing developed them further and advance other ones. First, she (1970:5) argued that the white supremacy drive is in fact like other neurotic drives for superiority or domination "founded upon a deep and pervading sense of inadequacy and inferiority." Secondly, she contends that the basis for this neurotic disorder is found in the "quality of whiteness (which) is indeed a genetic inadequacy or a relative genetic deficiency, state or disease based upon the genetic inability to produce the skin pigments of melanin which are responsible for all skin coloration."

Whiteness as the absence of color or "the very absence of any ability to produce color" is in the minority in the world given that "the massive majority of the world's people are not so afflicted." Thus, the color normality in the majority throws light on the abnormality of the colorless minority. Moreover, given that "color always annihilates' phenotypically and genetically speaking, the non-color, white," and given their numerical minority status, whites are faced with the constant fear of genetic extinction (1970:6). Therefore, Welsing continues, "an uncontrollable sense of hostility and aggression developed defensively which has continued to manifest itself throughout the entire historical epoch of mass confrontations of the whites with peoples of color."

Welsing contends that this "sense of numerical inadequacy and genetic color inferiority" led whites not only to dominate, destroy and deform Third World peoples, but also to alienation and self-hatred as well as defense mechanisms to handle these feelings. Among these are: 1) repression of the inadequacy-inferiority feeling by denying it; 2) discrediting and despising Black and other colors of skin; 3) suntaning and making up to acquire color; 4) elaborating myths of white genetic superiority as with Jensen's and other racist theories; 5) projection of their hate and sexual desires on Third World peoples, pretending it is they who hate and lust after whites; 6) obsessive focus on the body yet alienated from sex because of inability to produce color; 7) dividing Third World people into factions to make them minorities; and 8) imposing birth control on Third World people to limit or reverse their majority number. Welsing (1970:10) concludes that if Third World people are armed with the above insights, this will indeed reduce their vulnerability to manipulation, messages of white supremacy and contribute to their psychological liberation from the white racist ideology which so dominates their lives.

AMOS WILSON. Focusing on the psychological development of the Black child, Wilson (1981:1978), contributes to the project of defining the tasks and parameters of Black psychology. Wilson (1981:8) argues as Nobles and others that an understanding of the psychology of Blacks - adults and children, demands that the study of Blacks begin in Africa, not in slavery. Moreover, he (1981:10) argues that Black psychology must be extremely careful about the application of European based psychology and the use of its models. In fact, he suggests white psychology does not even adequately explain white people who "seem bent on destroying themselves as well as the rest of the world."

Drawing on the growing interest in melanin and its properties, Wilson (1981:10) contends, that the study of melanin is important in the study of Black people. Arguing that the history of Blacks are in their genes, he suggests Black superiority in the areas of mental development, neurological functioning and psychomotor development of the Black child which are all related to the possession of a high level of melanin. Melanin, he contends, is not simply a coloring agent, but "an integral part of the body system itself operating in the brain." In fact, the ability of the Black child to survive and the comparative long life of Blacks are related to their Blackness.

Wilson (1981:12) is also concerned that Blacks have been reduced to use only one side of their brain. This right side, he states "processes information...deals with the world in a holistic fashion and (also) processes music and art." The left side is the analytical side which develops technology, mathematics and so forth. But "the side of the brain an individual uses is determined by experience," therefore, "if we look at the history and experience of Blacks in America, we see essentially that the European has rewarded Blacks for using the right brain," i.e., singing, dancing, music and sports. On the other hand, because whites "are afraid of intellectually assertive Black people," Blacks are discriminated against and discovered from using the left side, i.e., the linguistic and analytical. The need is thus for a balance, for "the ultimate human being is the one who can balance between the use of both sides of the brain."

Finally, Wilson (1981:12) maintains that one of the major problems of Black child development "is determining how we can maintain the intellectual and psychological advance that nature has given our children." It is here, he states, that we see the inadequacy of white child psychology for "the issues and questions that the Black psychologist must address are distinctively different." This essentially demands the development of an educational psychology and methodology directed toward "the reconstruction of the personality and the orientation of our children" (Wilson, 1981:13).

Such a thrust would be directed toward educational and cultural change which not only stimulates the brain, but teaches children how to think, not simply prepares them for jobs but also facilitates and encourages high levels of self-development and service to their people. For "Blacks who are not conscious of their Blackness, who have no sense of destiny, and then go through (white systems of education) ultimately end up serving their own oppressors and become a means of oppressing their own people." Therefore, Black liberation depends on an educational system for Black children based on a psychological model which builds on and develops Black strengths in order "to create an intelligent, independent thinking, interpretive and critical person committed to working tirelessly in the interest of Black people."

BOBBY WRIGHT. Although Wright (1981; 1975) has written other pieces in Black psychology, his fundamental and most-known work is *The Psychopathic Racial Personality*. In this essay, he poses whites as the mortal danger to Black people and seeks to analyze their behavior to demonstrate this. The urgency of such an analysis, he suggests, is due to the fact that this period in history is critical to blacks' future. Using the analogy of a bull fight in which the bull finally stops charging the cape blindly, sees the "matador" and faces "the moment of truth," he (1975:3) argues that "this is indeed Blacks moment of truth and it is time for them to look at the matador."

According to Wright, European "matadors" have for hundreds of years held up various banners to distract and delude Black people, i.e., "such concepts as democracy, capitalism, Marxism, religion and education." But now these banners, Wright contends, have been reduced to one-genocide, as evidenced in the development of genetic chemical, electrical surgical and other behavioral control strategies. This emerges from the fact that due to technological development and the worldwide struggle for resources, "Blacks are now a threat and a liability to the white race." It is in such a context that the understanding of the white "matador" becomes imperative.

Wright (1975:3) states at the outset that the basic premise of his work "is that in their relationship with the Black race Europeans (whites) are psychopaths." Moreover, he states that this "behavior reflects an underlying biologically transmitted proclivity with roots deep in their evolutionary history." He defines a psychopath as "one who is constantly in conflict with others,...unable to experience guilt, completely selfish and callous and has total disregard for the rights of others."

Expanding his analysis, Wright focuses on evidence of behavior traits which he reasons proves his contentions and demands Black consideration. He (1975:5) asserts that key to understanding the psychopathic personality is its "almost complete absence of ethical or moral development and an almost total disregard for appropriate patterns of behavior." This is expressed in the fact that whites have "historically oppressed, exploited and killed Black people - all in the name of their God Jesus...and with the sanction of the churches" (Wright, 1975:6). The activities of the KKK, a white Christian organization and the Pope blessing Italian planes and pilots on their way to bomb Ethiopia without provocation are cited as examples.

Secondly, Wright maintains, the psychopath is also defined by the lack of "concern or commitment except to their own interests" and becoming indignant and angry when they are exposed or questioned. The unkept promises of the 60's by whites and their attitude toward Black liberation and progress are examples of this. Also, Wright argues that "the psychopath is usually sexually inadequate with a very limited capacity to form close interpersonal relationships." This is exhibited in whites in their constant projection of excessive sexuality on Blacks, although it is they "who 'streak,' 'mate swap,' participate in orgies, etc."

Fourthly, the psychopath has a marked "inability to accept blame (or) to learn from previous experience." Whites "never accept blame for Blacks environmental conditions which is clearly the result of white oppression" (1975:7). Instead, Blacks are held responsible. Also, attempts to sensitize and change them fail because of their inability fo feel guilt. Finally, the psychopath rejects authority and discipline. Even when their own laws are the authority, they reject them, if it is not in their interests as Blacks "who seek legal solutions to their problems" discover (1975:8).

Given this kind of adversary, "the inevitable question is what should Blacks do?" (1975:9). First, Wright suggests that Blacks must cast aside illusions that a psychopathic oppressor can provide strategies of liberation for those they oppress. Secondly, Blacks must recognize the oppressors as waging war against them and respond in equal measure. And finally, he (1975:11) states that they should seek the "answer to Blacks problems in the works and lives of Black heroes" and heroines "whose minds have moved past the psychopath's imposed boundaries and have begun to blaze new paths towards Blacks' rendezvous with destiny."

ETHOS

The stress on the radical restructuring of the consciousness of Black people and persons by Black psychologists finds its logical parallel and support in the Kawaida contentions concerning the need for a proactive and positive ethos among Afro-Americans (Karenga, 1980: Chapter VIII). Kawaida defines ethos "as the sum of characteristics and achievements of a people which define and distinguish it from others and gives it its collective self-consciousness and collective personality" (Karenga, 1980:90). Put another way, "the ethos of a people is often called its national or ethnic character which is not only defined by itself, but also assumed by others."

Now, ethos, or a people's self-consciousness and self-definition is defined by their thought and practice in the other six fundamental areas of culture, i.e., history, religion, social organization, economic organization, political organization and creative production. This means essentially that we know ourselves and are known by what we have done and do. And from our knowledge of self and others' knowledge or perception of us, we acquire our self-concept. Thus, the Egyptian-Africans contributions to the establishment of the major disciplines of human knowledge defines them in their own eyes as well as the world's. Moreover, the Moorish African contribution to the civilization of Europe, the African contribution to Olmec civilization and Afro-Americans' contribution to the social and cultural wealth of the U.S. and its political liberation and development, all indicate sources of positive self-consciousness and self-definition.

The achievement of a positive ethos lies then in historical and current struggle and achievement. The struggle can be seen as an ongoing struggle of humans, in this case Blacks, to realize themselves. In Kawaida theory, self-realization has a double meaning, i.e., to know *and* to produce oneself. To know oneself is to grasp the essences of one's past, one's present and especially one's future possibilities and thereby know who you are by what you have done and thus what you are capable of doing and becoming based on past achievement and current conditions. To produce oneself, is to create oneself through struggle against natural and social oppositions and through knowledge of what and who you can and ought to be. Thus, self-knowledge and self-production are at the heart of ethos and are clearly linked. For as a people struggles to overcome basic oppositions, then, it creates and defines itself and informs the world of its difference and distinctiveness, i.e., its ethos. Thus, *a people comes into being and knows itself by its achievements, and through its efforts to become and know itself, it achieves.*

Given this, it is a fundamental Kawaida contention that a people whose achievements are minor or whose knowledge of its history and the possibilities it suggests is deficient, develops a self-consciousness of similar characteristics. Moreover, in a social context which denies and deforms a people's capacity to realize itself, the problem of self-consciousness is not simply a problem of thought, but also a problem of practice (Karenga, 1982). For the demand to end a deficient consciousness must be joined to a demand to eliminate the conditions which caused it. This is why Black psychologists advocate the social intervention model of psychology advanced by Fanon (1967:11) who argued mental health demanded a solution on both the subjective (mental) and objective (social) level.

In conclusion, then, the problem of self-consciousness is solved in the process of solving the social problems which cause it. This essentially means that through *study, work* and *struggle*, building and becoming, Blacks' real self, hidden under layers of false roles and identities imposed by the dominant society, will emerge. Through these self-conscious efforts and the resultant achievements in the various areas of human thought and practice as well as the model of work and liberational struggle Africans in America establish, they will, as I (Karenga, 1980:114) stated, transform themselves into a distinct self-realized and "self-conscious historical personality, proud of its past, challenged by the present and inspired by the possibilities of the future."

STUDY QUESTIONS

1. Define psychology stressing the reasons for its human focus.

2. Give and historical summary of the development of Black psychology.

3. What are the defining aspects of the traditional school of Black psychology?

4. What are some defining aspects of the reformist school of Black psychology?

5. What are some defining aspects of the radical school of Black psychology?

6. Discuss critically the contentions of the traditional psychologists presented.

7. Discuss critically the contentions of the reformist psychologists presented.

8. Discuss critically the contentions of the radical psychologists presented.

9. Define and discuss the Kawaida conception of ethos.

10. Discuss the link between self-consciousness, social achievement and social struggle.

REFERENCES

Akbar, Na'im (Luther X Weems). (1974) "Awareness: The Key to Black Mental Health," Journal of Black Psychology, 1, 1 (August) 30-37.

_____ . (1981) "Mental Disorder Among African-Americans," Black Books Bulletin, 7, 2:18-25

_____ . (1976) "Rhythmic Patterns in African Personality," in African Philosophy, Assumption & Paradigms for Research on Black Persons, (eds.) Lewis King, et al, Los Angeles: Fanon Center Publication, pp. 175-189.

Baldwin, Joseph. (1976) "Black Psychology and Black Personality: Some Issues for Consideration," Black Books Bulletin, 4, 3:6-11.

_____ . (1980) "The Psychology of Oppression," in Contemporary Black Thought, (eds.) Molefi K. Asante and Abdulai S. Vandi, Beverly Hills: Sage Publications, pp. 95-110.

Clark, Kenneth. (1965) Dark Ghetto, New York: Harper & Row.

Cross, William E., Jr. (1980) "Models of Psychological Nigrescence: A Literature Review," in Black Psychology, (ed.) Reginald L. Jones, New York: Harper & Row.

_____ . (1971) "The Negro-To-Black Conversation Experience," Black World, (July) 13-27.

Fanon, Frantz. (1967) Black Skin, White Masks, New York: Grove Press.

_____ . (1968) The Wretched of the Earth, New York: Grove Press.

Grier, William H. and Price M. Cobbs (1968) Black Rage, New York: Bantam Books.

Guthrie, Robert V. (1970) *Being Black,* San Francisco: Canfield Press.

_____. (1976) *Even The Rat Was White,* New York: Harper & Row.

Jackson, Gerald G. (1982) "Black Psychology: An Avenue to the Study of Afro-Americans," *Journal of Black Studies,* 12, 3 (March) 241-261.

_____. (1979) "The Origin and Development of Black Psychology Implications for Black Studies and Human Behavior," *Studia Africana,* 1, 3 (Fall) 270-293.

Jones, Reginald. (1980) *Black Pscyhology,* New York: Harper & Row.

Kagan, Jerome and Ernest Havemann. (1976) *Psychology,* New York: Harcourt Brace Jovanovich.

Karenga, Maulana. (1978) "Chinese Psycho-Social Therapy: A Strategic Model for Mental Health," *Psychotherapy: Theory: Research and Practice,* 15, 1 (Spring) 101-107.

_____. (1980) *Kawaida Theory: An Introductory Outline,* Inglewood, Ca.: Kawaida Publications.

_____. (1982) "Society, Culture and the Problem of Self-Consciousness: A Kawaida Analysis," in *Philosophy Born of Struggle,* (ed.) Leonard Harris, Dubuque, IA: Kendall/Hunt.

King, Lewis M. et al (eds.). (1976) *African Philosophy,* Los Angeles: Fanon Center Publication.

Nobles, Wade W. (1980) "African Philosophy: Foundations for Black Psychology," in *Black Psychology,* (ed.) Reginald L. Jones, New York: Harper & Row, 23-36.

_____. (1976) "Black People in White Insanity: Issues for Black Commmunity Mental Health," *Journal of Afro-American Issues,* 4, 1:21-27.

Poussaint, Alvin F. (1972) *Why Blacks Kill Blacks,* New York: Emerson Hall Publishers.

Thomas, Charles W. (1971) *Boys No More,* Beverly Hills: Glencoe Press.

_____. (1978) "The Need for an Ethinically Specific Social Science," lecture, Tuskegee Institute, Tuskegee, Alabama, April 27.

_____. (1974) "The Significance of the E (thnocentrism) Factor in Mental Health," *Journal of Non-White Concerns in Personal Guidance,* 2, 2.

_____. (1979) "The Social Significance of Research," paper presented at Howard University Mental Health Research and Development Center, May 1-3.

Welsing, Frances Cress. (1980) "The Concept and the Color of God and Black Mental Health," *Black Books Bulletin,* 7, 1:27ff.

_____. (1970) *The Cress Theory of Color Confrontation and Racism (White Supremacy),* Washington, D.C.: C-R Publishers.

White, Joseph. (1980) "Toward a Black Psychology," in *Black Psychology,* (ed.) Reginald L. Jones, New York: Harper & Row, 5-12.

Williams, Robert. (1974) "A History of the Association of Black Psychologists: Early Formation and Development," *Journal of Black Psychology,* 1, 1 (August) 7-24

Wilson, Amon N. (1978) *The Developmental Psychology of the Black Child,* New York: Africana Research Publications.

_____. (1981) "The Psychological Development of the Black Child," *Black Books Bulletin,* 7, 2:8-14.

Wright, Bobby E. (1981) "Black Suicide: Lynching by Any Other Name is Still Lynching," *Black Books Bulletin,* 7,2:15-17.

_____. (1975) *The Psychopathic Racial Personality,* Chicago: Third World Press.

IX
CHALLENGES AND POSSIBILITIES

INTRODUCTION

Inspite of its established relevance, Black Studies now faces challenges which, depending on the process and effectiveness of their solution, will determine and shape its future on campuses across the country. Although these challenges suggest severe tests, the successful meeting of these challenges can only enhance the possibilities of further expansion and development of the discipline. These challenges are both external and internal to Black Studies, but are clearly interrelated. Although I use the category *challenge* here, many in the discipline consider the word, *crisis,* a more definitive category to express the problems and pressure now confronting Black Studies. I have, in fact, also used this category, but in keeping with the positive and proactive thrust of this work, I have decided to use challenge instead. This is essentially because a challenge by definition is a demanding task or problem which calls for special effort, dedication and struggle.

Surely, the problems and tasks confronting Black Studies demand special commitment and effort to solve and complete. Crisis on the other hand suggests a turning point and great dangers, but does not bring to mind for most people its other aspect, great possibilities through bold planning and action. Thus, the category challenge here is preferable, for it not only contains emphasis on tasks and problems, but also special dedication, effort and struggle to complete and solve them. A listing of these basic

350

challenges to Black Studies will aid in demonstrating the value of such an approach. In this context, two broad categories of challenges stand out: (1) the political challenge; and (2) the intellectual challenge. However, before discussing these challenges, it is important to put these challenges in historical perspective by providing a background of conditions which led to the current state of things.

BACKGROUND

The current challenges to Black Studies appear, upon analysis, to be rooted in the very process of its birth and development as a discipline. Three fundamental factors among others contributed directly and most definitively to the development of these challenges. The first of these was the fact that initially Black Studies was not simply an academic enterprise, but also a political one. As outlined in the Introduction, Black Studies was part of the overall demand of the Black community for meaningful and effective participation in every decision and process that affected their destiny and daily lives. In fact, the struggle for Black Studies was viewed and posed as part of the overall struggle to rescue and reconstruct Black history and humanity and free Black minds and labor for Black people's use and benefit. As Nathan Hare (1972:33) observed, "early advocates of Black Studies sought both the collective elevation of a people with education of, from and for the masses, and the training of a mass minded Black conscious middle class."

Also another expression of the political character and shaping of the Black Studies enterprises is that Black Studies rose, not from internal administrative enlightenment and decision to expand university offerings, but out of a struggle by Black students deeply immersed in the thought and movement of Black liberation. As I argued above, the demand for Black Studies is unavoidably linked to the rise of the militant Black Student Movement in the 60's. "In fact, it is no exaggeration to say that the establishment of hundreds of Black Studies curricula in colleges and universities across the land was a major achievement of the Black Student Movement..." (Allen, 1974:2).

This dual interrelated thrust to create Black Studies from the Black Liberation Movement in general and the Black Student Movement in particular was a political thrust as well as an academic one. This provoked cries of politicization of education and facile arguments against Black Studies by hostile administrators already eager to oppose what was considered an intrusion in the traditional academic arena. Also, this political thrust often led to the subordination of academic demands to political interpretations of relevance and to periodic halts in academic work and intellectual production. This, among other things, certainly interrupted necessary instruction and contributed to diminished production of literature in the field.

A second factor contributive to the current challenges to Black Studies is the fact that those who posed the issue struggled for and won a space for Black Studies on campus were and are not the same who were brought in and chosen for the administration of the programs or departments (Brisbane, 1974:223-237). The students who spearheaded and led the struggle were obviously incapable of administration of the programs they fought for and won. Likewise, their community-organization allies could only obtain temporary teaching positions, never administrative ones. Thus, their theoretical orientation, their principles and motivations never became a fundamental part of the spirit, thought or practice in the discipline of Black Studies. In the place of these principles and motivations were inserted the ideas, interests and orientations of four basic types of administrators who shaped Black Studies in their own images and threatened to bring it to the brink of impotence and irrelevance on several campuses.

The four types of administrators, i.e., chairs, coordinators and directors, which assumed leadership of Black Studies were: (1) the pragmatists; (2) the Continental and Caribbean Africans; (3) the integrationists; and (4) the opportunists. The pragmatists were essentially resistant to ideological emphases and necessities. Instead, they reduced Black Studies to what was essentially an administrative and public relations program. Their guiding principles were legitimacy, harmony and action-by-the-book. Brisbane (1974:239) described the product of the pragmatists when he spoke of the courses offered at leading Black institutions like Howard, Morgan, Atlanta, Fisk, and Lincoln. The courses these pragmatists put together to defuse the demands for Black Studies "consisted principally of the regular curriculum plus a few additional courses in Black history, politics, art, religion and the like." In fact, "none of them appeared to reflect a genuine long-term commitment to the teaching of the Black Experience." Afterall, the point for the pragmatists was not to be ideological or inventive, but rather to be successful in defusing the force of radical demands and reduce everything to efficient administration and effective public relations.

Many Continental and Caribbean African administrators often came with less stake and orientation in the struggle for Black Studies and/or Afro-American liberation and thus, with less commitment to build Black Studies in the image of the politically-oriented groups who demanded and fought for its existence on campus. They were usually more acceptable to white administrators because of their non-problematic nationality, i.e., non-American, which often mean less or no stake in the struggle and thus, less tendency to challenge or try to link what was considered to be essentially an academic enterprise to the embarrassing and disruptive demands of the Black community. Moreover, they were the prototype Blacks (Continentals) or at least considered not as "mixed" (Caribbeans) as "so-called negroes" and therefore, often exempt from the intense criticism Afro-American academic brokers in similar roles were subjected to by Afro-American radicals and moderates alike. In a word, they easily met the racial criteria and often escaped the political criticism in the name of Pan-African unity and through the naive assumption that Blackness was a function of geographical origin rather than cultural consciousness and political struggle.

It is this uncritical acceptance, the tendency toward accommodationist academics by many Continentals and Caribbeans, the lack of strong, viable links with the Afro-American community struggle among many of them and white administrator's apparent preference for them over Afro-Americans which began to prove problematic for Black Studies. Moreover, another problem was the tendency of many of the Continentals and Caribbeans to focus on Continental or Pan-African Studies rather than Afro-American Studies. This tended to create a problematic quandry of emphasis in a discipline which by origin and need should logically be and have been Afro-American centered. None of this is to suggest that all Continental and Caribbean administrators fitted into this framework. Many were committed to both the academic and social missions of Black Studies. But it does suggest that there were enough uncommitted to have posed a problem for Black Studies in its early striving to establish itself, even as there were many Afro-American administrators who posed similar problems for the discipline.

A third type of administrator is the integrationist who was embarrassed by what he/she considered the raucous political demands often placed on Black Studies to maintain its Afro-centric focus. The integrationist was split between the economic benefit of his/her position and the perceived liability of being a part of anything that reeks of separatism. Moreover, she/he is less prone toward community links which obviously would impose on her/him an identity and duty she/he would rather deny, downplay or dismiss. Like Frazier's (1970) Black bourgeoisie, they are defined and limited by their pathological attempts to escape identification with the Black masses and the resultant self-hatred engendered by their failure.

Finally, the administrators include a group best defined as academic opportunists. They entered Black Studies not because they believed in its principles or supported its academic or political objectives, but simply because of its personal benefit to them. Some were there because they could not be in the traditional departments due to institutional racism or their own incompetence. Since in the confusion of knowing with being, all Blacks are supposed to be competent in Black Studies, and since Black Studies is considered less than an academic enterprise, these Blacks often were appointed not so much on the basis of academic credentials as on the basis of racial identity and psycho-political orientation (Brisbane, 1974:241). Thus, they were appointed and promoted on levels and with a facility no other department would have allowed. In addition, they received increases in rank and step, not for theoretical production or professional achievement, but for non-problematic management of a pseudo-academic nuisance unscheduled for long endurance. It was this approach to Black Studies that led some to conclude that Black Studies was the first academic discipline "for which burial was in order before the labor pangs subsided" (Brisbane, 1974:239).

The third factor which has clearly contributed to the development of these challenges is opposition and ambiguous acceptance of Black Studies by campus administrations and traditional departments. Brisbane (1974), Walton (1974) and Hare (1972) all make this point and demonstrate how this opposition and ambiguous acceptance continues to plague Black Studies and pose for it a clear challenge. Actually, few administrations ever fully accepted Black Studies as a viable and valid academic enterprise. Generally, they conceded to its establishment only under various kinds of pressure and usually refused to grant it department status, conceding instead programs or just courses. Moreover, traditional white studies departments challenged its academic validity and viability and also felt threatened by the students it would take, the courses it would teach, the budget it would use and the challenges it would pose to traditional disciplines and to the paradigms and data on which they were based. Recognizing Black Studies does not have the level of active community and assertive student organizational support it had in the 60's, the administrative tendency is now to move to dismantle, reduce or merge it. These forces, then, never fully accepted Black Studies, opposed its establishment and are continuing to pose one of its most critical challenges today.

THE POLITICAL CHALLENGE

The political challenge to Black Studies begins with the continuing opposition and lack of support from campus administrations. This takes many forms, including dismantlings, subsuming Black Studies under Ethnic Studies, budget cuts, refusals to grant or support department status and other acts negative to the maintenance and development of Black Studies. As early as 1972, Hare, (1972:34) one of the leading theorists and activists in the struggle for Black Studies, had noted that Black Studies was being systematically dismantled and diluted in the areas of its identity, purpose and direction. He observed that not only were the college and university administrators opposing the liberational thrust of an incipient Black ideology, but they were also in large part successful in destroying or diminishing the community links component of Black Studies and "in restricting Black Studies to culture and the humanities to the mere study of Blackness."

By 1974, Allen (1974:2) would report that Black Studies was "in deep trouble" and fighting a rearguard battle even though it "began with such enthusiasm and optimism in the late 60's." This, he continued was due to the fact that "wholesale cutbacks in operating budgets and student financial aid, coupled with intellectual ambushes by academic critics, have crippled or destroyed dozens of Black Studies departments and programs around the country." In fact, he concluded, "In 1971 some 500 schools provided full-scale Black Studies programs; today that figure has dropped to 200." Although a rough estimate of existing programs still hovers around the figure 200, it is clear that many are on tenuous ground. The need, then, becomes one of building political support on and off campus for them.

In addition to cutbacks and dismantling, Black Studies faces the problem of establishing itself as a department. As Brisbane (1974:240) noted, one of the major problems at the beginning of Black Studies was the issue of "...whether the program should be administered by an autonomous department or by an interdisciplinary, coordinating committee." This problem has still not been solved. It was argued then and remains true that without departmental autonomy, a viable and effective Black Studies enterprise is difficult if not impossible. However, the vast majority of institutions resisted such autonomy and reduced Black Studies to programs managed by interdisciplinary coordinating committees.

Walton (1974:23) observed that it was this administrative crippling through the refusal to build departments and give economic security through tenure-oriented assignments that contributed greatly to the decline in the academic quality and stability of the Black Studies program. As he stated:

> ...unwillingness of the white controlled educational institutions to make any sort of long-term commitment to Black Studies created a situation wherein the academic quality of Black Studies programs was rapidly eroded by the fact of the unstable and temporary nature of the persons responsible for the implementation of the programs.

Moreover, instead of developing strong Black Studies Departments, colleges and universities have come up with three alternative structures: (1) courses only; (2) programs; and (3) institutes
which lack the legitimacy, structure and personnel to achieve goals
usually associated with departments (Smith and Yates, 1980:279).

A second political challenge is the need to firmly establish
support for and critical participation in a generally recognized
respected and effective national professional organization for
Black Studies. The National Council of Black Studies has assumed a
vanguard role in this respect and should be supported and further
developed. Whereas the tendency is to create more than one
professional society for a given discipline, such a step for Black
Studies now would tend to divide efforts to define, defend and
develop the interests of Black Studies as a discipline. It does not
mean that eventually there will not be space and function for more
than one national professional organization. But at this time, given
the newness of the discipline and the need to maximize and concentrate efforts to establish it as a viable and permanent discipline,
such a move would most likely prove counterproductive. It is in the
context of a strong and viable organization that collective strategies, a standard curriculum, rationales, resources, defense of interest, scholarly exchange will evolve. Without such organized efforts
and collective thrusts, separate structures will tend to be reduced to
struggle for attention, duplication of effort and negative division of
effort.

A fourth aspect of the political challenge is the underdeveloped or non-existent relations many Black Studies programs
and departments have with the community and students. In their
advisory, supportive and service responsibilities to the community
which were once posed as mandatory for Black Studies most programs and departments are deficient (Hare, 1972). Likewise, many
Black Studies departments and programs have similarly underdeveloped relations with the students. Again, in areas of support,

advice and service, they often are less than effective and/or involved. The irony of this is that it is students who stood at the center of the struggle to win, expand and save Black Studies and it is they who will,through their giving or denying support — academic and political — help determine the fate or future of Black Studies.

Finally, an important aspect of the political challenge is underdeveloped and/or negative relations with other Third World ethnic programs or departments (Allen, 1974:7). Relations are often characterized by antagonistic competition for resources, positions and administrative favor. In some cases, there are no relations at all which lead to the cultivation of negative myths on all sides, gratuitous distance and dismissal of the importance of mutually beneficial exchanges. Such distance and/or hostility makes Third World ethnic departments and programs more vulnerable to administrative manipulation and eventual cancellation or forced combining. On the other hand, operational unity around clear principles of cooperation and common objectives would add to the meagre strength most of these departments and programs have individually. It seems, however, that the forging of an effective operational unity among Third World ethnic departments and programs, and the development of positive and effective relations of these departments and programs with the community and students as well as the building and support of a national professional organization for Black Studies depend, in the final analysis, on the resolution of the intellectual challenge which would provide the necessary coherent set of views and values to initiate, sustain and develop such practices.

THE INTELLECTUAL CHALLENGE

Like the political challenge, the intellectual challenge is multidimensional and as mentioned above affects Black Studies' capacity to meet the political challenge. The intellectual challenge begi..s with the need of Black Studies to define itself, i.e., establish in clear terms in a body of critical literature its academic and social missions. The problem of self-definition is undoubtedly the core of the intellectual challenge for its resolution and has implications for all its other aspects. In fact, it appears that unless effective self-definition is achieved, the defense and development of Black Studies will remain not only a problem of theory, but also a practical problem as well. (Stewart, 1979)

At its inception, Black Studies was relatively clear about its broad objectives even if it were less so about specifics. As a product of the Black Liberation and Black Student Movements, Black Studies assigned itself two broad set of goals which overlapped and reinforced each other. These were the academic and social missions posed in the Introduction. As Hare (1972:33) expressed it, "Black Studies was (essentially) a mass movement and a mass struggle based on the notion that education belongs to the people and the idea is to give it back to them." Given this, Hare argues that "Most crucial to Black Studies, Black education, aside from its ideology of liberation, would be the community component of its methodology." This essentially involved a process of gaining and utilizing skills to teach and assist the community in its defense and development and, in turn, seeking assistance from the community in the thrust to become and remain a viable and relevant academic unit on campus.

However, these goals once so clear have been obfuscated by changes in the community and on campus which eroded clarity and called into question the very existence of Black Studies. Among these changes are: (1) decline of Black students' unions and their deterioration into social clubs or at best pale images of their once defiantly Black selves; (2) the lull in the Black Movement which inspired, informed and supported campus struggles; (3) the police

and intelligence agency suppression of Black leaders and organizations who led the community and campus struggles; (4) the resurgence of racism in the face of weakened campus and community
structures; and (5) the return to academic business-as-usual, given
the inability of Blacks to intervene effectively in the process to
introduce and impose their interests.

Central to the problem of self-definition is the issue of focus
and thrust which pose several dualities not easily reconciled. First,
there is the issue of whether Black Studies should be Afro-American
centered or Pan-African. Usually, a Pan-African emphasis means a
Continent centered program, but it may include Caribbean studies,
the study of South American and Islander Blacks or any other Blacks
as well. As Ford (1973:3) pointed out:

> ...The phrase "Black Studies" has become an acceptable designation for
> all studies primarily concerned with the experience of people of African
> origin residing in any part of the world. (Thus)... it includes the experiences of
> Africans, Afro-Americans, Afro-Asians, Afro-Europeans, and African des-
> cendants of the Caribbean and other island territories.

Such a broadly based focus, might satisfy some Pan-Africanists, but
it still leaves fundamental questions unanswered. For example,
which of these areas or peoples should get the most attention, and
if it is to be equally divided, why? If Black Studies is still to link the
campus to the community, how does it now define the community
given its expanded focus? Moreover, just as a point of departure
and sound procedure, does not logic demand a thrust which is not
over-ambitious, but begins where it is, in the U.S., among Afro-
Americans, and then as it grows stronger, expands outward? In
other words, is not the study of Afro-Americans the core of Black
Studies in the U.S., the study of an African people neglected more
than any other, certainly more than the study of Continentals or
Caribbeans? And finally, if Afro-Americans, do not place ourselves
as priority, can they honestly wonder why no one else does either?

This does not preclude Pan-African Studies, it only gives greater emphasis to the study of Africans in the U.S.

A second problem of focus revolves around values. By values is meant here, categories of commitment, categories of priorities and categories of possibilities. Stress is especially places on possibilities, for what a person or people is committed to and set as priorities dictate their human possibilities. Thus, the value focus of Black Studies is key to understanding the possibilities it offers its advocates and students. Among the value foci debated in the midst of the ideological crisis are: (1) critique and correctives vs. acceptance and perpetuation of the established order in study and research; (2) stress on Black resistance and construction vs. the virulent character of our oppression and the assumed pathologies it engendered; (3) education of change agents vs. the vulgar careerists which DuBois (1961:42-54) and Frazier (1970:71-76) abhorred and against whom they warned; (4) a multidimensional education vs. a one-dimensional education, and finally (5) program or department stress on development vs. stress on simple survival.

Especially important is the last question of value focus, for it is the tendency to stress the value for survival rather than development which has caused and sustains many, if not most contradictions and weaknesses in the Black Studies thrust. Programs for simple survival have never been effective in the long run, for the very act of survival demands development. As I have observed elsewhere "society develops, conditions change and the world is not what it was even yesterday" (Karenga, 1978:9). With new conditions come new challenges and the need for new strategies and tactics just to save former gains. Development is obviously the superior value, for not only does it stress the need for new competencies, but inherent in the concept of development, itself, is the assumption and insurance of survival.

It would seem safe to say that the way to handle the value dimension of the ideological crisis is to stress both aspects of the dualities, to stress alternatives and acceptance, resistance and oppression, change and careerism. However, such a position is not only dishonest, but negative to the clarity and strength necessary for Black Studies to successfully meets its challenges. As an African proverb says *"mpanda farasi wawili, hupasuka msamba"* (a rider of two horses is split in two), and we can add, in this case, both theoretically and structurally. Moreover, a challenge demands a clear and solid decision and that decision must, of necessity, be proactive rather than simply defensive or survival-oriented. Afterall, the cockroach has lasted longer than any other creeping, crawling thing, but at what level of life?

Another problem is that there is no standard rationale for the existence of Black Studies. The rationale for African (Continental) Studies and Caribbean Studies is provided by the white administrators and professors involved, but we have yet to develop a standard rationale for the study of Afro-Americans. In fact, it is the tendency to put more emphasis on Continental and Caribbean Studies which tend to delay, diminish the stress on the need for a rationale for Afro-American Studies.

The problem of rationale was engendered as mentioned above, by the over-ambitious expansion of focus, the value crisis, and the assumption of power by administrators who shared none or few of the motivations and objectives of those who launched and won the struggle for Black Studies. In addition to these problems was the problem created by the success of administrators in blocking the "incorporation of an ideology of liberation (particularly in scientific and technical courses) to replace that of acquiescing to the status quo,....rejecting the community component,... (and) restricting Black Studies to culture and humanities,..." (Hare, 1972:34). Such restriction of Black Studies to courses to appease emotionally, but not develop intellectually, of necessity called into question the validity and value of Black Studies even among its supporters. For indeed, few people, if any, could claim academic and political relevance and at the same time support self-indulgence as a substitute for critical knowledge of society and the world. Nor could advocates of Black Studies support its reduction to the music, drama, dance and history courses on how bad white folks treated us which were taught as isolated, unconnected and self-contained subjects and palmed off as the essence of the Black experience.

An equally fundamental problem of rationale was the theoretical and administrative thrust toward integration. The first thrust was a natural outgrowth of the introduction and the motivations of professors and administrators who, as mentioned above, saw assimilation as the highest goal and were embarrassed by their Blackness and the socially indelicate images of Black folks created by their rough and raucous struggles on campus and in the community to define, defend and develop their Blackness. On the other hand, the administrative thrust was a practical and often racist effort to deny autonomy or reality to Black Studies and subsume it under already existing disciplines and departments. Thus, they found ideological allies in the integrationists who argued that Blacks were more definitively Americans or humans, not simply Blacks and that thus, the need was for a good American or human education, not a Black one (Kilson, 1973).

The problem with this position, especially for the Black academicians, is that it puts them on shaky grounds, ideologically and practically. On one hand, they argue their essential American and human identities and on the other hand, they seek, of necessity, to justify their positions, or more specifically, their jobs in a discipline which by their own admission not only does not really exist, but also does not need to exist. Afterall, how can one argue she/he is most definitively human or American and then justify a department for the study and teaching of a less important or irrelevant sub-identity?

Another aspect of the intellectual challenge is the lack of and need for a standard curriculum. Every discipline is in great part defined and introduced in a practical sense by its curriculum. Often in Black Studies, courses seemed to be offered based on the teaching interest or area of the department's or programs' current faculty (Smith, 1971:265-270). Although there should always be room for innovative experimental courses, no serious discipline can establish itself or its academic legitimacy if all or the bulk of its courses are experimental and if it lacks a standard or core curriculum.

The problem of a standard curriculum can be traced back to the origins of Black Studies which as noted above was born in a time of confrontation and political urgency. Things were not always thought out, nor was the emphasis always on the academic. However, credit must be given to pioneers who were treading on new grounds and in times not conducive to long critical academic exchange. As noted above, in the academic year of 1967-1968, a Black Studies program was adopted at San Francisco State which included eleven courses in Anthropology, Dramatic Arts, Education, English, Psychology and Sociology. These courses were tentative and ad hoc, and were supplanted by a more extensive curriculum designed and developed by Dr. Nathan Hare. (Brisbane, 1974:226-227). Hare also built in a community component which included a Black Community Press, Black Information Centers and specific methods of faculty, student and community interaction. Although important groundwork was lain by Hare and the Black students at San Francisco State, it seems that it was the struggle for the program rather than its construction and development which became the model. Thus, in most cases, the wheel was reinvented in almost each Black Studies program and a critical study of curriculum and structure proposals was never made on a widespread level.

Added to the inability of subsequent Black Studies programs to learn from the first historical model is the recurring problem of self-definition and definitive focus it requires. For until Black Studies is able to establish a *priority focus*, it is logically and practically impossible for it to design and develop a standard curriculum. With advocates torn between an Afro-American centered focus and a general Pan-African thrust, a unified approach to curriculum is problematic, if not improbable. Moreover, without basic agreement on value focus, the same limitation on standardization is imposed on curriculum development. Thus, Walton (1974:27) is correct when he argues that:

> The offering of an uncoordinated patchwork of ethically oriented courses on an 'a la carte' basis will serve only to perpetuate the long term frustrations and problems that many institutions of learning experienced because they readily adopted uncoordinated courses and portions of Black students' program suggestions *prior* to the development of an *internally consistent* structure to support the implementation of such courses and programs.

The solution of this problem is obviously a major intellectual challenge and calls for serious and sustained critical thinking and exchange.

Finally, the intellectual challenge includes the task of developing a substantial and definitive body of literature for the discipline of Black Studies. It is obvious that teaching in and development of the discipline can only suffer, if such a body of literature is not produced. Such a body of literature not only introduces the subject areas of the discipline but also establishes its focus and rationale, develops and presents its special language and introduces its paradigms, models, techniques, methods, theories, research strategies and research designs. Without a substantial definitive body of literature in Black Studies, the worth and future of the discipline will always be in doubt.

TOWARD NECESSARY CORRECTIVES

The solution to both the intellectual challenge and the political challenge to Black Studies, begins with a definition of Black Studies in the U.S. as essentially an Afro-American centered enterprise. Departments and programs in Continental and Caribbean Studies already exist; the deficiency and need are in Afro-American Studies. Certainly, this does not suggest or imply that Afro-American Studies be isolated from the study of other African peoples throughout the world. On the contrary, to be relevant and real, the study of Afro- Americans, an African people, must include a critical grasp of their historical, current and possible future relations with other African peoples. However, the *priority focus* on Afro-Americans, as a people, gives Black Studies a core focus from which expansion can proceed in a systematic and effective manner. As Turner and Perkins (1976:10) noted, such an ideological focus on Afro-Americans and the development of: "a critical Afro-American social theory will also strengthen our intellectual work, by making our scholarship the study of *our* reality, as it is and has been, not as it might have been or as we would have liked it to have been." Moreover, they maintain that "it will create the kind of intellectual bases where the dimensions, problems, and tactics of the Afro-American struggle may be discussed, interpreted, and absorbed." This is obviously the self-defined task of Black Studies.

A priority focus on Afro-Americans will also contribute to the solution of the problem of developmental links with the community. For the community is most clearly and effectively defined as the Afro-American community. In this context, Black Studies can build on and continue the legacy of the political struggle in the 60's that defiantly and dramatically placed Black Studies on the academic agenda and charged it to be relevant to the people it must of necessity serve. Such linkage is vital, for as Chinweizu (1977:24) argues, "...The transmission of the gains and experiences of the struggle from one generation to the other is a vital task of education."

Moreover, such linkage facilitates the implementation of Hare's (1978:14) position that, "We must transform the community and make it relevant to the educational endeavor at the same time as we make education relevant to the Black community." In such a mutually beneficial relationship, the power of Black Studies and the Black community to define, defend and develop themselves is enhanced and consolidated. Power, as the ability to realize one's will even in opposition to others is, both in concept and practice, a collective expression which requires and assumes organization and united thrusts. Hence, the stronger the organization(s) and the alliances built and effectively utilized, the greater the power. The organization and alliance of Black Studies and the community can only enhance each other's power and unite them in an effective mutually beneficial project of the collective rescue and reconstruction of Black history and humanity.

The value focus for Black Studies must be proactive rather than reactive, toward social change rather than protest or servile careerism, toward critique and correctives rather than sterile statements on social pathologies and the oppression which assumedly engendered them. As Hare (1972:33) contended, "...Black education must be education for liberation, or at least for change. In this respect, it was to prepare Black students to become the catalysts for a Black cultural revolution." But to be an education for liberation and change, Black Studies must develop a new body of literature which reflects audaciousness and initiative in research, and critical and corrective intellectual production. It must challenge established disciplines, develop its own social science methodology, and give a new meaning to social science, i.e., the science of social change and reconstruction. As McClendon (1974:17) stated, "Black Studies, in remaining compatible with the assorted needs of Black people to obtain useful and purposeful formal education, is compelled to teach contrary to much of what has become customary and routine in a variety of disciplines."

The thrust of Black Studies toward contribution of a body of literature which will help bring into being a new social science and at the same time contribute to the rescue and reconstruction of Black history and humanity, must have at least four characteristics. It must be holistic, critical, corrective and committed (Karenga, 1977:50-54). Such an audacious and urgent task:

> ...must take place within a definite *analytical* and *value* framework. It must, in both inquiry and presentation, adhere unashamedly and unreservedly to a core of basic values that express our priorities, aid us in choosing the most important problems, assist us in selection of data most relevant to solving those problems and provide categories and concepts which inspire and inform our inquiry and assumptions (Karenga, 1977:52).

A holistic approach is a comprehensive inquiry into the core process and practices of Black life as well as an investigation into related internal and external factors which confront and affect us as a people. Such an approach recognizes and respects that fact that society or social life is an interconnected, interactive and independent whole and that failure to view it in its totality as far as possible limits perception and intellectual production. A holistic approach places Blacks in interaction with society and the world not in isolation. A holistic approach considers both race and class factors and their interrelatedness. It does not and must not sacrifice one for the other or fail to perceive that a fadist clamor for exclusive class analysis in no way can deny or diminish the fundamental role race has played in the shaping of the U.S. and has played and will play in the struggle to reshape this country in a more human image.

A critical approach is a concrete, rational and incisive approach. It seeks to avoid sterile "protest and pomposity — the temptation to indulge in the maudlin, moralistic enterprise of cataloging injustices and tragedies to elicit sympathy..." (Karenga, 1977:53). Critical intellectual production moves beyond the insubstantiality of free flows of consciousness and pitiful calls for survival, digs beneath the surface and raises that which is absent in traditional literature, i.e., the rich variousness and potential of Black life and the subversive content of our history. Its search is for possibilities as well as achievements, for contradictions as well as tendencies that will lead us beyond the established state of things.

A corrective approach strives to go beyong criticism to reconstruction. Thus, a corrective body of Black Studies literature must begin with a redefinition of the world in our own image according to our own needs. In fact, an essential, inevitable act of a people coming into consciousness of itself is to redefine the world and society in order to assure its rightful and true role them. Moreover, such a people must and does construct alternatives to the established order on the theoretical and practical level. For it under-stands that *the most severe and effective criticism of a society is self-conscious practice which transforms it.*

Finally, the intellectual production that contributes to a new social science and to the rescue and reconstruction of Black history must be committed. It must be unashamedly committed to a set of values contributive to its task — which in the final analysis — is both theoretical and practical. Committed intellectual work reflects the acceptance of one's role as an *unashamed partisan of one's people.* Moreover, it recognizes the fact that there is no pure research isolated and divorced from the urgencies of the day. In fact, "all cultural work takes place in a definite social context, thus, either reinforcing or challenging that context" (Karenga, 1977:52). Or as Chinweizu (1977:24) maintains, "There is no neutral, value-free research, especially in the unnatural, or so-called 'social', sciences. Even in the natural sciences, what gets researched, when, and with what priority and thoroughness, are all matters determined by political and economic considerations." Given this then, "Afro-American researchers and educators should organize in ways to permit them to research what is of value to Afro-America, rather than what is against the interest of Afro-America." Having accepted such a responsibility on the intellectual level, one cannot but recognize and respond creatively to the fact that a real and effective effort to rescue and reconstruct Black history and humanity in the social sciences must be at the same time a step toward doing the same thing in society. It is in recognition of this that Black Studies has defined for itself both an academic and social mission and is, thus, both an investigative and applied social science.

In terms of a standard curriculum, the seven core subject areas serve as a framework for that determination. A survey of Black Studies curricula shows that numerous variations are possible within such a curricular framework (Smith, 1971). Moreover, since most Black Studies programs already have courses within this framework, the standardization process would be less difficult to initiate. Also, as argued in the introduction, these seven core subject areas are most definitive of the various aspects of Black life and culture and thus, serve as core foci for inquiry and analysis. Finally, it is important in the standardization process to start with the establishment of core courses which mirror the core subject areas rather than the possible variations in them. For example, an introductory or advanced course in Black Economics per se should precede courses on specialized areas, i.e., Black Cooperatives, Black Capitalism, etc. Likewise, a course in Black Politics or its equivalent should precede and take precedence over a course in Urban Welfare Politics or the Political Ideology of Racism. This is curricular base-building as opposed to academic hang gliding, i.e., catching whatever wind faculty members can ride.

The question of rationale is more a problem of standardization than creation. That is to say, Black Studies has established its relevance as outlined in the Introduction; the need is for Black Studies literature and faculty to standardize its essential rationale. Obviously, I think that whatever its final form is should reflect the six basic contentions of relevance I advanced in the Introduction, i.e., that it is a contribution: (1) to humanity's self-understanding; (2) to the university's realizing its claim of universality, comprehensiveness and objectivity; (3) to U.S. society's understanding itself; (4) to the rescue and reconstruction of Black history and humanity; (5) to the creation of a new social science; and (6) to the creation of a body of conscious, capable and committed Black intellectuals who self-consciously choose to use their knowledge and skills in the service of the Black community and by consequence and extension, in the interest of a new and better society and world.

It is this last contribution that in fact is key to all the rest, for the development of such a Black intelligentsia insures the realization and expansion of the other contributions which are at the same time tasks. Thus, the central responsibility for the successful meeting of all challenges to Black Studies as well as those which confront Black people, rest as DuBois (1969) argues, with the best minds of the race. Both Cruse (1967) and Frazier (1973) were critical and doubtful of the consciousness, capacity and commitment of the Black intellectual. Frazier's (1973:60) criticism remains in great part valid. He contends that "they have failed to study the problems of (Black) life in America in a manner which would place the fate of (Blacks) in the broad framework of man's experience in this world." Moreover, he charges that "they have engaged in petty defenses of the (Afro-American's) social failure. Even worse, "more often, they have been so imbued with the prospect of integration and eventual assimilation that they have thought that they could prove themselves true Americans by not (even) studying (Blacks)."

Cruse (1967:455) is more optimistic concerning the Black intellectual, assigning them the vital task of intellectual production which leads to a critical explanation of the economic and institutional causes of Black oppression and the development of solutions to it. These contentions are obviously supportive of the academic and social mission of Black Studies. For they pose education as a narrow and invalid process and experience, if it is not placed in service of Black people and is not a contribution to the intellectual conception and practical building of a better society and world. And they also place hope and educational focus on the creation of a conscious, capable and committed body of Black intellectuals who will self-consciously intervene in social reality and history and shape them in the image and interest of Black people.

At the beginning of this chapter, I had advanced the proposition that challenges successfully met enhance possibilities. It is the history of humankind that overcoming social and natural oppositions strengthened them and pushed them further along the road to ever higher levels of life and daring. The struggle to defend and develop Black Studies offer similar possibilities of development in the academic world. *Black Studies' need to defend itself, is at the same time a demand to develop itself.* Moreover, whatever unsure steps or stumbling there was in the past offers a wealth of lessons for the future which will aid a quicker-paced development. For as an African proverb says, "To stumble is not to fall but to go forward faster." The need, then, is for bold and critical thought and planning, greater intellectual production, more vital research, effective organization, systematic exchange and development. In a word, the need is for self-conscious action which not only answers critics, but more importantly answers the critical questions the discipline continuously raises for itself in the constant refining and expanding of its capacity to carry out its academic and social mission.

STUDY QUESTIONS

1. Define challenge and crisis in relationship to Black Studies.
2. What are three fundamental historical factors which contributed to the development of the current challenges to Black Studies?
3. What are the basic political challenges facing Black Studies?

4. What are the fundamental intellectual challenges facing Black Studies?

5. What were the basic types of administrators which posed problems for the development of Black Studies as an established discipline?

6. What changes in the community and on campus contributed to a blurring of the original goals of Black Studies?

7. What are the four structural forms of Black Studies?

8. What are some problems of value focus within Black Studies?

9. What characteristics must Black Studies literature have, if it is to fulfill its academic mission?

10. Discuss, suggested correctives to meet the challenges to Black Studies.

11. How will the intellectual and political challenges to Black Studies serve to enhance its possibilities?

REFERENCES

Allen, Robert L. (1974) "Politics of the Attack on Black Studies," *The Black Scholar*, 6, 1 (September) 2-7.

Brisbane, Robert.   (1974) *Black Activism*, Valley Forge, N.Y.: Judson Press.

Chinweizu.   (1977) "Education for Power," *First World*, 1, 3 (May/June) 20-24.

Cruse, Harold. (1967) *Crisis of the Negro Intellectual*, New York: William Morrow & Co.

DuBois, W.E.B.   (1961) *The Souls of Black Folk*, New York: Fawcett Publications.

_____. (1969) "The Talented Tenth," in *The Negro Problem*, (ed.) Ulysses Lee, New York: Arno Press and the New York Times.

Ford, Nick. (1973) *Black Studies*, New York: National University Publications.

Frazier, E. Franklin. (1970) *Black Bourgeoisie*, New York: Macmillan.

_____. (1973) "The Failure of the Negro Intellectual," in *The Death of White Sociology*, (ed.) Joyce A. Ladner, New York: Vintage Books, pp. 52-66.

Hare, Nathan. (1972) "The Battle for Black Studies," *The Black Scholar*, 3, 9 (May) 32-47.

_____. (1978) "War on Black Colleges," *The Black Scholar*, 9, 8 (May/June) 12-19.

Karenga, Maulana. (1977) "Corrective History: Reconstructing the Black Past," *First World*, 1, 3 (May/June) 50-54.

_____. (1978) *Essays on Struggle: Position and Analysis*, San Diego: Kawaida Publications.

Kilson, Martin. (1973) "Reflections on Structure and Content in Black Studies," *Journal of Black Studies*, 1, 3 (March) 297-314.

McClendon, William H. (1974) "Black Studies: Education for Liberation," *The Black Scholar*, 6, 1 (September) 15-20.

Smith, William D. (1971) "Black Studies: A Survey of Models and Curricula," *Journal of Black Studies*, (March) 259-272.

Smith, William David and Albert C. Yates. (1980) "Editorial In Black Studies," *Journal of Black Studies*, 10, 3 (March) 269-77.

Stewart, James B. (1979) "Introducing Black Studies: A Critical Examination of Some Textual Materials," *Umoja*, 3, 1 (Spring) 5-17.

Turner, James and W. Eric Perkins. (1976) "Towards A Critique of Social Science," *The Black Scholar*, 7, 7 (April) 2-11.

Walton, Sidney F. (1974) "Black Studies and Affirmative Action," *The Black Scholar*, 6, 1 (September) 21-31.